THE
PLACE
TO BE

CONTENTS

Previous page: a local woman in Yúnnán, China. Opposite: by the Zambezi River in Zambia.

FOREWORD

 We'd set off an hour earlier in sea kayaks for a day of paddling around the Bay of Islands on the northeast coast of New Zealand and then they appeared, barely noticeable beneath us. Three powerful, black-and-white shapes were swimming slowly through the sapphire water – orcas, or killer whales, hunting for food. Two larger whales flanked a small one, which held a ray between its teeth. We were awash with emotions after the encounter: awe at seeing such majestic creatures in their natural habitat; exhilaration at how close they had been to us; and joy at experiencing the unexpected in such a beautiful setting. Such was the powerful effect of those feelings that, years later, the memory remains as clear as ever.

Whether we go for a weekend or a year, most of us travel to see unforgettable sights and enjoy new experiences. But, ultimately, we travel in search of a feeling. That feeling might be a sense of awe or wonder that we don't receive in our daily routines, or it might be a cossetting feeling of calm. We might want to experience an energising sense of exhilaration or to find the mental space for thoughtful reflection or to be inspired.

This book is a little bit different: it's an introduction to almost 250 places around the world based on how they might make you *feel*. Every destination in the following chapters, from the most remote Pacific islands to the

world's greatest cities, is intended to elicit one (or more) of a dozen emotions. Each chapter, beginning with Awe and ending with Reflection, visits 20 places around the world and explains how they might make you feel and the practicalities of getting there.

Along the way we will hear from experts who believe that experiencing many of these emotions – which may be in short supply in our busy day-to-day lives – is essential to our mental and physical wellbeing. These feelings can challenge our understanding of the world and of ourselves. They might make us feel small as we witness for the first time a whale breach (see page 12) or view the galaxy revolving overhead at a star party (see page 286), and more connected to the world and the people around us. Similarly, becoming absorbed by the intricate detail of a butterfly's wings or the decorative carving at Jaisalmer in India or the Alhambra in Spain, might cause us to pause for reflection or be enlightened. We don't neglect the spirit of adventure either, from venturing to the tribal heartlands of Papua New Guinea, diving into Bogotá's music scene or visiting New Zealand's Queenstown, the hometown of exhilaration.

However, although these wonderful destinations can be a shortcuts to feelings of joy, inspiration, serenity, passion or more, we also hope that this book inspires you to seek out these emotions close to home.

The Bay of Islands, New Zealand.

AWE

In the words of Dr Dacher Keltner, professor of psychology and a co-founder of the Greater Good Science Center at the University of California, awe can be defined as 'the experience we have when we encounter things that are vast and… transcend our current understanding of the world'. The emotion has been shown to 'lead people to be more altruistic, less entitled, more humble and aware of the strengths of others, and less stressed by the challenges of daily living'.

The world is full of places that have the potential to inspire awe: the feeling doesn't have to come from big things or expensive trips. As Dr Keltner notes, awe can be felt seeing snow cranes fly over a Buddhist temple in Bhutan or simply by backpacking in your local national park, wherever that may be. What matters is being open and receptive to the experience, finding the time and space to absorb and appreciate it.

Whump … Whump … Whump … Another wave at ❶ Waimea Bay in Hawaii detonates on the North Shore. The break is jacked up by an undersea lava shelf 100m beyond the headland. It's one of the largest, heaviest waves in the world, with 6-8m (20-25ft) swells on which pioneers such as Greg 'Da Bull' Noll then Eddie Aikau first tested the possibilities of big-wave surfing. When it's firing, the beach and road behind it fill with crowds

① WAIMEA BAY, HAWAII, USA

Waimea is on O'ahu's North Shore. Hawaii's main island, O'ahu welcomes lots of international flights to its capital Honolulu. You can get around using the island's bus service but you'll have more independence by renting a car. There are various accommodation options, from hostels to private lets and resorts along the North Shore in towns such as Hale'iwa, which is close to Waimea Bay and a 90-minute bus ride from Honolulu. There are also places to stay in Waimea Bay. Winter brings the big waves (and surfers) and summer attracts the sunseekers.

② ICEBERG ALLEY, CANADA

Newfoundland's international airport is in St John's. Carriers arrive from the US, some European cities such as London, and the rest of Canada. It's a two- to three-hour drive down the coast road to the southern tip of the Avalon Peninsula, passing sea-faring settlements, most offering motels, inns and B&Bs. One town that you will pass is Ferryland, which dates back to 1621. It offers incredible views from the lighthouse, though, as always, take care near the ocean edge. Icebergs can be spotted along the whole coast. Check www. newfoundlandlabrador. com for sightings.

watching the action. You may feel awe at the skill and bravery of the select few surfers but also awe at nature's power, the great unstoppable swells of water swirling around the planet.

Much of our planet is water. As some of that water crashes on Hawaiian beaches, elsewhere it is locked in the ice caps and glaciers, which gradually disintegrate into the ocean. ❷ Iceberg Alley lies just off Cape Race in Newfoundland, Canada. Each spring and summer, as the Arctic pack ice breaks up, chunks of ice 10,000 years old float along it, often visible from the shore. These bergs can be so large that they usher in a chill to the local weather. That's not all that's amazing about these icebergs: those that float through Iceberg Alley average 100,000-200,000 tonnes in weight and are the size of a 15-storey building (remember that 90% of the iceberg is submerged). However, the very largest can weigh 10 million tonnes. Small bergs, the size of a grand piano,

are called growlers. They can be just as dangerous to shipping as the larger icebergs.

We don't know whether icebergs inspired awe in the crew of the *Titanic* on its maiden voyage in 1912 but they clearly didn't inspire sufficient respect. Cape Race at the southeast tip of Newfoundland's Avalon Peninsula received the last radio call from the *Titanic* on the night of 14 April, as it sank 600km (370 miles) out to sea.

Just round the corner in Canada's ❸ Québec province, the waters of the Gulf of St Lawrence and the St Lawrence River's estuary are patrolled by another type of giant: whales. In fact, 13 species of cetacean visit the feeding grounds along a 1250km (775 mile) section of Côte-Nord from Tadoussac to Blanc-Sablon. You might see some of the largest creatures to ever exist on this planet, such as the blue whale and the fin whale, which each feed on tonnes of krill daily. Humpbacks, sperm whales and North Atlantic right whales also appear, followed by beluga, orca, smaller dolphins and porpoises. Whale watching – and this is one of the best places in the world to see them – is often a highly emotional experience. There might be a variety of reasons for the intense response that many people experience: firstly, wonder at seeing such massive and graceful animals in their natural environment, then perhaps a recognition of their intelligence, their family structures, their sentience. And finally, maybe an acknowledgement that humans hunted many whale species almost to extinction.

For Dr Keltner, a walk is all that it takes to conjure awe: 'I look for Awe Walks during my work day, with my family at night, and in rural and urban settings.' And from time to time, he takes a walk among ❹ redwoods in places such as the Muir Woods National Monument in Marin County, on the north side of San Francisco's Golden Gate Bridge. Here the sense of awe comes from numerous sources: the trees' height and 'the sense of peace they create high in the air above', then their very presence – these are trees that have lived for millennia.

The air in a grove of redwood trees seems to hum with energy. It might be the stillness or maybe the scent of year after year of needles on the forest floor. California is the natural home of some of the world's largest living organisms, giant sequoia trees and their relatives, the redwoods. The larger sequoia grows at heights of up to 2400m (8000ft) along the western slopes of Sierra Nevada in Central California. The taller redwood thrives along the coast of northern California. Both trees have national parks dedicated to them.

Of course, feelings of awe aren't limited to large things. Sometimes the beauty of nature lies in minuscule marvels. Only a little larger than the US state of Colorado, ❺ Ecuador, which straddles the Andes, is blessed with

③ CÔTE-NORD QUÉBEC, CANADA

The whale-watching route runs from Tadoussac to Blanc-Sablon, with lots of coastal towns and villages along the way in which to overnight and find provisions. Tadoussac is a three- to four-hour drive from Québec City and has a range of accommodation (www.quebecmaritime.ca). Whale-watching season is from May to October, which coincides with the best weather. Many towns offer excursions by boat and sea kayaking is also possible along most of the coast.

④ THE REDWOODS, CALIFORNIA, USA

Coast redwoods grow along the north coast of California and in southern Oregon. Numerous parks, state and national, protect them. These include Prairie Creek Redwoods State Park, an hour's drive north of Eureka off Hwy 101, the Avenue of the Giants. There are campgrounds in the park – book via www.parks.ca.gov. Adjoining Prairie Creek is Redwood National Park (www.nps.gov), which offers four campgrounds and also backcountry sites. There are no hotels or lodges, although there are options in local towns such as Orick, where you can also stock up on food supplies. Arcata and Eureka to the south have more choice.

Previous page: giant waves at Waimea Bay, Hawaii. Right: giant trees at Prairie Creek Redwoods State Park, California.

A whale dives in the Gulf of St
Lawrence, Québec, Canada.

Courting purple-bibbed whitetip
hummingbirds in Ecuador.

incredible biodiversity, and here you can be struck with wonder by some of the world's smallest creatures. Bird watching is one of Ecuador's big draws, a land where jewel-like hummingbirds flit from flower to flower.

In fact, Ecuador has probably the greatest number of hummingbird species of any country, with counts of more than 130 types. They have beautiful names too, such as the sapphire-vented puffleg; the viridian metaltail; the sparkling violetear; the rainbow starfrontlet; the amethyst woodstar; and not forgetting the spangled coquette. Hummingbirds seem to live their lives in fast-forward: they beat their wings from 50 to 200 times per second, their tiny hearts beat 1200 times a minute, and they must consume half their body weight (which may only be two or three grammes) in sugar daily.

You don't have to go far to start your search: privately owned Bellavista Cloud Forest Reserve, on the edge of the Mindo Cloud Forest, is just 90km (56 miles) northwest of the capital Quito and known for the number of hummingbirds that live among the trees and vines. Orchids, equally beautiful organisms, are also found widely there. Beyond Bellavista, there are many once-in-a-lifetime locations for birding in Ecuador.

Venture north to Central America for more mind-blowing marvels, this time of the amphibious variety. Costa Rica is home to some 140 species of frogs and toads and many of them live in the misty environment of ❻ Monteverde Cloud Forest Reserve, northwest of the capital San José. When Christopher Columbus made his fourth and final journey to the New World he landed on Costa Rica's Caribbean coast in September 1502. The Spanish named Costa Rica the 'rich coast' because of the tales of gold in the hills. The early Spanish settlers didn't find much gold, but they may have overlooked a more interesting treasure – the golden toad.

Up until the late 1980s there were thousands of these beautiful amphibians around Monteverde. However, the mountains are becoming less misty every year and the golden toad disappeared, not so much the canary in the mine as the toad in the forest. But many species of amphibian survive in Monteverde, including such amazing varieties as glass frogs (yes, with transparent skin) and dart frogs that secrete a deadly poison through their skin. Both are typically tiny, often around 2-3cm in length, so spotting them in the forest is a challenge. Fortunately, the Monteverde Frog Pond contains more than 20 species of native frog. Both the hummingbirds and the frogs invite us to find delight in life's details and to marvel at evolution's infinite variety.

In the rainforests of ❼ Daintree, Australia, evolution could be said to have stalled. Listen carefully as you walk through this Unesco World Heritage site and national park in the far north of Queensland. Snap! What broke that twig? It might be nothing. Or it could be a short-tempered 1.5m-tall throwback with dagger-like claws and a vicious kick: the southern cassowary. Dressed in long, hair-like black plumage with a hard crest-like helmet, a vivid blue neck and a red wattle, this bird's origins go back to the age of the dinosaur, about 65 million years ago. In fact, they're among the closest living creatures to dinosaurs. So, if you encounter one on a forest track, remember that as you back away slowly.

Cassowaries are not the only part of northeast Queensland that inspires awe. Gondwana was one of two Jurassic landmasses and about 180 million years ago it began to break up into the continents we know today. There are parts of Daintree rainforest where Gondwanan plants still survive, making this one of the most primeval corners of the planet. It doesn't take much imagination when hiking through somewhere like Mossman Gorge to picture a dinosaur – or at least its nearest living relative.

⑤ ECUADOR

Bellavista Cloud Forest Reserve is a 90km (56 mile) drive on good quality roads northwest of Quito, Ecuador's capital and transport hub. Cars can be rented in the city. Bellavista itself is a private lodge that can be booked direct or through agents (www. bellavistacloudforest. com), and hotel pick-ups from Quito for day trips or longer can be arranged. Beyond Bellavista, to the east, the parks become larger, wilder and less accessible (but no less rewarding). The dry season runs from mid-June to early October but note that humidity remains at an average 95% all year.

⑥ MONTEVERDE, COSTA RICA

The eco-community at the heart of this cloud forest reserve, full name Reserva Biológica Bosque Nuboso de Monteverde, has deliberately kept the immediate access roads unpaved to keep a check on the number of visitors. It's only partially successful – at weekends and in the high season this place gets busy. You'll need a 4WD to drive yourself to Monteverde (rental agencies won't hire a 2WD if you tell them you're going there). Bus services (five hours from San José) terminate in the nearby town of Santa Elena so you'll need a taxi to continue to Monteverde. Most of the affordable accommodation is in Santa Elena; more expensive lodgings lie in Monteverde itself.

This page: a butterfly in Monteverde Cloud
Forest Reserve, Costa Rica. Opposite: a
Kuku Yalanji guide in Mossman Gorge in
Daintree National Park, Australia.

A dawn search for tigers on a jeep safari in India.

In the forests of the night there's another creature that inspires awe, if not reverence and fear. The tiger is one of the world's iconic species but due to poaching for body parts that are used in traditional Chinese medicine they perhaps number about 3000 today. The Bengal tiger is the largest of the cat family, weighing up to 225kg (500lbs). One of its last refuges is ❽ Ranthambore National Park in eastern Rajasthan, India. This park is a figurehead in India's tiger conservation efforts and there are about 50 Bengal tigers in Ranthambore, making it somewhere you're most likely to see one in the wild.

Even the captive tigers of 18th-century England were able to instil in poet William Blake a sense of their 'fearful symmetry'. In the dry, scrubby forest of Ranthambore (or the nearby sanctuary of Sariska), the experience of watching one stroll languidly across the track is heart-stopping. It's the sharp alarm calls of nearby langur monkeys that often herald an appearance

⑦ DAINTREE NATIONAL PARK, QUEENSLAND, AUSTRALIA

Cairns is the regional transport hub of Far North Queensland. Given the vast distances in Australia, most people will arrive by air, from state capital Brisbane or from Melbourne, Sydney and other regional airports. From Cairns, there's a bus service operated by Trans North that travels north to Port Douglas, close to the Daintree National Park and Mossman Gorge. But most visitors will prefer the independence of renting a vehicle. Average temperatures are at their coolest from June to September, when the rainfall is also at its lowest.

⑧ RANTHAMBORE NATIONAL PARK, INDIA

To reach Rajasthan's top tiger-spotting destination you'll need to get to Sawai Madhopur, which is on the new Delhi to Mumbai main line and is also served by trains from Jaipur, which take two to three hours. Lots of accommodation options, from boutique lodges to standard hotels, suit all pockets but note that the best places book up quickly in the park's open season from 1 October to 30 June. Jeep safaris can be booked with the Forest Office via your hotel or online at www.forest.rajasthan.gov.in – again, demand is high during holiday seasons so plan ahead.

Water pours through lava rock
at Hraunfossar waterfalls in
Borgarfjördur, Iceland.

and then there's an awestruck hush if one emerges from the striped shadows of the forest.

In Africa, great wildlife spectacles are just as magical but on a massive scale. Tanzania's ❾ Ngorongoro Crater, which extends over 260 sq km (102 sq miles), was formed almost three million years ago when the caldera of a giant volcano collapsed. It is now an amphitheatre for a daily wildlife drama with around 25,000 ungulates such as wildebeest, eland, gazelles and Cape buffaloes sharing the crater with more than 60 Masai lions. In such a confined space, compared with the vast plains of the Serengeti, sightings of some of the 'big five' – the Cape buffalo, black rhinoceros, African elephant, lion and leopard – are guaranteed on safari here.

The entire Ngorongoro Conservation Area covers 8292 sq km (3202 sq miles) and walking safaris, with appropriate planning, are encouraged. To set foot on African soil, with no fences between you and any animals, is a uniquely thrilling feeling. In fact, the earliest hominids left their own footprints in Ngorongoro about 3.6 million years ago at Laetoli, west of the crater. In Oldupai Gorge, to the north, excavations have revealed remnants of four types of human descendent, each showing a gradual increase in brain size. This part of Africa was the 'Cradle of Mankind' and to walk here is to experience the world much as our ancestors did, though without a camera-phone and a waiting 4WD.

It took until the late 9th century for humankind to reach another volcanic location, ❿ Iceland. This island's landscapes inspire awe through their otherworldliness: black-sand beaches, glacial lakes such as Jökulsárlón where blue icebergs float, great thunderous curtains of water, active volcanoes that spit rocks and fire. You may as well have landed on another planet – or in another time-warping dimension.

A 2012 Stanford University study published in the journal *Psychological Science* suggested that experiencing 'jaw-dropping moments' led to participants feeling that they had more time available, which made them more patient and less materialistic; awe-inspiring experiences (especially travel) brought the participants into the present moment and made life feel more satisfying. If that's the case, then Iceland is a prescription that can benefit all of us. You don't have to venture far from Reykjavík: Gullfoss waterfall and Geysir are a 90-minute drive. And Silfra in Þingvellir National Park, where divers can swim in impossibly clear water between two tectonic plates, is 40 minutes away. But

there's a whole island to explore (see the index) by bike, pony, 4WD or snowmobile, so take your time.

The high-altitude landscapes of Chile's ⓫ Atacama desert are almost as otherworldly. They have stood in for the planet Mars in movies and NASA scientists have replicated tests here that were used by the Viking spacecraft on Mars, believing the Atacama to be the most arid and lifeless place on our world, 50 times drier than Death Valley. Standing on this 15-million-year-old plateau is certainly an awesome experience (just bring your own water). But is it truly beautiful? Perhaps you need water for that.

In North America, few places are as naturally and strangely beautiful as ⓬ Antelope Canyon, near Page, Arizona. It's one of many sandstone slot canyons in the American southwest, carved by flowing water into sinuous shapes that catch the light and shadows. Antelope Canyon is particularly pretty due to the colours illuminated by the shafts of sunlight, much like the stained glass of a cathedral's window (and the resulting feeling of reverence is similar in some people). Both the upper and lower portions of Antelope Canyon can only

⑨ NGORONGORO CRATER, TANZANIA

The local airport is at Arusha, which receives direct flights from Dar es Salaam. It's a three- to four-hour drive west to the crater – there are daily buses, or Arusha-based operators can meet you at the airport. The next closest airport is Kilimanjaro International, further west – there are shuttles between this airport and Arusha. The closest town to the crater is Karatu, which has a range of rooms, from backpacker guesthouses to luxury lodges. The crater receives fewer visitors during the rainy season from March to May, and the weather is cool in winter from June to August.

⑩ ICELAND

More and more transatlantic flights between North America and Europe are going via Reykjavík so Iceland has never been more accessible or affordable. Airlines range from budget to the big carriers so there's plenty of choice. Note that mid-June through August is the peak season with long hours of daylight. But spring and autumn also have plenty to offer visitors, not least cheaper accommodation (although some of the highland roads may be closed). See Lonely Planet's guidebook or online for the latest hotel recommendations and excursions.

be accessed on a tour in the company of a guide, and if you're craving some solitary contemplation you'll be out of luck. But there are lots of other less accessible but equally exciting (and risky) canyons in which to experience awe. One of the largest is Buckskin Gulch in Utah's Paria Canyon-Vermilion Cliffs Wilderness area, between Kanab in Utah and Page. It's a one- or two-day hike, which may require some canyoneering and wading (and as ever in a slot canyon, be aware of the threat of flash floods).

On the east coast of the USA, there are different types of canyons, those formed by the skyscrapers of **13** New York. So where is the awe in these man-made chasms that span Manhattan, more than 300m (985ft) deep? It lies not just in the realisation that humans built this place with their hands and ingenuity, but also in New York's place in American history and everything for which it stands.

The Statue of Liberty opened in 1886. New York had already been first a Dutch trading outpost with the Old World then a refuge for European immigrants, fleeing war, oppression and poverty, as documented in Tyler Anbinder's book *City of Dreams: the 400-Year Epic*

The Valle de la Luna in Los Flamencos National Reserve in the Atacama desert, Chile.

---

⑪ ATACAMA, CHILE

San Pedro de Atacama is the gateway to this desert. The tiny adobe town is dependent on travellers and has a wide range of amenities and accommodation. To reach it, take Hwy 23 southeast from Calama. If time is short, it's best to take one of the many daily flights from the Chilean capital Santiago to Calama. It's best to visit the Valle de la Luna as part of an organised tour and with a captive market some operators cut corners. Lonely Planet's guide to Chile will have the latest recommendations.

⑫ ANTELOPE CANYON, ARIZONA, USA

The closest town (and local airport) to Antelope Canyon is Page, a 15-minute drive to the northwest. To enter Upper or Lower Antelope Canyon you will need to be accompanied by a Navajo guide – there are outfitters in town or you should be able to meet a guide in the car park off Hwy 98. Upper Antelope is the more accessible from the car park (a 10-minute walk) and receives many more people. Lower Antelope is a more strenuous trip (involving some steps). The canyons were carved by water, which explains some of the safety constraints. Time is limited to an hour in either.

History of Immigrant New York. By 1860, 69% of voting-age New Yorkers were foreign-born: Irish, Germans, Russian Jews, Italians – all were now Americans. Each group had its own enclave in the city, such as Little Italy, and its own professions. Assimilation came slowly. Yet to wander through one of the world's greatest cities today and to notice the traces of its unique history is never less than an awesome experience. And if you want to amplify the awe, twice a year in May and July, the sun sets in perfect alignment with the city's urban canyons, so the sun is framed by glowing skyscrapers in a highly Instagrammable phenomena known as Manhattanhenge.

Some of the best streets in which to view the sunset are 42nd, 57th, 34th, 23rd and 14th. Interestingly, this is an entirely accidental spectacle; prehistoric people such as the Chaco did organise their settlements according to the movement of the sun and moon, but that didn't occur to New York's city planners.

New York is a man-made wonder but ⓮ Rio de Janeiro in Brazil is set in a harbour that is one of the great natural wonders of the world. Perhaps unusually, the city doesn't detract from its spectacular setting. Instead, the standard

Left: Upper Antelope Canyon in Arizona, US. Below, Cristo Redentor and Rio de Janeiro, Brazil.

response to standing atop Corcovado mountain and looking out over the bay, with its famous beaches and Sugarloaf mountain, is 'wow!' And behind you stands Brazil's most famous icon (with the possible exception of Pelé), the statue of Cristo Redentor, the 30m-tall Art Deco Jesus that was carved by French sculptor Paul Landowski and made with reinforced concrete and soapstone tiles in the 1920s. Tear yourself away from Ipanema and take the Trem do Corcovado funicular railway that runs up through rainforest to Christ's feet (tip: taking the first train means the fewest people around you at the top).

Corcovado is far from being the only awe-inspiring spot in Rio de Janeiro: witness the sun setting over both Sugarloaf and Corcovado mountains from Parque Natural Municipal José Guilherme Merquior. And for a glimpse into the future, check out the Museum of Tomorrow in an ostentatious building by Santiago Calatrava in the city's old port.

⓭ NEW YORK, USA

This city is on various airline routes, with John F Kennedy International Airport receiving most flights. However, LaGuardia is also useful for domestic arrivals and don't rule out Newark Liberty International Airport – it's connected by rail to Penn Station in New York and by bus to Grand Central Terminal. Accommodation is in demand all year round – beware of major events or holidays. Winter weekdays are often the most affordable. Getting around: the subway covers all Manhattan and extends out towards Brooklyn and Queens. You'll need a MetroCard, either as a seven-day pass or a pay-per-ride.

⓮ RIO DE JANEIRO, BRAZIL

Flights arrive at Galeão International Airport, which is about 20km (12 miles) from central Rio. Frequent buses (Bus Rapid Transport – BRT) serve the city (and other destinations), or you can take a taxi. For accommodation, the neighbourhoods behind the most famous beaches – Copacabana, Ipanema, Leblon – clearly carry a premium. Away from the beach, Santa Teresa, in the hills behind Lapa, is an appealingly arty neighbourhood with boutique hotels. There are also favela projects in what are known as 'pacified slums', such as Vidigal. Peak season is from December to March.

'From her beacon-hand glows worldwide welcome': the Statue of Liberty at the gates of New York.

One human feat that has weathered the test of time (in parts) is the **⓯** Great Wall of China. The Great Wall is really a collection of walls whose first fortifications – to protect the territory of the Qin dynasty – date from around 2300 years ago. Subsequent sections were built and maintained by the Han (2000 years ago), the Sui (1500 years ago) and in particular the Ming (from 1368 to 1644) dynasties. It is this Ming-era wall that is most visible today and it's the longest human-made structure in the world. In 1421, the Ming capital was moved to Běijīng, and it is around here that many well-preserved sections of the wall may be visited. Walking along this ancient construction meets Dr Keltner's definition of awe as an experience that gives you goosebumps.

In Greece there's another goosebump-inducing place: **⓰** Meteora and its monasteries. There is an ascetic school of thought among many world religions that certain places of worship should be built far from the distractions of other humans and as high as possible in order to allow for the proper contemplation of the divine (see also the cliff churches of Tigray in Ethiopia and the Tiger's Nest Monastery in Bhutan). In the Meteora region

of central Greece, 24 monasteries were built from the 11th or 12th centuries on top of rock pinnacles and cliffs: six still function, housing just a handful of monks or nuns. Access to the monasteries was deliberately made difficult, with most reached by a rope ladder or steps cut into stone – a certain amount of faith must have been required. Thankfully, it's a lot easier to reach this Unesco World Heritage-listed region from Athens these days.

On the other side of the world the indigenous Chacoan people of the Southwest USA dominated their region (now northwestern New Mexico) for thousands of years, their civilisation peaking from the 9th to the 13th centuries. During this pre-Columbian period they constructed extraordinary structures (houses, ceremonial and administrative buildings), linked communities by roads and trade routes, developed the sciences of astronomy, engineering and economics, and left behind some amazing rock art (with 1.5 million artefacts having been recovered already) at the **⓱** Chaco Culture National Historical Park, high in the desert.

The huge semi-circular houses were often aligned with the sun and moon; lines of sight allowed communication across the miles between houses and they had food and water storage. It's very isolated – all the better to allow your imagination to roam. The Chaco Culture Unesco World Heritage Site has been an International Dark Sky Park since 2013 so visitors are able to share in some of the wonder that the Chacoan people would have felt at the night sky; the Chaco Observatory at the visitor centre hosts public astronomy programmes from April to October and on the Winter Solstice.

John Muir, the renowned Scottish naturalist, activist and author who was the trailblazer for California's conservation movement, regularly experienced feelings of awe in the great wild spaces of that state and others. In *My First Summer in the Sierra* (the year was 1869), Muir discovered awe in not just groves of great pine and fir trees in the Sierra Nevada but in everything from the smallest squirrel to creeks rushing with 'champagne' water, the 'crystal' mountains around and even the 'stupendous' clouds above.

Of all the great places in the Sierra Nevada in which to experience awe, the most perfectly realised may be **⓲** Yosemite National Park. John Muir lobbied the US government to protect this wilderness of sheer rock walls, forest, meadows and waterfalls. The valley itself, just a tiny fraction of the entire park, is presided over by the 914m (2998ft) granite cliff of El Capitan, which may seem intimidating to some but inspires rock climbers to incredible feats on the various routes up its walls. It was first solo climbed by Royal Robbins in 1968; he later said 'a first ascent is a creation in the same sense as is

⑮ GREAT WALL OF CHINA

The wildest part of the Jiànkòu section of the Great Wall is best accessed from Xīzhàzi village, about 100km (60 miles) from Běijīng. You can take a series of buses from the Dongzhimen Transport Hub to first the town of Huáiróu then Yújiāyuán and finally Xīzhàzi. Or you can take a taxi from the regional capital or Huáiróu for extra cash. The wall runs along the top of the ridges around Xīzhàzi and you can access sections of it from various points along the valley. Note, however, that part of the wall has not been restored and may be dangerous; it is illegal to hike along the wall here.

⑯ METEORA, GREECE

The closest town to Meteora is Kalambaka, which can be reached by bus (with one change) or direct train from Athens, the latter being slightly quicker (five hours each way) and more comfortable. Most visitors stay in Kalambaka or the smaller village of Kastraki then walk to the monasteries (one to two hours away). There are accommodation options in both places, from campsites to hotels, but they do get booked up during Greek holidays. Peak season is from August (hot) to October (less so). Closer to Kalambaka than Athens is Thessaloniki, which is roughly a three-hour trip.

This page: the Great Wall of China. Overleaf: Rousanou monastery at Meteora in Greece.

a painting or a song'. And in June 2017, free climber Alex Honnold astonishingly pulled off the feat without a rope or safety gear. But you needn't scale rock faces to experience some of the wonder of Yosemite; if you don't want to join the crowds at the top of Half Dome there are numerous backcountry trails for multi-day adventures with fewer people (and more bears).

There are no bears on New Zealand's islands, nor any other large predators or venomous snakes. Instead there are plenty of strange indigenous critters (giant carnivorous snails, flightless birds, insects the size of your hand) and many intriguing pockets of wonder. ⓳ Waitomo Caves in King Country on the northwest of New Zealand's North Island is one such place. It's a huge network of water-filled channels, sinkholes and caverns, inhabited by constellations of glow worms only found in New Zealand. Visitors can float through the darkness of the caverns on inner tubes to view the illuminated cave ceilings. It's a popular trip so it might be difficult to focus on your surroundings, but as author Henry Miller once said: 'The moment one gives close attention to any thing, even a blade of grass, it becomes a mysterious, awesome, indescribably magnificent world in itself.'

One of the most mysterious and awesome natural

⑰ CHACO CULTURE NATIONAL HISTORICAL PARK, USA

This park in the northwest of New Mexico is remote, lying at the end of a dirt road (check the forecast for rain or snow); rangers suggest entering from the northeast on County Rd 7900. The small town of Bloomfield, with hotels and food shops, is about an hour's drive away. There are no supplies of food, water (or fuel) in the park, except at the visitor centre (open 8am-5pm). The park is open daily from 7am until sunset. Follow the Petroglyph Trail to discover the rock art. Bring binoculars.

⑱ YOSEMITE NATIONAL PARK, USA

San Francisco and Oakland airports are the international gateways to Yosemite, which lies a three-hour drive east. There are several entrances to the park from Hwy 140, Hwy 120 and Hwy 41; some access roads may be closed in winter through spring. Book accommodation via www.yosemitepark.com; camping reservations can be made at www. recreation.gov for spring, summer and autumn; note that peak season sites book up in minutes. Some campgrounds are first-come first-served.

Left: glow worms illuminate Waitomo Caves, New Zealand. This page: Yosemite Falls, California.

experiences is to witness the hatching of baby turtles. On remote, jungle-backed ➋ Sukamade Beach in Meru Betiri National Park at the eastern tip of East Java, Indonesia, sea turtles haul themselves up the sand to lay their eggs. After about two months the eggs hatch. Sukamade is a crucial nesting site for several species. You may see green, olive ridley, hawksbill and even huge leatherback turtles, which can grow to 2m in length and migrate 12,000km (7500 miles) between breeding and feeding areas.

However, it's the short journey across the beach, from hatching in its sandy nest to the ocean waves, that is the most dangerous of a turtle's life. Only a few hatchlings survive the gauntlet of crabs, gulls and poachers. The park rangers take a few eggs to hatch them safely and return them to the ocean. We don't yet know everything about sea turtles but being at Sukamade Beach on a tropical night, waiting for these tiny prehistoric creatures to hatch and inch their way down to the water under the moonlight will inspire viewers to learn more. Wonder, says Dr Keltner, is the aftermath of awe: 'Wonder is when we are delighted by that which surprises, and we are moved to find explanations and deep causes.'

⑲ WAITOMO CAVES, NEW ZEALAND

The caves are less than a three-hour drive from Auckland, New Zealand's largest city and main international gateway. They form a convenient sightseeing triangle with Rotorua and Lake Taupo in the centre of the North Island. Numerous operators offer trips through the caves on foot or by boat or inner tube. There are hundreds of caves in the area – the glow-worm cave tour takes about 45 minutes, but you can also see weta (giant insects) in Aranui Cave and stalagmites and stalactites in wheelchair-accessible Ruakari Cave. Visit November to April.

⑳ SUKAMADE BEACH, INDONESIA

The journey to Meru Betiri National Park involves river crossings and rough roads. The reward is 500 sq km of Java's finest rainforest, once home to the Javan tiger, and a coast that is a key hatchery for several turtle species including green turtles, hawksbills, olive ridley turtles and even giant leatherbacks. The dry season is from April to October; turtles may be present all year round. Approach the park from Jember or Banyuwangi by truck or 4WD vehicle. Stay overnight at a guesthouse at Sukamade to maximise the chance of seeing turtles, large or small.

Green turtle hatchlings race towards the ocean on Sukamade Beach in Meru Betiri National Park, Indonesia.

Anchored at Waewaetorea island in the Bay of Islands, New Zealand.

SERENITY

'How's the serenity?' asks Darryl Kerrigan in cult Australian film **The Castle**, enquiring after the Kerrigan family's holiday retreat. Well, there might have been serenity in Bonnie Doon but there's precious little elsewhere in our modern lives.

This chapter is about more than peace and quiet, important though that is. It's about disconnecting from the distractions of daily life (think how often you check your phone/social media/email), and getting better acquainted with yourself. A state of serenity means that your senses are receptive to the outside world but you're also opening up awareness of yourself. As Greek philosopher Socrates said, all philosophical teachings can be summed up in the commandment 'know thyself'. Serenity can also let your mind wander in surprising directions – a resting brain is known to aid creativity.

The calmest way to approach New Zealand's ❶ Bay of Islands is by boat, with the water splashing at the hull lulling you into a pre-emptively serene state. New Zealand is a famously nautical nation: many Kiwis keep a boat at their bach (or holiday cabin) and a significant proportion of the 4.5 million population are world-class sailors. So if you can inveigle your way aboard a boat, do so. As an archipelago of 144 islands lying on the northeast coast of the country around the towns

① BAY OF ISLANDS, NEW ZEALAND

The small local airport is Kerikeri. It's a 45-minute flight from Auckland, the nearest international airport. But it's only a three-hour drive north to the Bay of Islands from Auckland, through gorgeous scenery, so it might make more sense renting a car in Auckland and driving. There are also regular bus services in the region. Paihia has a good selection of budget accommodation and Russell a more boutique assortment. Peak season is December to March (plus the Easter holiday) and the coldest, wettest period is winter from June to August.

② LITTLE CORN ISLANDS, NICARAGUA

To reach Little Corn Island you must get to Great Corn Island. This big sibling has an airport with daily connections to Managua, the Nicaraguan capital, and the Caribbean hub of Bluefields. There are also regular if not reliably punctual boats from Bluefields to Great Corn Island, taking five or six hours. From Great Corn Island, take one of the daily pangas to Little Corn Island (bring waterproofing – it can be a rough crossing). On Little Corn Island, you can stay in the village or in one of the outlying and more exclusive abodes.

Top: almond trees blossom on Mallorca in February. Below: chill out in a hammock on Little Corn Island, Nicaragua.

of Russell and Paihia, the Bay of Islands is one of the hotspots of New Zealand yachting. The islands offer sheltered sailing from island to island, guided by warm breezes and often accompanied by bottlenose dolphins surfing the bow wave. In these warm, clear waters you might also encounter small pods of wild orcas feeding on rays they pluck from the sea floor. Lay anchor in a secluded bay and let the swell sway you to sleep.

Serene thought it may be, the Bay of Islands is far from undiscovered (not least because it was the site of the first British settlement in New Zealand) and tourism is a mainstay of the region. If you want fewer people around while you seek serenity, then you could head further up the coast to Cape Reinga (unsurprisingly

③ THE CYCLADES, GREECE

This group of more than 200 islands around Delos is southeast of the Greek mainland. The main holiday islands include Santorini, Mykonos, Ios, Paros, Naxos and Milos. The less-frequented outer islands include Sikinos, Kimolos and Anafi. Ferry services link most of the islands so visitors to the Cyclades tend to fly direct to Santorini (plenty of direct flights from European cities in the holiday season or via Athens) and take a boat onwards. Note that services to remote islands such as Anafi reduce in frequency outside July and August so check the timetables of Blue Star Ferries (www.bluestarferries.com) and ANEK Lines (www.anek.gr).

④ MALLORCA, SPAIN

Palma is a popular European tourist destination so there are lots of direct flights from all over the continent, with competitive prices. In the low season, there might be fewer flights but prices will still be keen. Likewise, although some places close in winter, it's still possible to find lots of great value accommodation from September to May. Palma is a chic and appealing city in which to stay but many people prefer to head north to Pollenca and its port resort on the north side of the island or into the Serra de Tramuntana in towns and villages such as Sóller and Valldemossa.

fewer people can tear themselves away from the Bay of Islands). Or you could go to some islands that are a bit further off the beaten track.

❷ The Corn Islands, about 70km off Nicaragua's Caribbean Coast, are a pair of equally idyllic retreats, peopled by a Creole population that makes its living from lobster fishing (and tourism). Great Corn Island is the larger but Little Corn Island attracts those on a quest for calm due to having no roads and therefore no cars. Instead, make your way from one palm-backed beach to the next via walking tracks beneath the mango and breadfruit trees. Just 750 locals live on Little Corn Island, often outnumbered by visitors during the high season, but it's possible to get away and find a quiet spot on a beach and soak up the tropical vibe. The north of the island is the most secluded and has the best beaches; the east coast is the more buffeted by wind and waves, perfect for beachcombing. To counterbalance the serenity – you can have too much of a good thing! – re-join the crowd at one of the bars or cafes, such as Habana Libre, for fresh lobster, drinks and dancing under the stars.

There's plenty of drinking and dancing on ❸ the Cyclades islands of Greece too. Mykonos might be known for its nightclubs and summer party scene but there are more than 200 islands in this group sandwiched between Greece and Turkey in the Aegean. You have to go a little further to find serenity – perhaps all the way to remote Anafi and its deserted beaches, or just to Naxos, the largest of the Cyclades, where it's easier to escape the crowds than on other islands and find a quiet corner.

For some serene retreats, it's not about where you go but when you go. For one third of the year the Mediterranean island of ❹ Mallorca is a heaving holiday isle. For the remainder of the year, from September to May, it's a tranquil haven of quiet coves, mountain hikes and bike rides, fruit, wine and blossom. The largest of Spain's Balearic islands is a diamond shape with, as a generalisation, sandy beaches to the east and the south, a modest mountain range called the Serra de Tramuntana running along the west coast, and central plains punctuated by hilltop monasteries. You can find pockets of peace in each during the autumn, winter and spring. After the sun-seeking crowds depart in August, expect warm autumn days, perfect for hiking along a rocky ridge-top path in the Tramuntana, where wild herbs and citrus trees fill the air with aromas. In late winter, from February, the almond trees, planted where the mountains meet the plain, come into blossom, their white petals floating in the breeze.

Mallorca must have been an especially devout place, judging by the number of monasteries and hermitages that dot the island. They were typically built at the

This page: sunset on Sanibel Island, Florida.
Overleaf: canoeing on Lac du Fou in La
Mauricie National Park, Québec.

tops of hills, perhaps to separate their residents from the lower orders, with the fortuitous advantage of also affording the monks the best views of the area. Some of these monasteries are now busy tourist attractions, such as the Santuari de Lluc, but others have escaped the limelight, such as the Ermita de Betlem. And at the Santuari de Sant Salvador and the Santuari de Nostra Senyora de Cura on the central plain, it's possible to stay overnight – they're as far from the Bacchanalian resorts as you can get. The latter lies at the summit of the Puig de Randa hill (those views again!), which has attracted hermits since the 14th century. Modern visitors can stay in one of 33 rooms for a very modest fee.

Say Florida to someone and they'll probably think of spring-break parties on the beaches, Miami's music scene or the numerous theme parks. But serenity can be experienced even in this most raucous of states. The wetlands are good place to start – the Everglades National Park has big skies and alligators, but the Chassahowitzka National Wildlife Refuge offers that most mellow of mammals, the manatee. On the Gulf coast of Florida, however, lies sleepy ❺ Sanibel Island, where the most demanding activity is hunting for seashells (the main street is named Periwinkle Way). This low-lying island is fringed by white sand beaches upon which fresh shells wash up after each high tide, in a sort of *Groundhog Day* for beachcombers. Focusing on a simple activity such as seeking seashells is a way of switching off from the hubbub of internal voices in our heads. But what about other distractions on Sanibel Island? It might be attached to the mainland by a road but it's not overrun by automobiles. And jet-skis are required to stay 300 metres away from the beaches. So, Sanibel is about as serene as Florida gets.

More than 150 placid lakes dot ❻ Park National du Canada de la Mauricie, one of Québec's most popular parks, and you only need to rent a canoe and dip in a paddle to experience some calming Canadian scenery. You might spy a moose splashing about the foreshore, common loons foraging for food, and if the season is right, gold, red and russet leaves of the birch, maple and poplar trees. This isn't one of Canada's wildest parks, but a well-run and accessible natural space that receives a lot of visitors. But in a canoe you can be your own boss and explore the five canoe routes (ranging from 14km to 84km (9 to 52 miles) in length) at your own pace. Lac Wapizagonke, with its waterfalls and beaches, is one of the most well-known lakes in the park (and has canoe rental facilities) but Alphonse, Écarté and Soumire lakes in the heart of the park are more secluded alternatives with fantastic wildlife-watching potential.

In Myanmar, ❼ Inle Lake is another famously serene body of water. This is a huge lake – 22km (14 miles) long and 10km (6 miles) across – and while it is a top fixture on Myanmar's tourist circuit, its size means that visitors can absorb its atmosphere without feeling crowded. The local Intha people, who live in houses standing above the water on stilts, get around in narrow wooden boats, and fish using conical baskets and the much photographed one-legged paddling technique. Using a long-tail motorboat, follow channels around the edge of the lake to discover sights such as the forest of stone pagodas on a hillside at the lakeside village of Inthein. These are largely Buddhist communities and 200 monasteries encircle the lake. On the west bank of the lake, north of Nampan, the Intha farm flowers, fruit and vegetables on floating trellises

If serenity is about being present in the moment then few activities encourage that feeling like surfing. Being out on the water, waiting for a pulse of energy that has

❺ SANIBEL ISLAND, FLORIDA, USA

Sanibel Island lies just off southwest Florida. Its closest airport is at Fort Myers, although international visitors will most likely arrive at Miami. You can drive onto the island over a causeway but note that parking is restricted (there's none on the roadside) and some areas will require a permit from the Sanibel Recreation Center. It's easier to get around on a rental bicycle. The local visitor centre (www.sanibel-captiva.org) maintains a list of available accommodation. For more information on visiting the JN Ding Darling National Wildlife Refuge, Sanibel Island's birdwatching hotspot, see www.fws.gov/dingdarling.

❻ LA MAURICIE NATIONAL PARK, QUÉBEC, CANADA

The main entrance to the park is St-Jean-des-Piles, near Shawinigan, which is about 160km (100 miles) east of Québec City. There's a second entrance at St-Mathieu. Both gates have information centres where you can pick up maps and the latest trail information – note that both centres are closed from late October to early May. There are three campgrounds (plus some tepees just outside the park), cabins, guesthouses and hotels in or near the park – see Lonely Planet's guides and website, and www.mauricietourism.com. Québec City receives international flights and it's easy to rent a car at the airport.

Left; fishing on Inle Lake in Myanmar and the stupas at Inthein.
Right: surfing at Noosa, Australia.

travelled thousands of miles before harnessing its power for a fleeting instant, is a zen-like experience that will develop a calm and confidence that carries over into your daily life. But it might help to have some surfing lessons first. **❽** Noosa on Queensland's Sunshine Coast has long attracted novice surfers. 'It's a magical place,' says former champion surfer Merrick Davis and founder of Noosa's Learn to Surf school. 'We can take someone who has never been on a surf board and by the end of a five-day programme they'll be able to take off on a green wave and turn left and right.' The natural features of this resort town's bay help: it's a warm-water point break with a sandy floor. 'A novice can go 200m on a 1-2ft wave here,' says Merrick.

With a grounding in the basics of board-riding, you're equipped to seek serenity on the ocean wave anywhere, if you can tear yourself away from Noosa's golden sunsets, blissful beaches and chilled-out atmosphere.

⑦ INLE LAKE. MYANMAR (BURMA)

Most people visit Inle Lake via Nyaungshwe, which isn't the easiest place to reach in Myanmar. Flying is one of the easier options: there's an airport at Heho, about an hour away by car. Daily flights arrive from Mandalay (one hour) and Yangon (two hours). There are also buses bound for Taunggyi that can drop you off, or private tour operators make the arrangements. Nyaungshwe has a growing number of guesthouses but book in advance from December to March. You'll need to pay a fee to enter the Inle Lake area, levied at the entrance to Nyaungshwe.

⑧ NOOSA. QUEENSLAND. AUSTRALIA

Noosa is about a 145km (90 mile) drive north of Queensland's state capital Brisbane, the closest international airport. The Sunshine Coast airport is a little closer for domestic flights. As one of Australia's top beach resorts, Noosa has a wide range of accommodation ranging from the laidback to the luxe (with the emphasis on the latter). Avoid school holidays and you might grab a bargain. The dry season is from May to November; September and October are prime picks, when the region is warming up again.

Scenes from a canalboat trip
on the Canal du Nivernais in
Burgundy, France.

Merrick's surf school also rents out kayaks if you want to
float away on another craft.

For a larger vessel and an even more sedate style,
take a canal boat down some of **9** Burgundy's 1200km
(745 miles) of waterways. Why Burgundy? Not only is
the French region home to tranquil canals and rivers,
including the Yonne, the Saone and the the Seille, but it
also produces wonderful wines, such as whites from the
terroirs of Pouilly-Fuisse and Puligny-Montrachet. When
the sun dips below the yardarm, open a chilled bottle
as you glide along, watching the world go by at walking
pace from your deck.

Canal boats can be hired from several operators in
the region. A favourite canal to explore is the Canal du
Nivernais, a 175km (109 mile) connection between the
Yonne river at Auxerre and the Loire at Decize to the
south, because it offers plentiful stop-offs at vineyards
and medieval villages. Take a day, a weekend, a week or
more to meander through the heart of France. Although
it takes only an hour to learn the basics of canal-
boating before you're set loose on the canal, avowed
land-lubbers might prefer to use a bicycle to explore
Burgundy's waterways – a bike path runs alongside most
of the Canal du Nivernais and you can always chill a
bottle of wine in the water after a day of pedalling.

The **10** Margaret River area of Western Australia is
another relaxing wine region worthy of slow exploration.
The wines are just as famed as Burgundy's, especially the
region's Chardonnay (from producers such as Vasse Felix
and Voyager Estate). Sadly, despite the name, you can't
tour Margaret River vineyards by boat, so wandering
wine seekers will have to use a car. But it's a beautifully
rural region with the added advantage of a long Pacific
shoreline from which to watch the sun go down.

Cruising Turkey's **11** Turquoise Coast on a *gulet* –
the traditional, broad wooden boats – adds a sense of
freedom to the serenity. Lie back on deck as the boat
rocks gently with the swell. A warm wind wafts the
scent of pine needles from the woods fringing the beach
just across the water, and the only other sound is the
distant rasp of cicadas. You can go to sleep on the deck,
under the bright stars, knowing that should another
boat intrude on your perfect bay, you can up-anchor
and move on to another quiet cove on this rugged coast
of Turkey's southwest. The heavily indented Turquoise
Coast features some familiar names: Bodrum, Marmaris,
Fethiye and Antalya. But it's easy to sail (or motor) away
from these hotspots and disappear around a headland.

There are dozens of options for cruising itineraries on
board a *gulet*, with plenty of sheltered bays around
Bodrum and a more exposed coast towards Antalya. But
one of the quieter stretches of coast is along the Kekova
region, where lie many Lycian ruins, relics of an ancient
(6th century BC) civilisation that pre-dated the Romans.
Look carefully into the clear sea when you're swimming
or snorkelling and you might spot submerged ruins.

On **12** Iriomote-jima, one of Japan's most distant
islands at the tropical southern tip of Okinawa
Prefecture, look out for something else beneath the
translucent waves: coral. This jungle hideaway, which
despite gaining popularity and boutique hotels in recent
years is still mostly covered by jungle and mangroves, is
surrounded by some of the best diving in Japan. There's
a curious serenity that comes with being absorbed in an
underwater world of colour and life, moving weightlessly
through an alien world. You don't need to be a scuba-
diver to appreciate this otherworld – just a snorkel and
a mask are enough to gain access, though you'll have to
take a boat trip out to the reef.

Away from Iriomote-jima's beaches, rivers lead inland

⑨ BURGUNDY, FRANCE

*This region's capital is
delicious Dijon, which
is just 95 minutes from
Paris by TGV and also
has direct rail links with
Charles de Gaulle airport,
Lille (connecting to
Eurostar from London),
Nice and other major
cities. Several motorways
also pass Dijon. Once
in Burgundy there are
local rail services (TER
Bourgogne) but a hire car
may be a better option
for visiting out-of-town
vineyards. There's a huge
range of accommodation
options from hotels and
self-catering to campsites
and canal boats – visit
www.burgundy-tourism.
com for bookings. Wine
town Beaune is an hour
south of Dijon by car.*

⑩ MARGARET RIVER, WESTERN AUSTRALIA

*Perth, capital of the state
of Western Australia
(and one of the world's
most remote cities) has
the closest international
airport. It's possible to take
a bus south to Margaret
River (up to six hours) but
easier to rent a car and
drive (three hours) if you're
going to explore. Margaret
River is a tourist hotspot at
weekends and especially
during holidays such as
Easter and Christmas. Visit
midweek for cheaper
accommodation and a
bit more peace and quiet.
There's a mild climate all
year round with more rain
in the winter.*

This page: cruising the Turquoise Coast at Kekova. Right: Pinaisara waterfall on Iriomote-jima.

⑪ TURQUOISE COAST, TURKEY

You'll need at least a week, ideally two, to sail Turkey's southwestern Turquoise Coast in a gulet. There are plenty of possible itineraries, from the sheltered bays around Bodrum to the more exposed coast towards Antalya. Many visitors fly to Bodrum or Dalaman, often transferring through Ankara or Istanbul. You'll need to book a berth on a gulet with a tour operator, so agree all the detailed arrangements in advance of payment. June and September, on either side of the hottest, busiest months, are ideal.

⑫ IRIOMOTE-JIMA, JAPAN

This Okinawan island is almost as far west as Japan extends. The nearest major regional airport is Ishigaki, on Ishigak-jima. There are few direct international arrivals so most travellers arrive via Naha, the capital of Okinawa, or Tokyo. From Ishigaki city, take one of the many daily ferries to Uehara port or Ohara port (taking about 30 to 40 minutes) on Iriomote-jima. Once on the island, there are affordable accommodation options, including four campgrounds, plus an increasing range of upscale hotels. Buses circle the island and many hotels also offer bicycles.

through watery mangroves and then up jungle-covered slopes. Some of the rivers can be explored by boat or kayak; if you paddle up the Hinai-gawa you will reach the base of the Pinaisara-no-taki, Okinawa's highest waterfall at 55m (180ft). The percussive power of the falls brings its own sense of calm, like a natural white-noise machine. Float or swim in the pool beneath the falls to benefit from swimming's known calming and therapeutic qualities, enjoying the connection with nature.

You may not wish to go swimming for as long in the seas off the southwest coast of England, but this surf-smashed shore is one of the most scenic parts of the country. As a result, it's hugely popular at holiday time – but there's a way around that. The ⑬ Roseland Peninsula is the region along the south coast of Cornwall around the River Fal and St Mawes and east towards Portscatho. It's arguably the most laid-back (and overlooked) corner of this beautiful county. And if you visit out of the summer season (July and August) the crowds thin further. Take a walk along a windswept clifftop and you could be all alone. Beaches here are hidden down narrow paths, sequestered between headlands – and there's a rich variety at hand, from broad sweeps of sand to secret coves of pebbles and rock pools. Seaside serenity is only a short walk away. But there are also tranquil places to discover inland. Head to the 13th- century St-Just-in-Roseland church, tucked away beside a quiet creek in a semi-tropical garden where you can hide behind huge leaves of

gunnera, to revel in a very green and serene setting.

At the opposite end of the British Isles you'll find beaches and a coastline that offers even greater serenity and beauty – largely because most people don't associate Scotland with sun, sea and sand. That's their mistake because Scottish beaches wow first-time visitors: when the sun is shining many have white sands, turquoise waters, and rich wildlife, including seals, otters and occasional cetaceans. And when the weather is inclement they display a steelier side, of vast grey-blue seas, raging white horses and buffeting gales that scour the daily grime from your mind.

You can find serene Scottish beaches on islands around the country, for example on the Summer Isles (reached via Achiltibuie) or on the Isle of Harris (check out Luskentyre Sands) but only one place combines beaches with ancient Viking settlements, shipwrecks and mystic stone circles: the archipelago of ⑭ Orkney. The beaches may have Caribbean colour schemes but the first settlers on Orkney will have had to have been a resilient bunch of seafarers from Scandinavia. They left behind a Neolithic site known as Skara Brae on the

⑬ THE ROSELAND PENINSULA, CORNWALL, ENGLAND

The Roseland Peninsula lies on the south coast of Cornwall; the Roseland Heritage Coast is to the east of Falmouth. It is studded with bays, beaches, headlands and tiny villages, which can all be reached via a rich network of footpaths. The National Trust (www. nationaltrust.org.uk) manages both locations. If you're driving, it's about five hours from London; there's also a high-speed train service to Penzance. Villages such as St Mawes get very busy during school holidays (July and August).

⑭ THE ORKNEYS, SCOTLAND

Kirkwall is the capital of the Orkney Islands, which lie off the northeast coast of Scotland. It has a small airport that receives flights from several British and European cities. You can also arrive by ferry, with regular services from Aberdeen on the mainland taking around six hours for the crossing. From Kirkwall you can also take ferries onwards to other Orkney isles and also the Shetlands. Check out accommodation options on the islands at Lonely Planet or www. visitorkney.com. The ideal time to visit is from May to October.

Strolling the broad sands of Pendower beach on Cornwall's Roseland Peninsula.

west coast of the main island that was revealed during a particularly savage storm in the winter of 1850. Also standing on Orkney's main island is the Ring of Brodgar, one of the most impressive stone circles in the British Isles. Standing here, surrounded by 36 of the 60 original standing stone circles, you can't help but let your mind wander.

The soft sugar-white sand dunes of New Mexico in the USA are far from the sea but their waves have the same mesmerising effect on visitors. The ⑮ White Sands National Monument protects much of this 700 sq km (270 sq miles) gypsum dune-field in the south of the state. It's an extraordinary place and there are a number of ways to experience its serenity. Five signposted day-hiking trails of varying difficulty venture across this vast sea of sand – the National Park Service notes that the longest, the Alkali Flat trail, is 'not flat'. But it should only take about three hours. If you want to stay longer, it's possible to camp at sites along the backcountry camping trail (with a permit). The silence and spectacle of the night sky in the desert is unforgettable. But take note of the Park Service's warning of unexploded ordinance because the National Monument is located on the edge of a US military missile range.

At 5.30am on 16 July, 1945, the desert's tranquillity was interrupted by the detonation of the world's first atomic bomb, codenamed 'Gadget', 100km (62 miles) north of what is now the White Sands National Monument. The crater created by this bomb test at the Project Trinity blast site spanned half a mile (0.8km) and the sand within it had been turned to glass the colour of jade. The fireball was 180m (590ft) wide and windows were blown in almost 200km (124 miles) away – which is something to think about if you're camping in the park. The next atomic device, Little Boy, was exploded over the city of Hiroshima three weeks later.

If you'd like to get an eerie sense of what a post-nuclear Armageddon sort of serenity might feel like, it's possible to visit the Trinity site twice a year, on the first Saturdays of April and October, courtesy of the White Sands Missile Range. Arrive very early in the morning because it's a popular open-day.

Sometimes, in the search for calm, it's not where you go but how you travel. Trains are perhaps the most relaxing mode of transport, with none of the hassle of air travel or the responsibility of driving. In 19th-century India, British colonists hop on board trains to the hill stations of the Himachal Pradesh, fleeing the heat of

Waves as far as the eye can
see at the White Sands National
Monument in New Mexico, USA.

The Rocky Mountaineer train
takes the scenic route through
Banff National Park in Canada.

India's plains. ⑯ Shimla was one such hill station and is still the most popular spot for holidaymakers. Until the British arrived, there was nothing at Shimla but a sleepy forest glade known as Shyamala (a local name for Kali, the Hindu goddess known as the destroyer of demons). A Scottish civil servant built a summer retreat here in 1822 and by 1864 Shimla was the official summer capital of the Raj. The Kalka-Shimla narrow-gauge railway was opened in 1906 and it's still the most relaxing way to arrive. The trains shimmy their way uphill through forest, passing through tunnels and over bridges; the journey takes about five very leisurely hours. The most civilised train to take is the Shivalik Express, which serves a meal each way and has wide glass windows for watching the scenery chug by. Shimla is a far more bustling place than it was back in 1820 but it's still cooler and slower-paced than the cities below.

In Canada, the ⑰ Rocky Mountaineer trains make

⑮ WHITE SANDS NATIONAL MONUMENT, NEW MEXICO, USA

The White Sands National Monument lies just to the west of Alamogordo, the largest local town. If you don't have your own wheels, it can be reached by Greyhound bus from Albuquerque and Roswell in New Mexico and El Paso, Texas. There's also a shuttle from El Paso International Airport. For accommodation, there's a Best Western and other hotels in Alamogordo plus a campsite at Oliver Lee Memorial State Park, which has views over the Tularosa Basin. There are basic campsites at the White Sands National Monument, for which you will need a permit from the visitor centre.

⑯ SHIVALIK EXPRESS TRAIN, INDIA

The Shivalik Express train, which runs from Kalka to Shimla, takes about five hours and leaves early in the morning (around 5am). It's almost uninterrupted with just one stop so breakfast is served en route (and dinner on the way back down from Shimla). Tickets can be purchased at any computerised Indian Railways ticket office – this is a tourist train so prices are higher than usual. Kalka can be reached by train from Delhi, the fastest taking just over four hours, although check timings and departures. Winter can bring snow but is also a great time to visit.

their way from Vancouver in British Columbia to Banff or Jasper in Alberta via some of the most sublime scenery in the world. The Romantic literary notion of the sublime – that heightened blend of awe, fear and delight, described by William Wordsworth in his poem 'Prelude' as he climbs Snowdonia in Wales – applies to this incomprehensibly vast and imposing landscape of snow-capped mountains, pine forests and glacier-fed blue lakes. But taking the train – as opposed to hiking or horse-riding through it as the Canadian pioneers would have had to – is the most serene way of experiencing it, that is, not too close but not too far. There's no hardship in lounging aboard a comfortable train with cinematically wide windows, although it might cross your mind that hundreds of navvies died laying these tracks.

There are several routes to take into Alberta but whether you disembark in Banff or Jasper, you'll be surrounded by national park wilderness where serenity is only a hike, bike ride or canoe trip away.

However, serenity isn't something only to be sought in wild landscapes. In a city it is perhaps an even more valuable commodity. Certain cities, even capitals, are naturally serene, for example ⑱ Vientiane. The languid capital of Laos is perhaps influenced not only by its French colonial occupiers, who left a legacy of delectable cuisine and boulevards lined with frangipani, but also by the Mekong River, which swirls implacably through the city and along Laos' border with Thailand. Vientiane is a city for *flâneurs*, who can absorb the city's sights, smells and sounds at walking pace (or, at most, by bicycle, freewheeling along the river bank). For a deeper sense of serenity, tap into the city's Buddhist traditions. Vientiane became a centre of Buddhist learning after King Setthathirat moved the capital of the Lan Xang kingdom to Vientiane from what is now Luang Prabang in the mid-16th century.

During this period many of Vientane's most beautiful *wats* (temples) were constructed. One of the oldest temples in Vientiane is Wat Si Saket but there are many other sacred spaces in the city in which to explore Buddhism's 'seven factors of enlightenment' – one of which is *passaddhi*, or tranquillity of the mind and body – that overcome Buddhism's 'five hindrances' of desire, ill-will, sloth, anxiety and doubt.

Serenity isn't only found in sacred spaces in a city; there are secular sources of it too. One of the most reliable – if a city has one – is a ⑲ botanical garden (or a physic garden). They're often green and exotic spaces where it is possible to slow down and smell the flowers in order to switch off from the stresses of the urban environment. Some of our favourite botanical gardens include Kew Gardens in London, where you can watch

The Shivalik Express
narrow-gauge train climbs
towards the town of Shimla
in the Indian Himalayas.

PASSION

Passion, the poster-child of 21st-century emotions, has travelled far from its origins. From the Latin 'pati' – to suffer – passion once described the suffering and death of Christ; transformed, it's now a millennial must-have, a necessity for a successful life.

Through history, passion's dark side – its uncontrollable nature, its tinge of madness – has been respectfully, even fearfully, acknowledged. In classical times, it was regarded with dubiousness. 'Subdue your passion or it will subdue you,' warned Roman poet Horace. By Benjamin Franklin's time ('if passion drives you, let reason hold the reins'), it was still being handled with care.

What happened to passion? Its edges rounded off, its wildness curbed, passion has been tamed for corporate seminars and self-help books. But as we travel the world we can see its mad traces – the romantic excesses, obsessive projects, wild desires, zealous pursuits. Although 'finding your passion' has become a cliché, when we travel it's easier to find ourselves in passion's path.

Commissioned in 1632 by Mughal emperor Shah Jahan as a mausoleum for his beloved wife, Mumtaz Mahal, the ❶ Taj Mahal – the world's best-known monument to romantic love – took more than 20 years, 20,000 workers and 1000 elephants to build. (Although some of the facts of the story are less than romantic. Mumtaz

① TAJ MAHAL, AGRA, INDIA

The Taj is in Agra, Uttar Pradesh, about 200km (125 miles) from Delhi. The fast train from Delhi takes two to three hours; many companies offer day trips but be aware that the journey is longer by road. The complex is on the right bank of the Yamuna River in a vast Mughal garden. It's open sunrise to sunset, every day except Friday. There are 12,000 visitors a day; to beat the queues, get there 30 minutes before the gates open. To avoid afternoon crowds and get beautiful sunset photos, take a car or rickshaw across the river to Mehtab Bagh gardens on the opposite bank.

② KHAJURAHO TEMPLES, MADHYA PRADESH, INDIA

Khajuraho domestic airport has connections to cities including Delhi and Varanasi, but getting there by other means is a challenge. There are few train connections (apart from one overnight train from Delhi), and bus journeys are long and arduous. Cycle- and auto-rickshaws can take you from Khajuraho village to the temples; a better option is to hire a bicycle from your hotel and roll through the rural byways, asking directions on the way. Guides can be hired at the temples but be choosy – go with a trusted recommendation or hire one via your hotel.

was one of three wives of the emperor – though she was his first and favourite – and she died giving birth to their 14th child, at the age of 39.)

Famed for its harmony, its scale, its symmetry and its craftsmanship, the Taj is often cited as one of the world's most magnificent buildings. Its interior, carved with Qur'anic verses, is inlaid with 28 types of precious and semi-precious stones – turquoise from Tibet, lapis lazuli from Afghanistan, sapphire from Sri Lanka. The exterior is made from marble mined in Rajasthan, some 250km (150 miles) away. It's this that gives the Taj its romantic glow, as the gleaming ivory-white marble changes colour throughout the day – dusky rose in the morning, milky white in the evening and glowing golden when the moon shines.

Not far away – in Madhya Pradesh, near the heart of India – is a different angle on passion. The temples at ❷ Khajuraho stand in imposing ochre-coloured clusters. Move in close, and you'll see that there's more going on than first meets the eye: carved into the soft sandstone are innumerable scenes of sensual pleasure, a little chipped and worn in places but remarkably pristine given they're over 1000 years old. Erected by Hindu and Jain kings between the 10th and 12th centuries, the temples and their erotic carvings are not for the prudish. Joyfully depicting a startling array of amorous activities from classic to contortionist, by man and woman, horse and elephant-headed god, in twos and threes and more, it's a giant orgy in stone.

Theories about the meaning and purpose of the carvings abound – are they the expression of a Hindu tradition treating sensual passion as a normal and essential part of life? Are they a depiction of Tantric sexual practice? Whatever their purpose, seeing these ancient figures cavorting as they glow yellow in the late afternoon sun is a unique combined experience of the sacred and the fleshly.

Of course, there are places whose page in the world atlas of passion is not earned by purpose-built edifice. Places where history, way of life, looks and reputation combine to spin an air of pure romance, a sense of magic. Places such as ❸ Venice. Blazing pink sunsets over canals darkening to purple, moonlit reflections shimmering on medieval facades, echoes of music floating along tranquil winding lanes – Venice is a city built for swooning, a damp monument to romance.

Enhanced, perhaps, by traces of the amorous escapades of its famous son, Giacomo Casanova. When he was born in 1725, Venice was the pleasure capital of Europe, celebrated for its gambling houses and beautiful courtesans. Casanova dabbled in careers from trainee priest to professional gambler, but it's as a lover he found his true talent and dubious immortality. His behaviour became too much for Venetian authorities – the final straw perhaps his affair with a nun on the island of Murano – and he was thrown in prison at the Doge's Palace for 'crimes against decency'.

You can trace his swashbuckling escape over the palace's roof – legend says that he stopped for a coffee on Piazza San Marco before fleeing by gondola. Today, the gondola ride for two complete with crooning gondolier is the clichéd climax of a Venice honeymoon, but our advice is to wander, half-lost and hand-in-hand, through the labyrinth of medieval alleyways and canals, imagining the hedonistic Venice of Casanova's day.

Across the top of Italy's boot is ❹ Cinque Terre, five tiny towns on the Ligurian coast, perched on rugged cliffs above the azure sea. Built over hundreds of years, starting around the 11th century, the impossibly picturesque villages are pastel-hued jumbles tottering

③ VENICE, ITALY

Spring in Venice is damp; summer – high season – is hot, crowded and expensive. Autumn brings warm days, thinning crowds and lower rates. In winter, expect chilly days, sociable nights and the fewest visitors. Flights arrive at Marco Polo airport, 12km (7.5 miles) outside Venice. A taxi from the airport costs around €50, alternatively you can take a bus or water shuttle. Transport around Venice is on foot or by vaporetto (public ferry) and the faster motoscafi. For a perfect romantic experience, take a vaporetto to peaceful Giudecca island, far from the tourist crush, find a secluded bench, and enjoy the view over the lagoon back towards central Venice.

④ CINQUE TERRE, ITALY

Genoa is the closest airport to Cinque Terre, being about 90km (55 miles) to the north. A train line connects all five villages directly with Genoa, Pisa and Rome. The villages are only between three and 20 minutes apart by frequent train. There are hiking options aplenty; the Sentiero Azzurro (Blue Trail) is the most popular. It's about 12km (7.5 miles) long, takes you to all five villages and requires about five hours, not including stops, to complete. High season starts after Easter and lasts through October, with May through August the busiest months. Cinque Terre is very popular, so book your accommodation at least three months in advance.

Previous page: the Taj Mahal in India. This page: the island of Burano, the best-kept secret in Venice, Italy.

This page: Manarola in Italy's Cinque Terre. Over the page: scenes from Yorkshire's Brontë Parsonage Museum.

on walls of rock, tumbling down into idyllic rocky inlets you can swim in, or just admire from a waterfront terrace, glass of chilled local white wine in hand.

Adding to the romance is their feeling of remoteness – the villages are largely inaccessible by road. Centuries-old walking trails criss-cross the region, so you can hike at leisure from one village to the next, pausing for refreshing dips in the ever-present sea. The coastal footpath from Riomaggiore to Manarola is called the Via dell'Amore, or Way of Love, just to clear away any doubts that the truly romantic way to explore the villages is on foot. It's a short walk significantly extended by the number of stops necessary to enjoy breathtaking views of wild sea, terraced farms and coastal forests.

5 Taormina, sitting on the eastern coast of far-flung Sicily, in a landscape of long beaches, rocky coves and tiny islands with spectacular Mt Etna as its backdrop, has held a dramatic allure for artists from Cervantes to Oscar Wilde. Perhaps its most famous conquest was the author DH Lawrence, who lived in a house (which is now a B&B) above the town during his voluntary exile from Britain after WWI.

It's believed that here he found the inspiration for his most notorious novel, *Lady Chatterley's Lover*, basing the title character on a local woman who scandalised the town by frolicking naked in olive groves with her lover. Another theory claims that the frolicker was actually his wife, Frieda, having taken up with a local mule-driver who became the model for Mellors the gamekeeper in Lawrence's racy book.

Infamous for his writing about sex, shockingly explicit for the time, Lawrence called himself a 'priest of love'. In Taormina, with its ancient Greek and Roman ruins, medieval winding streets and wild ocean views, the distant smoke from Mt Etna a constant reminder of the restless Earth, it's easy to understand how he found a temporary parish here.

If you set your mind to finding a landscape the direct opposite of southern Sicily, it's not unthinkable that you'd settle on the desolate, windswept moors of **6** Yorkshire. The literary contrast is striking too – while the exploits of Lawrence's characters got his novels banned for obscenity, the tale of Emily Brontë's *Wuthering Heights*, set on these stormy hills, is one of unconsummated passion. Despite its Gothic darkness and tragic turns, it's one of English literature's most loved romances.

Literary pilgrims come from around the world to hike their way across this stark landscape, where the Brontë sisters lived and wrote in the early- to mid-1800s. In *Wuthering Heights*, the moors' whirling wind and slashing hail symbolise the characters' uncontrollable passion for each other and the madness of their love.

Cathy and Heathcliff's undying love is a touchstone for romantic devotion, and the dramatic Yorkshire moors are its perfect, immortal backdrop.

It's just a hop across the Irish Sea to the site of a different kind of literary passion. James Joyce, then in exile from his hometown, once said: 'I want to give a picture of Dublin so complete that if the city suddenly disappeared from the Earth it could be reconstructed out of my book.' And in *Ulysses*, that's what he did.

The book distils the quotidian life of the city, as its hero, Leo Bloom, drifts across it. Joyce's evocation of Bloom's inner voice, the working mind of an ordinary man on an ordinary day, was the radical feat that made him the great modernist author. As he follows his characters from the post office on Westland Row to Barney Kiernan's pub to Sweny's chemist, Joyce preserves the soul of the city in stream-of-consciousness amber.

7 Dublin today can seem, to the literary traveller, like a Joyce-themed amusement park. Plaques bedeck the

---

⑤ TAORMINA, SICILY, ITALY

The nearest airport is at Catania, about an hour's drive to the south, with frequent bus connections to Taormina's centre. If you're travelling from mainland Italy, the train is shunted on to the ferry to cross from Calabria to Messina, one of the few train ferries left in southern Europe. The train from Messina to Taormina takes about an hour. Taormina is at its best out of season, especially in early spring (which starts in February this far south) or late autumn, for magnificent views of snow-capped Mt Etna framed by hibiscus, narcissi and orange blossom, and to avoid the summer crowds.

⑥ THE YORKSHIRE MOORS, ENGLAND

Wuthering Heights-related sights include buildings thought to have inspired those that feature in the novel, such as Top Withens near Haworth and Stanbury's Ponden Hall (now a B&B where you can stay in the room where Cathy's ghost knocked on the window). The Brontës' former home, the Parsonage in Haworth, is a museum to the lives and work of the sisters (www.bronte.org.uk). The nearest airports are at Manchester or Leeds, both about an hour from Haworth by car. Keighley is the nearest mainline train station, from there you can catch a steam train to Haworth, operating on weekends, holidays and during the summer months.

This page: Montmartre in Paris, France. Previous page: Isola Bella beach at Taormina, Italy.

city, on places he once lived (there were 19 of them) and those that feature in *Ulysses* and his other Dublin books. Joyce left Dublin aged 22 and never really returned; his evocation of his lost homeland is the passion of the absent son. Asked late in life whether he might ever return to Dublin, he answered, 'Have I ever left it?'

Joyce finished writing *Ulysses* in 1921 in Paris, a city still wearing the glow of La Belle Époque, an era that did much to earn it the title 'City of Love'. From the late 19th century to the start of WWI, a group of artists both French and foreign-born – among them Claude Monet, Henri de Toulouse-Lautrec, Pablo Picasso and Vincent van Gogh – settled on the hill of ❽ Montmartre and conjured the romantic image of bohemian life.

Annexed by the City of Paris only in 1860, Montmartre attracted middle-class pleasure seekers with its tax-free wine, *guinguettes* (dance halls) and cabarets (the can-can was born here at the famous Moulin Rouge).

⑦ JOYCE'S DUBLIN, IRELAND

Flights arrive at Dublin Airport, 12km (7.5 miles) from the city; the ferry from Holyhead in Wales takes about three hours. May, June and September are the most reliably sunny months, but summer can equally be a washout. Winter brings a charming contrast between chilly streets and cosy pubs. Joyce fans should visit on Bloomsday, 16 June, when devoted Joyceans don Edwardian costume, follow in the footsteps of the characters from Ulysses, and perform readings in locations such as the National Library and Glasnevin Cemetery, largely unchanged since Joyce wrote about them.

⑧ MONTMARTRE, PARIS, FRANCE

Winters in the City of Love can be brutally cold but atmospheric; summers can be gorgeously warm but crowded. Spring and autumn, which bring different varieties of beauty (choose from blossoms and tulips or golden red leaves), are best. Montmartre overlooks the city from a hill on the Right Bank and can be glimpsed from all over town, thanks to the opulent Sacré-Coeur Basilica on its peak. Metro line 12 runs to Abbesses, from where you can wander Montmartre's charming streets. Or take line 2 to Anvers and walk to the steps leading to Sacré-Coeur.

San Francisco's historic streetcars run along Market St from the Castro to Fisherman's Wharf.

Artists came for the cheaper rents, village feel – still palpable today – and picturesque views, and to live *la vie bohème*: a life of romantic poverty, passionate love affairs and ardent creativity, often fuelled by absinthe, which was devotedly hedonist.

Immortalised in the works of many of its denizens, the spirit of Montmartre is best captured in the posters and paintings of Toulouse-Lautrec, who lived and worked on the hill, frequenting its bars and dance halls, vividly capturing local impresarios, prostitutes and cabaret stars, imbued with the drama, movement and joie de vivre of his milieu.

It's not too long a bow to draw parallels between *fin de siècle* Montmartre and San Francisco in the 1950s, where a small group of writers created a community and a lifestyle based on art and hedonism, rejecting materialism and exploring sexuality. These new bohemians lived boldly and wrote about their wild lives, uncensored, in madly expressive prose and poems. They were the people Jack Kerouac describes in his 1957 book *On the Road*, as '…the mad ones, the ones who are mad to live, mad to talk, mad to be saved, desirous of everything at the same time…'.

Their traces are easily found in today's San Francisco, especially around ❾ North Beach – Caffe Trieste where they hung out (and is unchanged since); Vesuvio, where Allen Ginsberg drank as he wrote his epoch-defining poem *Howl*; and the legendary City Lights Bookstore, which published it (cue more obscenity charges). Find one of the city's numerous spoken-word events or poetry slams – direct descendants of the Beats' performances – to chase a fix of their artistic zeal. You may even see some of Ginsberg's 'angelheaded hipsters', updated for the modern world.

Artists who devote their lives to their passions have a habit of coming to tragic ends. Jack Kerouac was dead from alcoholism at 47; Toulouse-Lautrec, that plus syphilis, at 36. Vincent van Gogh exemplifies this story, and he left behind a stunning body of work that translates passion into form and colour.

Of course, Vincent van Gogh's story is not so simply explained. He was an artistic genius who, it's believed, was probably suffering from what would today be recognised as a mental illness. Some retrospective diagnoses suggest his periods of intense focus and gargantuan output could signify mania, others believe that the steady labour of painting was his method to keep the demons at bay.

The Dutch artist spent just over a year near the end of his life – he shot himself in 1890, aged 37 – in ❿ Arles, where he painted about 200 works that are seen as the pinnacle of his career. Whatever the nature of his inner struggle, he was deeply inspired by the landscapes of Provence. The intense sun, big skies, pastel-coloured houses and lush landscapes – sunflowers, cypress trees and verdant fields – filled his canvases with a rush of intensity. In Arles today, you can explore the places he painted, and marvel at the power of his artistic vision.

We can only wonder what kind of hallucinatory magic Vincent van Gogh would have made of the spectacle at ⓫ Namaqualand, South Africa's outback – the reality is more vivid, more stunning than even his most vibrant palette. Every spring, the normally arid plains burst into a kaleidoscope of colour, as a carpet of wildflowers covers the gently rolling landscape. It's a volatile exhibition – an estimated 4000 different species of plant (more than 1000 of which are found nowhere else) may appear, depending entirely on the weather. Every year brings a different formula, a different selection of flowers. It's as if all the florists in the world have congregated

⑨ NORTH BEACH, SAN FRANCISCO, USA

Planes fly into San Francisco International Airport, a 30-minute BART (train) ride from downtown SF. North Beach is in the northeast, adjacent to Fisherman's Wharf. With its long-standing Italian heritage and status as one of the city's happening nightlife spots, it squeezes cabarets, jazz clubs, galleries, red-tableclothed restaurants and gelato parlours into less than a square mile. Climb to Coit Tower, atop Telegraph Hill, for breathtaking views over the city and bay. San Francisco's weather is unpredictable. Visit in spring or early autumn, when clear sunny days are most likely.

⑩ ARLES, PROVENCE, FRANCE

Arles is close to the south coast of France, about four hours from Paris by train. The closest airports are at Marseilles and Nimes, both around 30 minutes by train. You can walk the same streets as van Gogh did, where the places he painted are marked by steel-and-concrete 'easels' displaying photos of his paintings, for fascinating comparison. The Fondation Vincent van Gogh (www.fondation-vincentvangogh-arles. org) is a must-see, with its rotating van Gogh-themed exhibitions. Arles is also famous for its Roman ruins, which include an amphitheatre, theatre and baths.

⑪ NAMAQUALAND FLOWER ROUTE, SOUTH AFRICA

The wildflower display is showcased on a series of drives centring on the towns of Garies, Springbok, Kamieskroon and Port Nolloth, roughly 500km (310 miles) north of Cape Town. Specialist tours are popular and should be booked in advance; you can take a day trip from Cape Town but this will only reach the southern end of the route. Precise timing depends on the weather, but the display appears mainly in August and September. As well as the driving route, hiking and cycling trails allow up-close enjoyment, some providing picnic spots and overnight facilities.

⑫ VALLÉE DES ROSES, MOROCCO

El-Kelaâ M'Gouna, the village at the heart of the rose cultivation area, is roughly a six-hour drive southeast of Marrakesh, crossing the Atlas Mountains to Ouarzazate, the gateway to the Sahara. The highlight of the harvest is the Rose Festival, drawing some 20,000 people to the village for three days of song and dance, feasting, markets and a chariot procession through a shower of rose petals. Timing depends on the harvest, but the festival is usually in early May. As there are few hotels in El-Kelaâ M'Gouna, you may need to stay in Ouarzazate and travel up the valley for the festival.

to throw open their doors on the biggest Valentine's Day celebration on Earth.

It's the rose that is the classic flower of love, reeling in poets from Robert Burns to Robert Frost with the beauty of its flower, its swoon-inducing scent, and the thorns on its stem, a sharp reminder to those who underestimate the dangers of passion.

No one is sure how roses first came to the M'Goun Valley, high in Morocco's Atlas Mountains. Legend says they were carried here centuries ago from Damascus – the species that grows here is the Damask rose, cultivated for its intense perfume. During the main growing season between April and mid-May, the ⑫ Vallée des Roses produces more than 3000 tonnes of wild roses. They sprout from hedgerows, bloom along stone walls, and tangle the borders between farmers' fields, filling the air with their entrancing, treacly perfume.

Every day before dawn, women gather the roses by hand and sell them to co-operatives dotted along the valley, where the petals are distilled into rose oil, for use in the finest perfumes. And some are enjoyed by the rose pickers as tea, when they take a well-deserved break from their fragrant toil.

The original passion came with a definite article and a capital P. The Passion refers to the end of the life of Jesus Christ – his arrest, trial, torture and death. The most pious and devoted Christians, those destined for sainthood, have imitated this agony. One of them began his life in late 12th-century ⑬ Assisi, born into a prosperous

Left: Berber women from the rose-growing villages of Morocco. This page: Skilpad Wildflower Reserve, Namaqualand.

family, and ended it in devout poverty, surrounded by followers (the first Franciscan friars) and, it's believed, displaying the stigmata – a spontaneous recreation of the wounds suffered by Christ during the crucifixion.

Saint Francis of Assisi is perhaps most widely known as the patron saint of animals. There are many stories about his love of the natural world – how he preached to birds about God's love for them (he's often depicted with a bird perched on his hand), how he tamed a savage wolf, convincing it to stop attacking local villagers and lie sedately by his feet.

As the birthplace of the most beloved of saints, Assisi has been a place of pilgrimage for centuries. Framed by the long, undulating hills of Umbria, it's a Unesco-listed treasure crowned by the enormous Basilica of Saint Francis, constructed immediately after his death and packed with frescoes by medieval masters. Soaking up the serenity at dusk, when the day-trippers are gone and the town is shrouded in reverent silence, is when the spirit of Saint Francis can most truly be felt.

Passion leads people in all kinds of unlikely directions. What moves a young woman born into middle-class

The hilltop town of Assisi in Umbria, Italy; this region has suffered recent earthquakes.

London suburbia to spend most of her life in the jungles of Africa, living among wild chimpanzees? Jane Goodall's two passions – animals and Africa – made it inevitable. An unlikely researcher with no academic training, she made one of the 20th-century's most important scientific observations when, one day in 1960, she witnessed a chimpanzee take a twig, bend it, strip it of leaves, stick it into a nest and use it to spoon termites into his mouth. In that moment, humans lost their perceived unique position as toolmakers, and the rules of nature changed.

This happened in ⑭ Gombe Stream National Park in Tanzania, a long-term living laboratory of primate behaviour as well as home sweet home to groups of well-observed chimps – and you can take a chimp-tracking safari to see them. It may take hours of hiking through thick vegetation, and there's no guarantee of a sighting. However, all going well, you'll find yourself in the midst of 30 wild chimpanzees, unconcerned by human presence, going about their daily lives in their jungle home. It's a magical experience.

A single-minded passion such as Jane Goodall's can change our understanding of the world. Or it can create something truly marvellous. The ⑮ Basilica de la Sagrada Família has been under construction since 1882; there are hopes that it will be finished in 2026 to mark the centenary of the death of its designer, Antoni Gaudí, who worked on it for 43 years. Great cathedrals have always taken centuries to complete and, as he said, 'My client is not in a hurry' – referring to God.

Gaudí's inspiration for La Sagrada Família came from the natural world – its colours and curved forms, but also its geometry, which he translated into incredibly complex and detailed designs. He wanted the interior to be 'like a forest'. Columns twist up to a ceiling decorated by vast geometric stars; greens, blues, yellows and reds pour in through stained-glass windows, casting dappled light over stone carved with grapes, cherries and flowers.

As work has continued over the decades, the basilica's tourist-pulling power has grown and the cult around the architect strengthened. Some say he should be sainted. The determination to remain true to Gaudí's vision is intense. So you can be sure when you stand inside this fantastical structure that you're experiencing something close to how the artist's singular vision was intended.

Frida Kahlo and Diego Rivera are the great obsessive love story of the art world. When they met in 1928, he was a celebrated established artist, she a novice of raw and original talent. Despite him being already married,

⑬ ASSISI, UMBRIA, ITALY

There is a small airport serving Perugia close to Assisi, but you're more likely to fly into Rome, about three hours away by train. It's also possible to visit Assisi as a day trip from Rome or Florence, though you'll miss the chance to soak up the ambience of peaceful, crowd-free streets at dusk. Central Italy can get very hot in summer, while spring and autumn are often warm and pleasant. Assisi is a pilgrimage town and there are religious festivals and holidays through the year, when crowds surge. Christmas is a lovely time to visit, with nativity scenes in every nook and cranny of the town.

⑭ GOMBE STREAM NATIONAL PARK, TANZANIA

From Tanzania's largest city, Dar es Salaam, you can fly to Kigoma; from there, the only way to Gombe is by boat. The safest, most comfortable (if expensive) option is to arrange a charter with an established company. Gombe is best visited during the dry season, from May to October. There is a daily fee simply to be in the park. Overnight facilities are rugged and camping is restricted in order to protect visitors from aggressive baboons. But those travellers willing to put up with such challenges are almost certain to be rewarded with glimpses of chimps.

Left: the interior of Gaudí's Sagrada Familia in Barcelona. This page: a portrait of Frida Kahlo in Mexico.

A samba school parades in the Sambadrome during Rio de Janeiro's annual carnival.

and his unattractiveness (Frida herself described him as a frog standing on its hind legs), her multiple health issues, and their 20-year age difference, they commenced a torrid love affair.

They divorced, and remarried. Each had many affairs: she with Leon Trotsky and Josephine Baker, he with her younger sister. And they continued to create outstanding works – his were grand political murals (both artists were committed Communists), hers folk-Mexican, surrealist, hyper-confessional paintings, which made her among the most beloved and collectible of modern painters.

Frida and Diego are inextricable from ⑯ Mexico City, and visiting there is a discovery tour of their lives. You can see many of Rivera's lavish, colourful murals, including those that include a portrait of his wife among crowds of revolutionary workers and costumed revellers. And you can visit places in which they lived together, decorated with their art and belongings, arranged as if

⑮ GAUDÍ'S SAGRADA FAMÍLIA, BARCELONA, SPAIN

The basilica looms over Barcelona from the Eixample district, a grid of graceful streets in the city centre. While you're there, visit other, smaller-scale Gaudí masterpieces Casa Milà (aka La Pedrera) and Casa Batlló; further afield is Parc Güell, his fanciful public park. Many companies run tours of Gaudí sites; queues can be long so buy tickets online. La Sagrada Família's continued construction is now funded by tickets bought by visitors, plus some private donations. Barcelona airport is 12km (7.5 miles) southwest of the city, there are bus and train links as well as taxis.

⑯ FRIDA AND DIEGO'S MEXICO CITY, MEXICO

Rivera's mural depicting the history of Mexico is at the Palacio Nacional. And one of his most famous, Dream of a Sunday afternoon in Alameda Central Park, is in what is now the Museo Mural Diego Rivera. Look carefully and you'll find Kahlo among the painted figures in both. La Casa Azul (The Blue House), where she grew up, is now the Frida Kahlo Museum, displaying her paintings and mementoes. The Museo Casa Estudio Diego Rivera y Frida Kahlo is the couple's former home – two modernist buildings, one for each artist, joined by a walkway.

the two could return at any moment to continue working together in death as they did in life.

Head south, way south, to Tasmania, an island 240km (150 miles) south of the Australian mainland, and the last stop before the South Pole. In sleepy Hobart, rising like a rusting hulk from the Derwent River, is the ⑰ Museum of Old and New Art, an adult Disneyland that could be the world's most unlikely, unique and challenging collection of art.

The single-minded vision of a maths prodigy, polymath and professional gambler, MONA could only exist as a result of personal obsession. No art council or group of curators could assemble a collection as daring and irreverent as David Walsh has created. A waterfall whose droplets spell out the day's most-Googled words, a wall of plaster-cast vulvas, a giant mechanical digestive system that produces one perfect bowel movement each day – this is art designed to question, to challenge, to provoke. A day spent at MONA is by turns bamboozling, awe-inspiring and hilarious – 'a mashup of the lost city of Petra and a late night out in Berlin', in the words of writer Richard Flanagan.

Rather than a display of discrete acquisitions, the effect of MONA is that of a complete work of art in itself. Walsh has said that the art is not important to him, and perhaps it's the act of collecting that's his true passion; or perhaps the museum is his insistent, obsessive search for an answer to the question: 'what is art, anyway?'

Beyond the wild devotions, unpredictable voyages and incredible achievements our passions can produce is the simple, sensual pleasure of being alive in the moment. Almost nothing does it better than dancing, and there's no more passionate dance than tango. Conceived in the mid-19th century in the port neighbourhoods of Argentina and Uruguay, influenced by African and European immigrants, tango is a mixture of the joyful and the melancholy, both totally elegant and incredibly sexy. And it's the ardent spirit of ⑱ Buenos Aires, expressed in movement.

You'll see street tango dancers, all high kicks and low dips, lightning-fast footwork and spins. But to find the heart of tango, visit a tango dancehall, or *milonga*, where you'll find *tangueros* from toe-stomping amateurs to old-time local *milongueros*, who've been gliding across the same boards for decades.

Things don't really get going until well after midnight; after 3am at some places. If that's too late, there's Milonga del Indio, every Sunday at San Telmo after the famous market. Professional dancers put on an impressive show, then amateurs from near and far gather on the dance floor as dusk falls, beneath trees hung with coloured lights, for a steamy open-air tango. Why not join them?

It takes two: learning to tango at a
dance class in Buenos Aires.

While we're on the dance floor, let's twirl by **19** Seville, the home of flamenco. Unlike tango, flamenco dancing is a performance art rather than a social dance, and in western Andalucía it's in the blood, a living culture, mixing the gypsy music of the Romani people with the rhythms of North Africa that were brought to southern Spain by the Moors.

At the heart of flamenco is *duende* – an untranslatable word that speaks of a passionate state of emotion and expression. It's easier to recognise than to define, and in Seville you hear it everywhere. You can see highly choreographed, quality performances at a *tablao*; but for something rougher and more rambunctious, go to a *peña* (a small private club) or a bar. There you'll find something more like a party, with mad jamming and spontaneous outbreaks of dancing. It may not be note perfect, but it's the expression of flamenco at its most raw and its passionate best.

It's time to hit the world's biggest party. At heart, the festivals known as 'carnival' are Catholic feasts to mark the start of Lent and its 40 meat-free days. It's all in the name: in Latin, *carne* means 'meat' and *vale*, 'farewell'. And there's nothing like impending deprivation to inspire a full-blooded free-for-all.

In **20** Rio de Janeiro, this traditional celebration merged with the popularity of local samba schools in the 1930s. Samba music is rapid-fire, with African influences and an infectious beat; the dance styles are varied but unmistakably samba: swaying, lively, dramatic. Today, the parades of the 100-odd local schools, all deeply connected to their communities, form Carnival's extraordinary set piece, which is held in Oscar Niemeyer's purpose-built Sambódromo stadium – extravagant floats, brilliantly costumed performers and an audience of 72,000.

But the real party is in the streets, where hundreds of free-spirited gatherings (*blocos*) turn Rio into one enormous dance party. Each centres on a band playing samba, or maybe old-school bossa nova, hip-hop or funk. Each is followed by hundreds or thousands of costumed revellers, moving to the intoxicating drumbeat under a pulsing sun, closing the city down to all but dancing, caipirinha-drinking revellers. It feels as if all the world is here, and all the world is a party.

---

17 MUSEUM OF OLD AND NEW ART, HOBART, AUSTRALIA
Flights arrive into Hobart from mainland Australia. A shuttle bus runs from the airport to central Hobart. MONA is 11km (7 miles) north of the city; the most scenic way to travel there is on the dedicated fast ferry along the Derwent River, departing from Hobart's picturesque waterfront. The museum's semi-rural compound includes a winery, brewery and fine-dining restaurant, so there's sustenance in easy reach. Allow a full day to see and taste everything on offer; or stay on site at one of the art-filled luxury pavilions. mona.net.au

18 TANGO IN BUENOS AIRES, ARGENTINA
Flights arrive at Argentina's main airport, Ezeiza, 22km (14 miles) southwest of Buenos Aires. A taxi to the centre takes around 45 minutes. Pick up the Tango Map from a tourism kiosk to find a list of all the city's milongas; note that most charge an entry fee and be sure to dress the part. Be aware of the rules – in some milongas, men and women sit on opposite sides of the room, inviting and accepting dances purely by eye contact. Never block anyone's view, especially that of a woman who is sitting by herself, and avoid eye contact – unless you want to dance.

19 FLAMENCO IN SEVILLE, SPAIN
International and domestic flights arrive at Seville's airport, or a train from Madrid takes about two and a half hours. Visit in spring, before the intense summer heat hits. Try flamenco at the Museo de Flamenco (www.museoflamenco. com), where the nightly shows in an intimate, elegant space are excellent and you can take a half-hour class if you get there early. The cultural centre Casa de la Memoria de Al-Andalus (www.casadelamemoria. es) has a good reputation for its performances in a 16th-century patio with skilful musicians who are unafraid to improvise.

20 CARNIVAL, RIO DE JANEIRO, BRAZIL
The date of Lent and thus Carnival changes each year (it's usually in February) but blocos are held throughout the city's party season, beginning in mid-January. Temperatures can reach 30-35°C and anything goes, so dress up as much – or as little – as you want. Around one million visitors hit Rio for Carnival, so book accommodation well in advance (and Sambódromo tickets if you want to see the big parade). Blocos are organised by neighbourhood, so it's easy to stumble across parties close to wherever you stay.

JOY

For Monet, it was all about colour. For Da Vinci, it lay in understanding the ways of the universe. To Emily Dickinson, it was in 'the mere sense of living'. We're talking about joy, that most sought-after of feelings. It's sometimes used as a synonym for happiness, and it can be that. But it can also be more, a deeper, more profound sense of physical, emotional or spiritual wellbeing. Research has shown that while achieving something – winning an award, finishing a marathon, buying a fancy car – brings a fleeting happiness, it's the journey to get there that brings the joy. Shakespeare wrote, 'Things won are done, joy's soul lies in the doing.' We've collected a list of 'doings' that will help you find your own joy.

As Louis Armstrong sang, it's a wonderful world, and there's no better way to feel that joy in your bones than by immersing yourself in the jazz vibes of Satchmo's birth city. Because really, is there any place with more joie de vivre than ❶ New Orleans? The Big Easy has had it anything but easy, from yellow fever epidemics to Hurricane Katrina to federal neglect.

But despite – or perhaps because of – these hardships, the city has a culture of exuberance, of celebrating life out loud. This is a city where, on any day of the week, a parade might materialise seemingly out of nowhere, with hundreds of revellers in sherbet-coloured suits and

① NEW ORLEANS, LOUISIANA, US

You can fly directly to Louis Armstrong New Orleans International Airport from most major cities in the US as well as several international ones, including London and Toronto. Though there's no bad time to visit, summer can be oppressively hot. If you want to get there for Jazz Fest, that's in late April to early May. If you want to hit (or miss) Mardi Gras, that can fall on any Tuesday between 3 February and 9 March, depending on the year, though celebrations start in January. Preservation Hall (www. preservationhall.com) has concerts nightly at 8pm, 9pm and 10pm.

② HAVANA, CUBA

Thanks to President Obama's easing of the US's longtime embargo against Cuba, you can now fly to Havana from 10 US cities, including New York, Miami and Los Angeles. As always, you can also fly to José Martí International Airport from major cities in Canada, the UK, Europe and Latin America. A Florida–Cuba ferry service is coming soon. December through May is the best time to visit, weather-wise, while summer through October is hurricane season. Watch Afro-Cuban dancing and drumming at the Centro Cultural El Gran Palenque, or catch its folk festival in January or July with a cohort of fans.

Previous page: Daniel Farrow at Preservation Hall, New Orleans. This page: scenes from Havana, Cuba.

feathered headdresses rolling down the streets to the boisterous clanging of a brass band. Anyone can join in these so-called 'second lines', strutting through the streets just to feel the ecstasy of being alive.

Catch world-class jazz at places like the venerable Preservation Hall, a weather-beaten 18th-century building where the house band cuts loose every evening to uproarious applause. Or shake it at any one of dozens of clubs in the French Quarter, where trumpets and trombones wail late into the night, and fans sip chilled drinks. In spring, the city explodes with jazz, zydeco, gospel, blues and more at Jazz Fest, attracting some half a million gleeful music fans.

Then, of course, there's Mardi Gras, that immense outpouring of joy and music (and alcohol) that marks the beginning of Lent each year. Just try not to be happy with a po' boy sandwich in your hand, a string of cheap purple beads around your neck and an entire marching band in full feather parading past.

---

③ CANAL ICE SKATING, AMSTERDAM, THE NETHERLANDS

Fly to Amsterdam's Schiphol airport from major cities across the world. From the airport, take a direct train to the city. Or arrive by rail at the Centraal Train Station from other European cities. Canal skating only happens when there's an extended cold spell, which is unpredictable. January and February are generally the coldest months. Check the local weather ahead of time; it will report canal freezings. If you don't get lucky, there are a number of outdoor ice rinks open all winter. The huge Jaap Eden rink and entertainment complex is open October to March, with disco skating on Saturday nights.

④ CHRISTMAS MARKETS, GERMANY

German cities hold Christmas markets from late November to Christmas Eve and sometimes beyond. Nuremberg's Christkindlmarkt is especially famed. You can reach the Bavarian city by air from a number of European and Turkish cities, or travel by rail via larger German ones. Cologne's markets are also famous worldwide. Fly to Cologne Bonn Airport from many major European and Middle Eastern cities, and a handful of American ones. Or go by train to Köln Hauptbahnhof. If these cities don't suit your itinerary, there are terrific markets in Berlin, Munich, Frankfurt, Dresden, Stuttgart and almost any other city you could think to visit.

Across the Gulf of Mexico you'll find a similar full-throated exuberance on the streets of old ❷ Havana. There's nothing quite as life-affirming as watching Cuban dance, whether it's traditional *danzón*, hip-circling *casino* (Cuban-style salsa), or – as is most common among young Cubans – gyrations to the rhythms of reggaeton. Cubans have a reputation as some of the world's best dancers, for good reason. Here, children learn to dance on the feet of their parents before they've even learned to walk, and dance is part of the national elementary school curriculum.

You can see the cream of the crop in action at professional venues such as the Centro Cultural El Gran Palenque, where you'll be hypnotised by hours of energetic Afro-Cuban dancing. Or go ahead and dig the kitschy vibes of old-school cabarets like the Tropicana, where feather headdress-wearing señoritas kick up their legs beneath the stage lights. Or just wander the streets of Habana Vieja on a steamy Saturday night and listen for music. This is a city where any front stoop gathering or park BBQ can easily turn into an impromptu dance party of the highest order.

Swap the sultry Cuban weather for the face-chapping cold of a Dutch winter to experience a joyful rush unique to a cold climate: ❸ outdoor ice skating. When the temperature drops below 4°C for at least four nights in a row, Amsterdam officials block off boat traffic on some of the city's famed canals. Then everyone – young couples, parents with parka-clad children, grandmothers in hand-knitted scarves – straps on their skates. As snow sifts like icing sugar from the winter white sky, fly past 17th-century row houses and modern glass shop facades, stopping only to tighten your laces or fuel up with a deep mug of hot chocolate.

Canal skates are always spontaneous – no one knows much ahead of time when or if the weather will cooperate. Sometimes the city goes years between freezes cold enough for canal skating. So when it does happen, it's all the more magical and spontaneous. Sometimes an unexpected joy is the best kind of all.

Experience more winter joy across the border in Germany, with one of the loveliest Christmas traditions on the books. For weeks leading up to December 25, cities across the country host ❹ Christmas markets in their central squares, providing a haven of warmth and light amid the chilly dark evenings. These markets are enchanting affairs, with twinkly stalls selling traditional handicrafts such as nutcrackers, wooden toys and blown-glass ornaments against backdrops of cobblestones and medieval cathedrals. Sip a tankard of clove- and anise-spiced Glühwein ('glow wine', a wonderfully appropriate name) while wandering the Christkindlesmarkt of old town Nuremberg, which has been drawing visitors for nearly half a millennium. Or pick out *baumschmuck* (tree ornaments) while munching warm roasted chestnuts at Cologne's Alter Markt, its stalls trimmed with fir branches and fairy lights.

There's something primal about our need for light in the darkness of winter – the candles of the Hanukkah menorah, the yule logs of the ancient northern European pagans, the lamps that decked Roman halls during Saturnalia. Germany's Christmas markets give us that light in darkness as well as something else crucial during the blackest months of the year – togetherness.

Next door in Austria, ❺ Vienna offers another one of life's most uplifting experiences: world-class live classical music. The grand city has been home to an inordinate number of the world's top composers – Mozart, Beethoven, Haydn, Schubert and Brahms, to name a few – and its Baroque concert halls are still some of the most transporting places to hear a symphony or concerto. Head to the Neoclassical-style Musikverein, whose opulent Golden Hall feels like being inside a giant's music box. The hall was inaugurated in 1870, and has hosted most of the great composers of each era since. At the 1441-room Baroque-style Schönbrunn Palace, once the imperial summer getaway, luxuriate in an evening of architecture, dinner and music. You'll tour the richly decorated apartments of Emperor Franz Joseph, dine by candlelight on the terrace, then savour music by an ensemble from the Palace Orchestra. They specialise in light, delightful Mozart overtures and arias, the kind of music almost guaranteed to raise your mood several notches.

In the summer, parks across the city become open-air concert venues, and many of the city's most dazzling cathedrals host regular performances as well. Top it all off with that other venerable Viennese delight: pastry. Music is a joy for your ears, but rich chocolate Sachertorte or warm, yeasty Apfelstrudel is a joy for the belly.

But if you really want a hardcore sugar rush, then head back across the Atlantic. No place enjoys its sweet treats with more childlike joy than the ❻ United States (Americans eat more than 126g of sugar per day, more than twice the global average!). Chocolate, in particular, contains a number of mood-lifting chemical compounds, including the stimulant theobromine and the amino acid tryptophan, which the brain uses to create serotonin.

You can build an entire vacation around chocolate at Hersheypark, in Hershey, Pennsylvania, home of the iconic Hershey Chocolate Company. The century-old theme park has all the usual thrill rides, plus music and firework displays, while the adjacent Hershey's Chocolate World features a build-your-own chocolate bar station, a 4D 'chocolate mystery' experience, and a tram ride through a mock chocolate factory full of manically singing characters. And then, of course, there's the airplane hangar-sized gift shop, where you can buy a Reese's Peanut Butter Cup the size of a dinner plate or a pillow shaped like a Hershey bar.

If that's not enough sugar for you, head north to Vermont for a tour of Ben & Jerry's ice cream factory, which includes a free sample and a gander at the 'Flavor Graveyard', a mock cemetery honouring bygone pints (RIP Rainforest Crunch). Or head south to Atlanta, the home of that most iconic of sugary American exports,

⑤ CLASSICAL MUSIC, VIENNA, AUSTRIA

Vienna International Airport connects the city to pretty much any major destination in the world. From the airport, take the Vienna S-Bahn line S7 or the City Airport Train to reach the city centre in 15-25 minutes. The Wien Hauptbahnhof is the city's main train station and has connections all over Central and Eastern Europe. There's live classical music throughout the city on any given night, everywhere from the vast Baroque concert halls to tiny wine bars. The Vienna tourism department's website (www.wien.info) has a calendar and plenty of information about the various venues.

⑥ AMERICAN SUGAR RUSH, USA

Hersheypark (www. hersheypark.com) is in the Eastern Seaboard state of Pennsylvania. The nearest airport is Harrisburg International Airport; the park is a 20-minute drive away. There's also an Amtrak station in Harrisburg. Or drive in from Philadelphia (2 hours), Washington DC (3 hours) or New York (3 hours). The Ben & Jerry's Factory (www. benjerry.com/about-us/ factory-tours) is in the New England town of Waterbury, Vermont, a 15-minute drive from the tiny state capital of Montpelier and a 3-hour drive from Boston. The World of Coca-Cola (www.worldofcoca-cola. com/) is in downtown Atlanta, a city connected to many international destinations by air.

Skating on Amsterdam's frozen
Prinsengracht in the Netherlands.

Coca-Cola. Here, at the World of Coca-Cola, a half-hour Coke propaganda tour is the price of admission to the real fun, a tasting area where you can sample dozens of Coke products from around the world. You'll leave burping, buzzed and sugar-high.

For a sense of childlike joy, head up to Rochester, New York, to the ultimate playroom: the ❼ Strong National Museum of Play. The 9,300 sq metre (100,0000 sq ft) museum claims the world's largest collection of toys, dolls, children's books and games, many of which are part of interactive exhibits. Some of the exhibits have a more historical bent – check out the handmade first-ever Monopoly game, or displays of classic toys like Erector Sets and teddy bears.

Other items are just about the pure fun of being a kid – riding the carousel or the old-fashioned mini train, dancing to moving electronic display screens in the DanceLab, walking through a giant kaleidoscope. Or wander through the steamy indoor butterfly garden, waiting for a shimmer-winged butterfly to land on your shoulder. Children will be in a state of bliss; ditch your adult preoccupations and join them.

But perhaps you're looking for joy of a more adult variety? In that case, Kentucky's ❽ Bourbon Trail may be the jolliest trip of your life. Made from at least 51% corn and distilled in charred oak barrels, real Kentucky bourbon is practically a religion in the American South. Which makes the Bourbon Trail – a collection of Kentucky distilleries offering tours and tastings – a

Right: a distiller at Willett Distillery in Kentucky. Left: Monarch butterflies gather in Mexico.

particularly spiritual pilgrimage.

Sip a golden glass at Buffalo Trace, the nation's oldest continuously operating distillery, sample a single barrel bourbon amid the Spanish Mission-style buildings of Four Roses, or savour the spicy notes of a double oak aged Jim Beam. Tour guides will teach you all you ever wanted to know and more about the liquor, which was first distilled in Bourbon County around 1789. But this isn't just about the distilleries, this is also about the road trip through the glorious Elysian landscape of central Kentucky. From Bardstown to Lawrenceburg to Frankfort, you'll drive down empty stretches of road winding through the limestone-rich bluegrass hills, passing fields of goldenrod, stands of tulip poplars, and million-dollar thoroughbreds grazing behind stone fences. On a clear day, puffy cumulus clouds dotting the blue sky as if sheep in a meadow, you don't need a drop of liquor to feel entirely content in the world.

⑦ THE STRONG. NEW YORK. USA

Rochester is a post-industrial city in far upstate New York. It's served by the Greater Rochester International Airport, which has flights to a dozen US cities as well as Toronto. A flight to New York City takes just over an hour, whereas the drive is about 5.5 hours. Frigid temperatures and snow make for frequent travel delays in the area in winter. The Strong Museum of Play is open Monday through Thursday 10am to 5pm, to 8pm on Friday and Saturday, and from noon-5pm on Sunday. General admission is $14.50. See www.museumofplay.org for more details.

⑧ BOURBON TRAIL. KENTUCKY. USA

Many distilleries on the Bourbon Trail are clustered around either Frankfort or Bardstown, Kentucky. Both are within an hour's drive of Louisville, home to an international airport, your best bet for flights from the central or eastern United States. The Kentucky Distillers' Association's Bourbon Trail website has information on distilleries, hotels, and safe ride services for after you've been imbibing. It also has info about tour companies and organised trips if you'd rather not drive at all. Expect higher prices in the two weeks before the Kentucky Derby on the first weekend of May. See www.kybourbontrail.com.

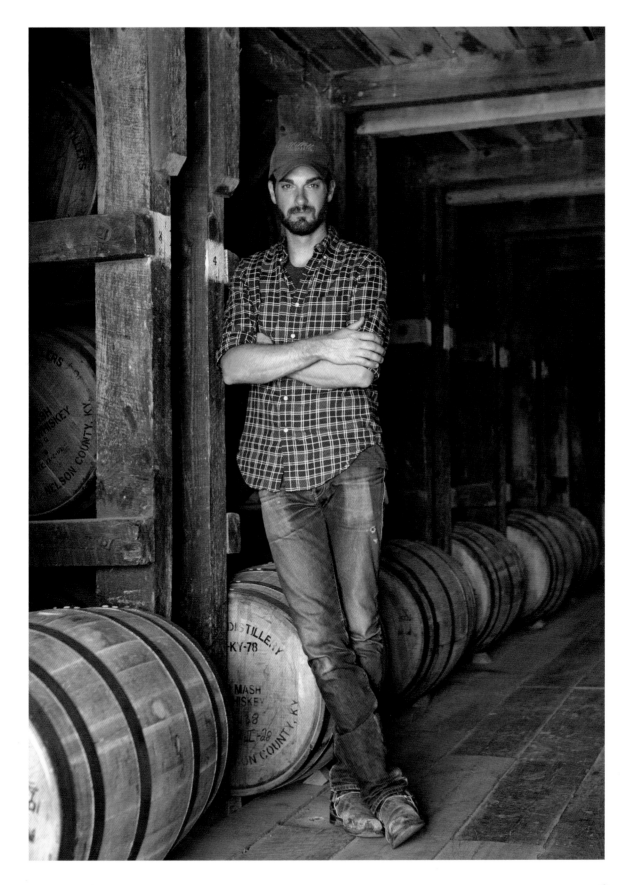

The space shuttle Discovery blasts off from the Kennedy Space Center in Florida in 1988.

Head down to Mexico for another kind of journey: the end of the monarch butterflies' long migration south. Each fall, millions of the iconic orange and black butterflies travel nearly 5000km (3000 miles) from the northern United States to the state of Michoacán in Mexico's central western highlands. Travel to the mountainous ❾ Monarch Butterfly Biosphere Reserve, where constellations of the butterflies cluster on dense stands of oyamel firs like strange fluttering flowers. In the mornings, as the sunlight begins to stream down through the thin mountain air, the butterflies warm and take to the skies in clouds of shimmering colour. To see them rising together, orange wings glinting in the chill morning air, is truly an occasion for wonder. No butterfly will make the entire migration, as their life spans are only about a month long. Their children, grandchildren and great-grandchildren will complete the trip back to the US and Canada. Which is another lesson about joy, isn't it: enjoy life while you can, for it is as fleeting as it is beautiful.

Witness flight of a different sort at NASA's ❿ Kennedy Space Center in Florida, where rockets depart Earth for the heavens. Just try to not tremble with excitement when you see the eruption of flame and feel the rumble of liftoff as thousands of kilograms of aluminum alloy streaks spaceward across the calm Florida waters. It's technology, but it sure feels like magic. No matter how troubled the world may seem, there's something deeply cheering about the fact that man can make this happen. From the Kennedy Space Center Visitor Complex, you can see launches from Kennedy Space Center and the nearby Cape Canaveral Air Force Station. You've got to be flexible to catch a launch – schedules are rarely set in stone, as technical issues and the vagaries of weather can easily scuttle plans. If you don't get lucky enough to arrive on a launch day, you can geek out at the visitor centre's exhibits. Gawk at the shuttle Atlantis, retired after 126 million miles in space. It's suspended in a vast building, but you can get close enough to nearly smell the jet fuel. Or make like Neil Armstrong on the simulated shuttle launch ride.

Speaking of flight, here's an item for the top of your joy bucket list: ⓫ learning to pilot a plane. In the words of airplane inventor Wilbur Wright, the feeling of flying is 'one of perfect peace mingled with an excitement that strains every nerve to the utmost'.

Imagine taking off from an airstrip in a single-engine Cessna or a Piper PA-28, the tiny plane trembling like a hummingbird as you rise into the thin morning air, sunlight streaming sideways through your windshield, fields unfurling like a quilt below. Not only is it beautiful and thrilling, but there's something incredibly gratifying about mastering a machine like this, of bending steel to your whims. Whether you just take an intro flight with an instructor, or commit to the whole licensing process, going airborne is an unmissable experience. As Wilbur Wright's brother and co-inventor Orville said, 'The exhilaration of flying is too keen, the pleasure too great, for it to be neglected as a sport.'

But maybe water is more your medium than air? Then head to Victoria Falls, the thunderous sheet of water crashing 108m (354ft) into the ⓬ Zambezi River, on the border of Zambia and Zimbabwe. The rafting beneath the falls is some of the best in the world – class V rapids that boil like a witch's cauldron, tossing boats like bath toys. Join a guided expedition, which will lead you through the narrow Batoka Gorge and down rapids with names including Oblivion, Gnashing Jaws of Death and Devil's Toilet Bowl. Longer expeditions will allow you time to camp on the sandy river banks, looking out for hippos, baboons and slit-eyed Nile crocodiles, and

⑨ MONARCH BUTTERFLY BIOSPHERE RESERVE, MICHOACÁN, MEXICO

The butterflies begin arriving in the reserve in late November, peak in number in February, and are gone by the end of March. There are three areas open to the public: El Rosario, Sierra Chincua and Cerro Pelón. The nearest large cities are Morelia, the capital of Michoacán, and Mexico City, both about a two-hour drive. You can take a bus from either of these cities to Angangueo, the gateway town to the reserve. In Angangueo you can join a group tour, or hop on one of the truck taxis that shuttle tourists to the reserves in high season.

⑩ KENNEDY SPACE CENTER, TITUSVILLE, FLORIDA, USA

The Kennedy Space Center Visitor Complex is located on Florida's central Atlantic coast. The city of Orlando is less than an hour's drive away and has an international airport that serves cities across the globe. There is no public transportation. From the visitor's centre you can see launches from both the Kennedy Space Center and the nearby Cape Canaveral Air Force Station. A one-day adult admission ticket costs $50, while children are $40. Check out the website ahead of time for launch schedules, but know that everything is tentative: www. kennedyspacecenter.com.

A rainbow arcs over Kalalau Valley
on the Na Pali Coast of Kauai, Hawaii.

toasting your narrow escapes with gin and tonics. Yes, it's a treacherous trip, but that's the point – a recent study showed that people who are more willing to take risks are happier with their lives. So plummet into Gnashing Jaws of Death and come out elated on the other side. Oh, and go now – a controversial proposed hydroelectric dam some 54km (34 miles) downriver from Victoria Falls threatens both the whitewater and the waterfall itself.

But yes, we understand that gut-churning rapids are not to everyone's taste, and that's just fine. One of the most joy-sparking places in the world is one of mellow hills, sun-bleached lighthouses and fields of lavender. And the animals are of a rather gentler variety too. No man-eating crocs here, just wallabies, seals and tiny blue fairy penguins.

We're talking about South Australia's ⓭ Kangaroo Island, a 4400 sq km (1700 sq mile) chunk of land between mainland Australia and the Southern Ocean.

⑪ LEARNING TO PILOT A PLANE

You can learn to fly pretty much anywhere in the world. But it makes sense to choose a place with good weather, or you'll risk being grounded for more days than you're aloft. Central Florida is popular for this reason, as are parts of Australia and South Africa. America's Federal Aviation Administration requires 40 hours of training to earn a private pilot's licence, though most students train for significantly longer. The average cost of the training hovers around $10,000 (£7750), but will vary greatly depending on the location, the school and the instructor.

⑫ RAFTING THE ZAMBEZI, ZIMBABWE OR ZAMBIA

Trips down the Zambezi depart from both the Zimbabwe and Zambia sides of the river. If you start in Zimbabwe, you'll be based in Victoria Falls town. If you start in Zambia, you'll leave from the city of Livingstone. Both have airports serving a handful of large African cities, including Cape Town, Johannesburg, Addis Ababa and Harare. Dozens of guide companies work the river; it pays to go with one of the older, more established ones. Day trips cost around $200 (£150), while week-long expeditions can run to more than $2000 (£1500).

A slow, rambling road trip around the island brings a new delight with every turn. Here is a sugar sand beach full of slumbering sea lions. Here's a small farm selling smoke-perfumed honey from bees that feast on the blossoms of the stringybark tree. Here's Little Sahara, a patch of giant sand dunes you can hurtle down in a rented toboggan. Here's a hiking trail meandering through a meadow populated by curious wallabies and western grey kangaroos. Spend your morning paddling a kayak along the rocky coast, eyes out for dolphins, fur seals and snowy white fairy terns. Then fuel up at one of the island's simple country cafes, gorging on local marron (a type of crayfish), and cheese from sheep that graze the banks of the Cygnet River. In the evening, join a tour to visit one of the fairy penguin colonies. Then head back to your campsite to sip a glass of local shiraz and gaze up at the Southern Cross, a feeling of perfect bliss settling over you from head to toe.

If you were to ask a child to draw a picture of 'joy', we're guessing they might hand you a wobbly drawing of a rainbow. Hop halfway across the Pacific to another island, Hawaii's Kauai, to see the most elusive species of the genre: the ⑭ double rainbow. One of Hawaii's many

Left: Pennington Bay on Kangaroo Island and, below, one of the islands' namesakes reclines on the beach.

nicknames is 'the rainbow state', thanks to the unique blend of climate and topography that makes rainbows more common here than practically anywhere else on earth. Of the archipelago's eight main islands, Kauai has the most prime rainbow-spotting location: the majestic scalloped cliffs of the Na Pali Coast. Getting here takes commitment: there are no roads along this 24km (15-mile) stretch, so the only way to enter the emerald-shrouded cliffs and wild canyons is by foot, kayak or helicopter. Which makes it all the sweeter when you spot an enormous rainbow arcing from mountain to ocean. The rainbows tend to appear just after a rainstorm, when the sun begins to gleam again. Luckily for rainbow-spotters, Kauai is one of the wettest places on the planet, so you'll have plenty of chances. Double rainbows can be a daily occurrence here, and keep your eyes out for triple rainbows as well – once thought to be a myth, they were substantiated by science in 2011.

Catch rainbows of a different sort in San Francisco, at the city's annual ⑮ Pride Parade. More than one million people gather each June, many marching exultantly down Market Street – vest-wearing 'dykes on bikes' revving Harleys, drag queens peacocking in glitter, beads and feathers, municipal employees riding elaborate floats, leather daddies cracking whips. It's a noisy, gleeful celebration of being yourself, and it's been

⑬ KANGAROO ISLAND, SOUTH AUSTRALIA,

Kangaroo Island is part of the state of South Australia. You can either take a 30-minute puddle jumper flight from the capital city of Adelaide, or drive from Adelaide to Cape Jervis (2 hours), then take a 45-minute ferry. Either way, you'll want to either bring a car or hire one on the island. The township of Kingscote is the island's main centre of tourism, while Penneshaw is the ferry port. There are a handful of inns and B&Bs around the island, though you'll have to book well ahead. There's also plenty of camping.

⑭ RAINBOW HUNTING, KAUAI, HAWAII, USA

There are direct flights to Kauai from the US mainland, as well as from Honolulu and Kahului. As there are no roads on the Na Pali Coast, you'll need to park at a trailhead and then hike. Permits are necessary for some parts of the trails. An easier way to visit is via an organised boat tour. Half-day catamaran trips run at about $150 (£115) per person, and include lunch and snorkelling. You can also kayak the coast, either on your own or as part of a tour. As for rainbows, whether or not you see one is down to weather and luck.

Right: revellers at San Francisco's Pride parade. Left: a musician of the San Francisco Lesbian/Gay Freedom Band.

going on for nearly 50 years, long before corporations such as Facebook and Home Depot would have dared sponsor floats. Join the crowds cheering them on, and feel free to express yourself to the max: unicorn suits, tutus and jockstraps are all valid dress choices. The event has grown into a celebration beyond the parade – shake it at a warehouse dance party, join an open-air sunset cruise or hum along to the Gay Men's Chorus' renditions of '90s R&B.

An equally colourful and joyous celebration happens on the other side of the planet every year. In India, Nepal, and other places with large Hindu populations, the beginning of spring means **16** celebrating Holi, aka the 'festival of colours'. The festival celebrates the triumph of good over evil, the forgiveness of wrongdoing, the joys of love and the coming of spring. Revellers toss coloured powders in the air and shower each other with water via water balloons and squirt guns, turning everyone into walking works of rainbow art. Afterwards everyone cleans up and enjoys special Holi treats – date-stuffed pastries, condensed milk sweets, spiced lentil puffs.

The colour-throwing aspect of the celebration has become famous worldwide, with people of all creeds joining in colour parties or 'colour runs', where runners are coated in powder as they pass mile markers. But these celebrations overlook the larger meaning of the festival, which emphasises love, tolerance and forgiveness as well as new starts. It's a time to pay off debts, to mend fences, to cleanse oneself of negative emotions. It's this aspect, perhaps, that brings the most joy – while tossing coloured chalk is fun, science has shown that forgiveness lowers anxiety and makes people healthier. 'Forgiveness has a lot of long-term benefits,' says Everett L Worthington, a psychology professor and author of several books on the subject. 'So in the long-term it no doubt contributes to more happiness.'

In Japan, the beginning of spring is marked in a very different way: with the arrival of the fragile pink **17** cherry blossoms. No place in the world celebrates a flower with such reverence; aristocratic Japanese have been picnicking beneath the blooming sakura trees for a thousand years. Today, everyone joins in the custom, arranging *hanami* (viewing parties) to take in the flowers from the best angle.

The *sakura* season begins in the southern island of Okinawa and slowly spreads northwards, reaching the ancient capital of Kyoto by late March and the northern city of Sapporo in late April. A few weeks later, they're

15 PRIDE PARADE, SAN FRANCISCO, USA

San Francisco Pride is a weekend festival held at the end of June each year; the parade is on the Sunday of the festival. There's a Trans March on the previous Friday, and a Dyke March on the Saturday night. Watching the parade is free; there's a voluntary donation requested if you enter the adjacent Celebration area. If you want to march yourself, you need to register your group ahead of time. Get to San Francisco by flying into San Francisco International Airport, 21km (13 miles) from downtown. It's connected to the city centre by BART train and bus. See www.sfpride.org.

16 HOLI, INDIA, NEPAL & WORLDWIDE

Holi takes place between late February and mid-March, depending on the year, but the exact dates can vary by region. While the night before Holi is about cleansing and prayer, the day of Rangwali Holi is all about colour. It's observed throughout India and Nepal, and wherever there's a sizeable population of Hindus. London, Singapore and Toronto all have various large, commercialised, secular celebrations over the day. If you want to view a traditional village Holi celebration in India, there are a number of tour companies based in large Indian cities offering just that.

gone. While they're here, ascend Mt Yoshino, whose slopes have been covered in sakura trees for some 1300 years, stopping to gaze down at the clouds of pink that carpet the valley. Stroll through Kyoto's Imperial Palace Park, its winding gravel paths blanketed with fallen blossoms. Or join the crowds in Tokyo's Ueno Park, who turn *hanami* into raucous, beer-fuelled parties. For the Japanese, the cherry blossoms symbolise the ephemeral nature of the seasons and of life itself, an attitude connected to Buddhist notions of celebrating the impermanent. So feel free to meditate on that, or simply lay beneath the frilly branches of a *sakura* tree, delighting in the joy of nature.

The fleetingness of life is faced with head-on boisterousness during ⓲ Day of the Dead, celebrated across much of Latin America. This may seem a strange addition to a chapter on joy, but journey to Mexico to find out why it's not. Here, every 2 November, families travel to local cemeteries to decorate loved ones' graves with colourful crepe paper, sugar skulls and wreaths of marigolds. They'll dance, sing and tell funny stories about the departed, and give offerings of tequila, candied fruit and any other foods the dead might have enjoyed in life (say, Fanta, or McDonald's French fries). The festivities are a mashup of pre-Hispanic beliefs and Catholic rituals.

Previous page: Holi in India. Right, a Day of the Dead parade in Mexico City. Above: cherry blossom below Mt Fuji, Japan.

Recently, celebrations have expanded to include enormous parades, with revellers dressed as Catrinas (skeletons in large hats) dancing to wild drum music. This isn't about mourning; it's about celebrating a reunion with the dead, who are said to travel back from the world beyond for just one day. Join the festivities and find your attitude towards death transform.

Travel to Sweden to partake in another festival with pre-Christian roots. In Sweden, June's ⓳ Midsummer Eve is the country's most beloved holiday, celebrated since the Middle Ages. If you've ever experienced an icy, sunless, monochromatic Swedish winter, you'll understand the intoxication (literal and figurative) with which the Swedes greet the nearest Friday to the longest day of the year.

Stock up on traditional Midsummer fare – new potatoes, herring, cream, strawberries and, of course, bottles and bottles of schnapps – and make for the Stockholm archipelago, a cluster of nearly 30,000 rural islands and islets dotting the Baltic Sea. This is where seemingly all of Sweden gathers to celebrate the sun with an abandon worthy of its Viking ancestors.

¡PA'L PANTEÓN!

In the morning, children skip through the golden fields, gathering clover, cow parsley, daisies and other wildflowers to make crowns and adorn the maypole, the pagan symbolic phallus central to the fete. Later, everyone dances around the maypole, singing ribald songs, feasting on fish, berries and cake, and downing shots of schnapps. If the spirit moves them, they might leap into the sea for an impromptu swim. Since the sun barely goes down, the party goes on into the morning.

Another Nordic country, Denmark, regularly tops the list of 'Happiest Countries in the World', making it a go-to place for experiencing joy. The best way to do it? That most Nordic of pastimes, **20** cycling. Hop on for a tour of Copenhagen, perhaps Europe's most bike-friendly city, where everyone from pre-schoolers to the prime minister cycles to school or work. Fly past the rainbow terraced houses of the Nyhavn waterfront, stop to say hello to The Little Mermaid statue on the Langelinie promenade and try to glimpse the royal family at Amalienborg Palace. Is cycling the reason Danes are so happy? Scientists suggest the real reason may be their excellent work-life balance, strong social safety net and egalitarianism. But the feeling of gliding down cobblestone lanes, fresh salt air in your lungs, must have something to do with it.

Below and right: midsummer festivities in Stockhom's archipelago.

⑰ CHERRY BLOSSOM VIEWING, JAPAN

Cherry blossom season runs from March through April, with blossoms spreading south to north. The Japan Meteorological Corporation releases an annual cherry blossom forecast of bloom dates, usually in January. Tokyo and Kyoto, both classic blossom-viewing locations, are highly accessible – for Kyoto, fly to Osaka's Kansai International Airport and take a 70-minute train to Kyoto Station. Cherry blossom season draws enormous crowds so hotels may be booked years in advance.

⑱ DAY OF THE DEAD, MEXICO

The Day of the Dead is technically two days. Departed children – angelitos – are honoured on 1 November, whereas 2 November is for adults. While observing Day of the Dead has become common across the country, it's especially traditional and prevalent in central and southern Mexico. Some events, such as Mexico City's enormous parade (first held in 2016), are public, but other aspects, for example in local cemeteries, are observed privately. Sit in a plaza to catch music and dancing.

⑲ MIDSUMMER EVE, STOCKHOLM, SWEDEN

Midsummer Eve is celebrated on a Friday between 19–25 June. The holiday is all about the countryside, so expect cities to empty out. For Stockholmers, the most popular destination is the Stockholm archipelago, where most of the larger islands are served by public ferries. You can also book a private water ferry. The archipelago's tourism website (www. stockholmarchipelago. se) provides links to boat companies and their timetables. Midsummer is about celebrations with family and friends rather than public events, so join a local friend or even throw your own party.

⑳ CYCLING, COPENHAGEN, DENMARK

Copenhagen has a city bike share programme called Bycyklen, with GPS-equipped electric bikes. Rental is 30 Danish Krone per hour with dozens of pick-up and drop-off locations. There are also traditional rental companies all over the city. Or you can join an organised bike tour, which will take in many of the city's major sights. Be aware that cycling is not allowed in the famous Tivoli Gardens. Fly into Copenhagen Airport from many major world cities, or take the train into Copenhagen Central Station from many European destinations.

ENLIGHTENMENT

What are we searching for when we travel? According to author Alain de Botton, we 'hang on to the idea that certain parts of the world possess a power to address our ills'. All travel takes the outward shape of a quest, whether it's for the fleeting relaxation of a warm beach or a 30-day solo trek in search of self-discovery, of enlightenment.

Our world is filled with light: the dancing luminosity of the Northern Lights; multicoloured sunlight streaming through the rose windows of Notre Dame Cathedral; the changing colours of Uluru under an electric blue sky; the dazzling neon of a Hong Kong night. From the eternal to the ephemeral, our fascination with light in all its forms is hardwired. Whether we're after the glistening sunlight of a Greek island or the bright suffusion of inner understanding, when we travel, it's often a movement towards the light.

Since the Beatles landed in ❶ Rishikesh in 1968 and generations of self-knowledge seekers followed in their footsteps, India has been synonymous with enlightenment tourism. Long one of Hinduism's holiest cities, it sits in the foothills of the Himalayas, where the sacred Ganges River is clear and fast flowing. On its banks sit dozens of temple towers and shrines; hundreds of orange-clad sadhus and thousands of Hindu pilgrims drink and bathe in the holy waters here, believing that

① RISHIKESH, INDIA

Rishikesh is 20km (12 miles) from the nearest airport at Dehradun, and 240km (150 miles) northeast of Delhi – a car ride from Delhi airport should take six to seven hours. As the self-styled 'World Capital of Yoga', it's a popular place for yoga courses and teacher training; the Sivananda Ashram is particularly renowned, and an International Yoga Festival takes place every year in the first week of March. There are budget hotels and guesthouses aplenty, and Rishikesh is a popular backpacker hangout as well as a whitewater rafting centre and gateway for treks in the Himalayas.

② BODHGAYA, INDIA

The nearest airport, 14km (8.5 miles) away at Gaya, is not well served; better to arrive at Patna – 115km (70 miles) away, with daily flights from Delhi, Kolkata and Mumbai – and take a train or a taxi to Bodhgaya. Alternatively, there are overnight train and bus services to Gaya from Kolkata. The weather can be hot from March to September; if you're travelling at this time be sure to book a room with air conditioning. From November to February, Bodhgaya welcomes a community of exiled Tibetans, often including the Dalai Lama, and with them a cohort of international fans and supporters of Tibet.

This page: travelling Kerala's waterways. Previous page: a statue of Buddha at Bodhgaya.

to do so will bring them closer to attaining moksha, freedom from the cycle of death and rebirth. Hundreds of thousands of travellers join them each year, drawn by the ashrams, yoga schools and meditation retreats, and the promise of spiritual discovery.

Every sunset, priests lead processions of chanting, saffron-robed monks to the edge of the river, where the devotional ritual Ganga Aarti unfolds. Flower-filled, candle-lit bowls are pushed out into the current, as locals join with pilgrims, travellers and seekers of all kinds to give thanks for God's light throughout the day.

Of course, India was a place of pilgrimage long before the psychedelic age. It's believed that in ❷ Bodhgaya, also in the country's north, in the 5th century BC, Prince Siddhartha, after an intense period of mediation underneath the Bodhi Tree, became the Buddha – 'the Enlightened One'. This small town is known as 'the place of enlightenment' and the birthplace of Buddhism, and it draws millions of Buddhist pilgrims each year, to study

and meditate at the sacred Mahabodhi Temple complex.

Spiritual travellers may find themselves drawn to the complex's inner courtyard, known as the Jewel House, where the Buddha is believed to have spent the fourth week after enlightenment. Nearby, monks perform prostrations while others meditate, sitting on wooden boards placed on the grass under a huge banyan tree. Join them as the sun sets and the trees overhead fill with birdsong, while gentle chanting and wafting incense create an atmosphere of quiet contemplation.

If the Buddha's 49 straight days of meditation seems too arduous a path to enlightenment, shortcuts are available. Amma, the famous hugging guru of Kerala, partly owes her fame to her auto-enlightenment – she is said to have achieved full enlightenment on her own, making her a divine soul in a human body. Her devotees describe a hug from her as an infusion of pure, unconditional love that brings about a higher state of consciousness, instantly. They say it's like a transfusion of light, and it's one from which more than 30 million people around the world have benefited.

Her ❸ Ashram, once just a few huts in Kerala's lush tropical backwaters, now includes highrises and more than 5000 residents, welcoming visitors and new adherents. It's a mini-city built on spirituality, a shining symbol of India's enlightenment industry.

You don't have to go to India on your search for higher consciousness. On California's wild, iconic Big Sur coastline is ❹ The Esalen Institute, a spiritual getaway that attracts about 20,000 visitors each year. Founded in 1962, as beatniks became hippies and the Western fascination with Eastern religions edged towards the mainstream, Esalen fused Eastern and Western spiritual traditions, enormously influencing the wave of countercultural energy that helped define the decade.

Today, Esalen is the perfect expression of the modern American quest for enlightenment – all-embracing spiritualism, mystical self-improvement and radical open-mindedness. Six hundred workshops annually offer a smorgasbord of mind-expansion, from shamanic cosmology to 'the energetics of consciousness'. From its weekend retreats to month-long live-in experiences, Esalen aims to illuminate the path to self-realisation, with accommodation for a range of budgets.

While Esalen styles itself as a modern-day pilgrimage centre, the pilgrims of the past did without four-star rooms and sweeping views of surf and coast. They faced multiple dangers on their quest to mitigate their sins and secure their place in heaven: often travelling in groups to discourage outlaw attacks, they suffered food deprivation while making long, arduous journeys on foot. According to Alain de Botton, they 'were not being

③ AMMA'S ASHRAM. KERALA. INDIA

Amritapuri is Amma's world headquarters, and its rose-coloured high-rises are a strange thing to encounter in the middle of Kerala's languid, tropical backwaters. This network of lakes, lagoons, rivers and canals extends almost half the length of the state, which sits at India's southern extremity. Towns and villages nestled in this verdant landscape form the jumping-off points for backwater cruises, the classic Kerala travel experience. The airports at Trivandrum and Cochin are respectively 110km (68 miles) south and 140km (87 miles) north of Amritapuri; it's a three or four hour taxi ride to the ashram. For a cheaper option, take a train to Kayamkulam and then a short auto-rickshaw ride. www.amritapuri.org

④ ESALEN INSTITUTE. CALIFORNIA. USA

Esalen runs a programme of weekend, five-day and seven-day workshops throughout the year. 'Rustic' accommodation is provided on its 50 hectares of spectacular grounds, between mountain and ocean, with natural hot springs and a canyon stream. Take a workshop, or self-style your own 'Time to Reflect' retreat over a week – if that's insufficient, there are work/study programmes of 28 days available. The closest airports are in Monterey and the San Francisco Bay Area; depending which one you arrive at, the drive will take from 75 minutes to five hours. There's a shuttle service available from all three airports on Fridays and Sundays. www.esalen.org

perverse in their insistence on slowness and difficulty… Our attempts at inner transition can be cemented by a protracted and hazardous progress. If inner change is difficult, then we may need a commensurately difficult outer journey to inspire and goad us.'

Pilgrims to ❺ Mt Kailash in the far west of Tibet have made a sacred journey of notorious difficulty for thousands of years. Followers of the Hindu, Buddhist, Jain and Bon faiths come to this striking mass of black rock to complete a circumambulation, or kora. Some believe that the 52km (32 mile) walk must be made in a day – 15 hours of altitude sickness and extreme cold in this remote and inhospitable corner of the Himalayas.

Others make the circumambulation while performing full-length prostrations the entire way: bending down, kneeling, stretching out at full length and making a mark with the fingers, rising to the knees, praying and then crawling forward to the mark made by the fingers before repeating the process – over and over and over again. Done this way, the kora will take two to three weeks of extreme physical endurance. One time around the peak erases the sins of a lifetime; to achieve moksa, 108 circumambulations are required.

Christians, too, have long walked the weary road to enlightenment. The most celebrated Christian pilgrimage route is the ❻ Camino de Santiago (or Way of Saint James), which crosses southern France to end at the cathedral in Santiago de Compostela in Galicia, northern Spain, the burial place of Saint James. Santiago can lay claim to being the world's first major tourist destination – at the pilgrimage's peak during the Middle Ages, up to two million people a year (around 5000 a day) arrived at the cathedral, coming not only from Spain but from France, Britain, Germany, Italy and Scandinavia. In what's widely regarded as the world's first travel guide, the Codex Calixtinus, dating around 1140, gave pilgrims advice about making the trek.

Massive infrastructure developed – bridges were constructed leading to nearby towns, hospices offered accommodation, all kinds of businesses were established – both to support and to cash in on the passing pilgrim trade. It was, if you like, a glimpse into the future of modern tourism. Today, the Camino's popularity is resurgent. In 2016, almost 280,000 pilgrims earned a compostela or certificate of completion at the cathedral in Santiago. Although not quite the 5000 per day pilgrims of the Middle Ages peak, it's 100 times more than in 1986. Whatever brand of enlightenment we're seeking, we're seeking it in ever-growing numbers.

Modern-day Camino pilgrims speak of the therapeutic benefit of leaving everything behind to do nothing more than put one foot in front of the other, every day for 20,

Making a pilgrimage along the Camino de Santiago in Spain. Previous page: the coast of Big Sur, California.

30, 40 days. They talk of blisters and sprains, faltering willpower, the small miracles and camaraderie of the trail. They talk of magical Galician forests, griffon vultures hanging in the sky above the Pyrenees, fields of poppies, hilltop villages in the distance, coming slowly, slowly closer.

We don't all have the time, or the funds, for a long holiday, even if it does provide spiritual illumination. American Christians can give thanks, then, for the opportunity to get closer to the light in their own backyard, at ❼ The Holy Land Experience in Orlando, Florida. Here, in the theme park capital of the world, Christianity gets the Disney treatment – minus the rollercoasters and with a much older demographic. You can see all the best bits of the Bible – the Last Supper, the Crucifixion, the Resurrection – performed on slick sets by attractive and appropriately costumed actors. Plus you can play Christian-themed mini-golf next to Noah's

⑤ MT KAILASH, TIBET

To enter Tibet, you'll need a valid Chinese visa, as well as a Tibet Tourism Bureau (TTB) permit. To obtain this, you must book a guide for your entire trip and pre-arrange private transport for trips outside Lhasa. Plus, there are other, specific permits needed to travel to Mt Kailash, as it's in a restricted area. In short, you'll need to do your pilgrimage on an organised tour – the tour company will arrange all your permits for you. Tours to Kailash depart from Lhasa and generally take around two weeks, starting with a couple of days in Lhasa to acclimatise to Tibet's lofty altitude.

⑥ CAMINO DE SANTIAGO, SPAIN

Your first decision is where to start. In the Middle Ages, the pilgrimage began the moment the pilgrim stepped outside their front door; a multitude of different 'ways' begin from all over Europe. The most popular route today is the Camino Francés (the French Way), starting in St Jean Pied de Port, just over the French border. To complete this 800km (500 miles) route, allow four to six weeks of walking 25 to 30km (18.5 miles) per day, including a few rest days. You'll find villages and towns with accommodation every five to 20km, and lucky modern-day pilgrims can have their luggage transported ahead.

Ark and get a lamb kebab for lunch.

Drive west for some 3200km (2000 miles) and you'll hit ❽ Monument Valley, on the border of Utah and Arizona. If you've ever seen a Western, you'll know this landscape well – it's that iconic, rugged part of the American West where monolithic, flat-topped buttes rise out of the red-hued soil. You're on tribal land in Monument Valley, sacred land to the Navajo, and the best time to feel the full force of its otherworldly power is as the sun goes down and drains the light from the valley in a riot of colour. The sky turns rose behind the setting sun, shifting to deeper red and darker shades of violet, as it forms layers of vivid light in the sky, mirroring the sedimentary layers of the buttes and pinnacles below.

You'll find a similar natural light spectacular on the other side of the world, at ❾ Uluru, in the middle of Australia's outback. Here, an immense red sandstone rock, 3.6km (2.2 miles) long, rises a towering 348m from the surrounding sandy scrubland. Daily, it performs a remarkable transformation: at dawn it's a rich pink; in the afternoon, deep orange, blazing against the endless electric blue sky. The setting sun illuminates the rock, bringing out the red ochre hues it's famous for, developing to a deepening series of darker reds before it fades to charcoal.

This is Australia's red heart, located almost exactly in the centre of the giant continent, and its remoteness is impressive – at some 450km (280 miles) from the closest major settlement, Alice Springs, getting to 'The Rock' is a kind of pilgrimage in itself for modern visitors. For its traditional owners, it has been part of a sacred journey for thousands of years.

All around Uluru are caves, patterns and features that local Aboriginal tribes see as marks left by their hero ancestors during the Dreamtime, when the Earth was created. It's part of the sacred geography formed by ancestral beings who emerged from inside the Earth and wandered over the land, creating the features of the landscape as they went, which is at the core of Aboriginal belief. Sacred places of power such as Uluru are stops on dreaming tracks, or songlines – the paths the ancestors made across the landscape, remembered in song, story, dance and painting. For the Aboriginal people, songlines are a way of navigating the land and regenerating the Earth; making journeys along the songlines is a way of living their Dreamtime heritage.

We shift our focus upwards, to the heavens in the world's northern extreme, for the hallucinatory spectacle of the Aurora Borealis, or ❿ Northern Lights. This otherworldly phenomenon of bright, dancing illuminations that spread surreally across the night sky at the Earth's magnetic poles is caused by electrically

© Justin Foulkes / Lonely Planet

The rock spires of Monument Valley, viewed from the Hunts Mesa, USA.

charged particles from the sun bombarding the upper atmosphere. Both eerie and magnificent, the gleaming lights are usually pale green and pink, but sometimes red, yellow, green, blue and violet.

In Iceland, just below the Arctic Circle, the northern lights may be seen during the months from October to April, especially on clear, dark nights. While it's possible to catch a particularly strong aurora blast from downtown Reykjavík, the world's most northerly capital city, it's best to escape the ambient light and experience the show in full darkness, and one of the best viewing spots is the Jökulsárlón glacier lagoon in the country's southeast. There you see the glowing lightshow as it hangs above a starkly beautiful landscape, dancing strands of light reflected in the water and ice of the lagoon.

Just a few degrees north and you hit the Arctic Circle, where you'll find Norway's ⓫ Svalbard Islands, Europe's northernmost inhabited region – the regional capital,

⑦ THE HOLY LAND EXPERIENCE, FLORIDA, USA

Off Interstate 4, 6km (four miles) from Universal Studios, a Colosseum-esque edifice beckons the theme-park seeker with a more enlightened variety of fun. Live performances dramatise Bible parables such as The Prodigal Son; on the Golgotha Walking Tour, you'll see artifacts that explain the crucifixion of Christ. Feast at Esther's Banquet Hall, or just grab a foot-long at the 'Last Snack'. Souvenirs of your day spent closer to God are available at the Gold, Frankincense & Myrrh Shop or Solomon's Treasures. You're not permitted to bring your own food or drinks, weapons and pets.

⑧ MONUMENT VALLEY, USA

Entry to the Monument Valley Navajo Tribal Park is during daylight hours and a fee is payable at the visitor centre. Stay overnight to make the most of sunset, and stargaze at the incredibly clear night skies – there's accommodation in gateway towns Bluff and Mexican Hat, and a hotel and campground within the Navajo Nation Tribal Lands (book in advance). Your trip to Monument Valley will involve plenty of driving; depending on where you're coming from and how much time you have, you can visit other natural wonders such as Moab, the Grand Canyon, Canyonlands National Park and Lake Powell.

Left: the red rock of Uluru. Right:
the aurora borealis in Iceland.

Longyearbyen, is only around 1200km (750 miles) from
the geographic North Pole. Summer here brings the
midnight sun, when the sun stays in the sky for 24 hours
each day. The light of the midnight sun glows golden
over this rugged archipelago, more than half of which is
covered by glaciers, a wilderness where there are more
polar bears than people.

The extended twilight is a golden hour without end –
a prolonged sunset and sunrise at once, colouring sky
and earth in a reddish yellow light. The sun never really
sets, but hangs low on the horizon, creating impossibly
elongated shadows before swinging back into sunrise.
Midnight glacier walks, dogsledding, whale safaris – the
already remarkable experiences offered by travelling in
northern Scandinavia are dialled up a notch when you
do them in the middle of the night in broad daylight.

For a very different experience of extreme light,
travel to ⑫ Lake Maracaibo, a 13,000 sq km (5000 sq
miles) tidal bay in the north of Venezuela, famed for its
dramatic lightning displays. The high heat and humidity,
and wind whipped up in the surrounding Andes, create
the perfect crucible for the most intense and predictable
lightning in the world. Sometimes called 'the everlasting
storm', Catatumbo lightning (named for the Catatumbo
River which opens out into Lake Maracaibo, the point
where the lightning is most intense), hits an average
of 260 nights each year, with shows lasting for up to
10 hours. During the peak of the wet season around
October, lightning strikes 28 times a minute.

Bright enough that it can be seen 400km (250 miles)
away, up close the Catatumbo lightning is a lightshow
like no other. Backlit by sheet lightning, gigantic storm
clouds swell, red-orange or blue-purple, depending on
the amount of dust particles or moisture in the air. Then,
forks of lightning explode in all directions, the most
intense burning their impressions on to the retinas; the
strikes, too many to count, transform the world into one
gigantic strobe light.

We can imagine that Benjamin Franklin would have
liked to see it. His experiments, linking lightning with
the power of electricity, were a step along the path to
where we can all, like gods, produce light at the flick of
a switch. But it was a long and dimly lit road to get here,
a road depicted in Raoul Dufy's luminous 600 sq metre
opus, La Fée Electricité (The Electricity Fairy). Originally
painted for the 1937 International Exposition in Paris,
the fresco celebrates 110 scientists and inventors who

⑨ ULURU,
AUSTRALIA

*Formerly known as Ayers
Rock, Uluru is found in
the Uluru-Kata Tjuta
National Park. (Kata
Tjuta is a striking group
of 36 boulders huddled
together about 35km (22
miles) west of Uluru. The
tallest of them is 200m
higher than Uluru; some
visitors find them more
captivating than their
neighbour.) To hear the
native Aboriginal people's
Dreamtime stories about
Uluru, visit the Uluru-Kata
Tjuta Aboriginal Cultural
Centre, or take a tour
with Aboriginal guides.
You can fly into Ayers
Rock Airport in about
three hours from Sydney.
Otherwise, it takes about
four and a half hours to
drive from Alice Springs.*

⑩ NORTHERN
LIGHTS, ICELAND

*Most visitors to Iceland fly
into Keflavík International
Airport (48km from
Reykjavík), flights from
within Europe take three
to four hours. A ferry
leaves from Hirtshals
in Denmark once a
week. Iceland is an
expensive place to travel
– one benefit of borealis-
chasing is that you'll be
there out of high season
(which is June to August)
and accommodation
prices will be lower.
Hire a car to get out of
Reykjavík and access
more remote places away
from artificial illumination
where the Norther Lights
will be brighter; or use one
of the hop-on, hop-off
bus services that follow
the island's Ring Road.*

contributed to the development of electricity, in a riot of colour combining mythology and technology, nature and gadgetry.

It's fitting that it lives in **⑬** Paris, la Ville Lumière, 'the City of Light'. Many believe this honorific was bestowed in the 19th century, in praise of the gas lighting then spreading rapidly across the city. The Champs-Elysées and the city's elegant covered passages were gas-lit by the middle of the 1800s; by the Paris Universal Exposition of 1900, when the eyes of the world turned to the city, it boasted 50,900 gas streetlamps. That Exposition helped cement Paris' reputation as the world's most modern city; one of its main attractions, the Palais de l'Electrique, was fitted with 5000 multicoloured incandescent lamps, truly ushering in the age of artificial light.

Paris' other claim as La Ville Lumière dates further back, when it was the epicentre of the Enlightenment. Also known as the Age of Reason, this explosion of revolutionary thinking in the 18th century heralded the birth of concepts of reason, liberty, equality, democracy and the scientific method. It stands as one of the most significant periods in the history of human thought.

---

⑪ SVALBARD, NORWAY

There are daily flights to and from Svalbard throughout the year. Most flights are to and from Tromsø in Norway's north, but during summer season you can fly direct from the capital, Oslo. The flight from Oslo takes around three hours. The midnight sun appears from April through late August. Midnight glacier walks, kayak tours and dogsledding are popular activities – even night-time golf. The average temperature over summer (June-August) is 1°C to 5°C, dropping to -14°C to -17°C over winter – when, of course, the opposite effect to the midnight sun occurs, and the islands are sunk in perpetual night.

⑫ LAKE MARACAIBO, VENEZUELA

The second largest city in Venezuela, Maracaibo is in a region known for its oil industry and drug trafficking. Flights arrive at La Chinita International Airport, taking about three hours from Miami. There are bus connections from Caracas, San Cristóbal and Mérida, and across the border to Colombia. A number of operators run lightning tours, usually starting at Mérida and passing through wildlife-rich jungle – the region is home to howler monkeys, alligators, iguanas and exotic birds. Observing the lightning requires an overnight stay – the show starts at around 2am and lasts for a few hours.

© Jøran Skaar / 500px

The tundra landscape of Svalbard in the Norwegian arctic archipelago.

Coffee houses, the ancestors of Paris cafe society, emerged as meeting places where prominent Enlightenment figures such as Voltaire, Denis Diderot and Jean-Jacques Rousseau debated and discussed the latest revolutionary ideas. Religion, monarchies and hereditary aristocracy were questioned, even attacked.

Stand in the magnificent forecourt of ⓮ Versailles, just outside Paris, home at the time to King Louis XVI, and consider how the absolute power and extraordinary wealth of the monarchy embodied by it appeared from the cafe tables of the Enlightenment. Seven hundred rooms, 67 staircases, 2153 windows, untold amounts of gilt – even today, the profligate luxury and overweening self-glorification of the royal rulers is apparent. French historians date the end of the Enlightenment to 1789, the start of the French Revolution; four years later, King Louis XVI was sent to the guillotine.

Revolutionary humanist ideas had flourished before, of course. Three centuries earlier, for example, in ⓯ Florence, Italy. The word 'Renaissance' literally means rebirth, and it describes how the world re-emerged into the light of classical Roman and Greek thought from the darkness of the Middle Ages. Florence, rich thanks to its innovative merchant class and robust enough to have survived the Black Death that wiped out two-thirds of its population in the 1340s, became the cradle for a new humanist and artistic revolution.

Early figures such as the poet Dante Alighieri (author of *The Divine Comedy*) and the painter Giotto had led the way, but it was with Filippo Brunelleschi's dome of the Florence Cathedral, officially completed in 1436, that the Renaissance can truly be said to have taken hold. A miracle of engineering at the time – no dome so high or so big had ever been built – its soaring interior marked a move towards light and openness from the sombre, often simultaneously breathtaking and forbidding Gothic interiors of the past. It's a spatial expression of Renaissance humanism, an emergence into light. With its completion, the ground had been cleared for the Florentine masters of the High Renaissance – Leonardo da Vinci, Botticelli, Michelangelo – and the first stone of the Enlightenment had been laid.

Back in Paris, in the years between the Enlightenment and the Exposition of 1900, a new school of artists emerged, preoccupied with the depiction of light. ⓰ The Impressionists used short, broken brushstrokes and pure, unblended colours – some of which, vibrant

shades like cerulean blue and cadmium yellow, had never been seen before and were now possible due to new synthetic pigments – to focus on their obsession with the mercurial, ephemeral qualities of light.

They were initially shunned by the art establishment. The annual art show, the Salon de Paris, rejected their works throughout the 1860s, leading them to establish their own independent artists' association. But today, Impressionists such as Claude Monet, Pierre-Auguste Renoir, Camille Pissarro and Paul Cézanne draw enormous crowds to the city's most loved museums. In a world of Monet tea-towels, where Cezanne's paintings fetch hundreds of millions of dollars at auction, it's hard to believe that these were once radical and controversial departures from the accepted version of painted reality. Immersing yourself in the collection at Paris' Musée d'Orsay is the most sublime art history class imaginable.

On the other side of La Manche (the English Channel), another painter had long before staked his claim to the title 'the painter of light'. Born in the midst of the Enlightenment, JMW Turner is now recognised as an Impressionist before Impressionism; some of his works

Left: the Hall of Mirrors in the Palace of Versailles. Below: the painted ceiling in the palace's Salon d'Hercule.

are even thought to prefigure 20th-century abstract painting. While his subjects were often dramatic human scenes – fires, ships in high sea, Hannibal's army crossing the Alps in a snowstorm – his real mission was making light seem to emanate directly from his canvas. Famously, his final words are said to have been: 'The sun is God.'

You can see for yourself how well he succeeded in invoking it, as he bequeathed to the British public more than 300 works, held today in London's stately ⓱ Tate Britain. Turner's stature in Britain is giant and the display of his paintings is reverent and eye-opening. Art historian Andrew Graham-Dixon says that Turner was saying in his paintings 'that the things we think are solid – ourselves, the objects with which we surround ourselves – they're not real. The only thing that's real is the thing that seems most transitory, the most fugitive – namely, light itself.'

When Turner was painting, humans had fire and

⑬ PARIS, LA VILLE LUMIÈRE, FRANCE

Find La Fée Électricité in Musée d'Art Moderne de la Ville de Paris (MAM; www.mam.paris.fr), where it curves around the walls of its own private room. MAM sits on the Seine's Right Bank, a short walk from the Grand Palais, built for the Exposition of 1900. The Palais' main hall has a glass barrel-vaulted roof, necessary for exhibitions before electricity. It sits just off the Champs-Élysées. To experience Paris by gaslight, visit the passages couverts – Galerie Vivienne, Passage des Panoramas (the first of Paris' public areas lit by gas in 1817), Passage Jouffroy and Passage Verdeau.

⑭ PALACE OF VERSAILLES, FRANCE

The Château de Versailles is an overwhelming display of royal wealth and a masterpiece of French 17th-century architecture. Originally constructed as a hunting lodge in 1624, it was embellished by successive kings up to 1789 when a revolutionary mob marched on Versailles, forcing Louis XVI and his family to flee. The town of Versailles is 17km (11 miles) southwest of Paris, and easy to reach from the capital by taking an RER train on Ligne C. It's worthwhile taking measures to avoid the massive queues – book online and visit in the early morning or late in the afternoon.

Right: Cerith Wyn Evans' light installation 'Forms in Space... by Light (in Time)' at Tate Britain. Opposite: the Boboli Gardens in Florence, Italy.

⑮ RENAISSANCE FLORENCE, ITALY

Peretola Airport, 8km (five miles) away from the city, is connected to Florence's SMN Novella central station by a half-hourly bus, but Pisa, an hour away by train, offers many more (and cheaper) flight options. Florence is emminently walkable, with key sites like the Duomo and Giotto's Campanile hard by eachother on the Piazza del Duomo, and Giotto's famous frescoes a ten-minute walk away in the Church of Santa Croce. And nearby on the banks of the Arno the Uffizi Gallery (www.uffizi.org) houses a Stendhal Syndrome-inducing collection of Renaissance masterpieces.

⑯ IMPRESSIONIST PARIS, FRANCE

Paris's Charles de Gaulle airport is 23km (14 miles) north of the city, but if you can, arrive by train; its stations are a perfect introduction to the City of Light. So perfect that in 1986 one was converted into the Musée D'Orsay (www.musee-orsay.fr), home to one of the world's best collections of Impressionism. Approach it from the Tuileries Garden opposite on the Seine's Right Bank, where Monet's Water Lilies dazzle at the Musée de l'Orangerie (www.musee-orangerie.fr), then take a westbound RER C train to the Musée Marmottan Monet (www.marmottan.fr) for the world's largest collection of his paintings.

⑰ TURNER'S LONDON, UK

Tate Britain is home to the world's largest collection of paintings by JMW Turner, including some of his masterpieces such as Peace – Burial at Sea and Norham Castle, Sunrise. The exhibition in the museum's Clore Gallery is constantly changing (there is only room to display a selection of the collection), and like many of London's museums, access is free. The Tate is close to the River Thames in Millbank, central London; the best way to arrive is by boat. The Tate Boat runs between the Tate Britain and Tate Modern further east; other river services run between Millbank Pier and Bankside Pier. www.tate.org.uk

⑱ SHINJUKU, TOKYO, JAPAN

Shinjuku is Tokyo's transport hub, home to the world's busiest railway station (3.5 million passengers a day) and a long-distance bus terminal. To the west of the station is a cluster of skyscrapers and government buildings; to its east, one of Tokyo's most energetic nightlife districts. Golden Gai is a warren of alleyways hiding 150 or so shoebox-sized bars and restaurants with room for only five or six guests, popular with hard-drinking salarymen. For an aerial view of all those lights, hop the lift to the free observatories on the 45th floor of the Tokyo Metropolitan Government Building.

This page: carefully restored lights
at the Neon Museum in Las Vegas.
Overleaf: Adam's Peak in Sri Lanka.

gaslight. Capturing light in paint was an act of magic – it's all but impossible for us to grasp how astounding his work seemed at the time. We, who can jump on an airplane and land in Tokyo.

Let Tokyo show you how well humans learned to make light. Stand in ⑱ Shinjuku at night and feel tiny and insignificant beneath the flashing walls of light that drape and wrap its streets. It's the verticality of the street lighting here that makes it different from other neon cities: flashing kanji signs reach towards the sky from the surging streets in narrow vertical streams, forming vast illuminated canyons. It's the ultimate commodification and celebration of light, and can make you feel as dwarfed and awestruck as a lightning storm.

As with the gaslights of 19th-century Paris, even our most cutting-edge attempts to turn night into day are destined to be outdone, to find their way to history. Take neon. Created by a French engineer in 1902, just a few years after neon gas had been discovered by British chemists, it was in America where neon lighting really hit the zeitgeist. Drawing the motorists of a new, car-centred culture off the highway and into diners, hotels and gas stations, by the 1930s neon was everywhere.

In time, the allure faded. Neon is high voltage, handmade and expensive. Businesses migrated to cheaper alternatives and, by the 1950s and '60s, neon began to be associated with the seedier side of life – dive bars, cheap hotels, sex shops. Since the 1990s, cheaper, more energy-efficient LED bulbs have gained prominence in the world's big neon cities – Shanghai, Hong Kong, Las Vegas.

But according to neon devotees, the brightness and vivid colours of neon, the deep purples and ambers and reds, can't be reproduced by new, lower-cost alternatives. Fortunately, the ⑲ Neon Museum exists to preserve them. Exactly where it should be – in Las Vegas, the brightest city in the world from space – the museum collects iconic signs for posterity and aesthetic admiration. So it goes: an invention blinked into existence by a chemical reaction became a flare of ephemeral commercialism, faded, and was transformed into a cultural treasure, adored for the special quality of its glow.

From the frivolous to the sublime, we arrive at a light show from nature, in a place of pilgrimage for more than 1000 years. Here in Sri Lanka's southern Hill Country is the site of a sacred footprint. For Christians and Muslims, the pointy, 2243m pinnacle cradles the spot where Adam first set foot after being cast from paradise.

Hindus believe it's the print of Shiva. For Buddhists, it's that of the Buddha.

Whoever made it, the curious depression at the summit of ❷⓪ Adam's Peak is the object of a multidenominational pilgrimage. It's traditionally made by night, when hundreds of tiny lights illuminate the steep route of more than 5000 steps and teahouses offer sustenance. It's an exhausting 7km (4.3 mile) trek that usually starts at about 2am in order to reach the summit by sunrise. As the sun rises and floods across the mountaintop, one can briefly see the shadow of the peak – a strange triangular apparition, not at all the same as the shape of the summit. (Buddhists explain it as a miraculous representation of the sacred 'Triple Gem', comprising the Buddha, his teachings and the community of Buddhist monks.)

We experience a moment of illumination where physical light changes our perspective. Maybe a fleeting appreciation of the irony that we often travel to find enlightenment, when spiritual teachings all seem to agree that it is to be found inside ourselves. These small moments of insight may be all travel can offer us. And they may be enough.

⑲ NEON MUSEUM, LAS VEGAS, USA

The museum launched with the installation of its first restored sign, the Hacienda Horse and Rider, at the junction of Las Vegas Blvd and Fremont St. Since then, classic signs – among them the Bow & Arrow Motel, The Silver Slipper, the Landmark and 5th Street Liquors – have been installed along the boulevard, functioning as public art that co-exists among the Strip's contemporary flashing lights. The museum also runs the Neon Boneyard, which can be visited by guided tour seven days a week, see www.neonmuseum.org. Many international airlines fly to Las Vegas airport.

⑳ ADAM'S PEAK, SRI LANKA

Most flights to Sri Lanka arrive in the capital, Colombo. Pilgrims leave from the small settlement of Dalhousie, 33km (20 miles) southwest of Hatton, which is on the Colombo–Kandy–Nuwara Eliya train line. Buses run to Dalhousie from Kandy, Nuwara Eliya and Colombo in the pilgrimage season, which begins in December and runs until May; January and February are the busiest times. There are budget and mid-range guesthouses in Dalhousie and around. Consider taking a walking stick (or two) for the hike – many pilgrims say the descent is harder than the climb – and take plenty of water.

ALONE

'I find it wholesome to be alone the greater part of the time. To be in company, even with the best, is soon wearisome and dissipating. I love to be alone. I never found the companion that was so companionable as solitude.'

So wrote Henry David Thoreau in 1854 in his classic tome on backwoods living, Walden: Or, Life in the Woods. It's a book that elevates the experience of being alone to a semi-existential state, and a century and a half later, in a world of social media and information overload, it's a book that seems more prescient than ever. In the book, Thoreau abandons his comfortable city life for a rustic cabin in the Massachusetts woods, and in so doing, learns the benefits of self-sufficiency and self-reliance: the simple pleasures of chopping firewood, foraging for food and sitting in silent, solitary contemplation of nature.

But the thought of solitude – let alone the prospect of travelling solo – is something that many people still find deeply daunting. And there's no doubt that it has its challenges. There's no one to watch that early-morning sunrise with, or discuss the day's adventures over a late-night beer, or lend you some spare cash when you just can't quite scrape enough together to buy that must-have Moroccan rug in a Marrakesh souk.

But, as Thoreau realised, solitariness has its own subtle pleasures. Your days are your own. You're a free bird. A

① ANTARCTICA

The only way for most ordinary mortals to visit Antarctica is on organised expedition ships, which run during the Antarctic summer between November and February (there's too much ice the rest of the year). Make sure your operator is accredited by IAATO, the International Association of Antarctic Tour Operators, www.iaato. org. It's also possible to fly to the South Shetland Islands and rendezvous with your ship there, thus avoiding the infamously rough stretch of ocean known as the Drake Passage. Visit later in the season, when the ice has warmed and wildlife is more plentiful.

② THE EMPTY QUARTER, OMAN, YEMEN, SAUDI ARABIA, UAE

Most visitors to the Empty Quarter fly to the Omani town of Salalah, and then travel onwards into the desert by 4WD. It's important to travel with an experienced guide, as it's extremely easy to get lost. Most operators, such as Arabian Sand Tours (www. arabiansandtoursservices. com), carry all the equipment you'll need, including tents, sleeping bags and food supplies. Evening meals are cooked for you over the campfire.

This page: Chinstrap penguins on Deception Island, Antarctica.
Previous page: Oman's Empty Quarter.

lone ranger. There's no negotiating your next destination, no waiting around for anyone else's luggage, no one to ask permission of or answer to. You can pick a point on a map, and just go. There's a sense of freedom in travelling on your own that, by definition, can't be matched when you're travelling with others – as Alastair Humphreys, a professional adventurer, serial solo traveller and bestselling author of a series of travel books including *Microadventures* and *Grand Adventures*, explains.

'Being alone is a really important part of my journeys,' he says. 'It forces me to be resilient and flexible. There can be no coasting, letting somebody else make the decisions, work out the route and find somewhere safe to sleep. And there are no ties, constraints or compromises. I can do what I want, go where I want, be who I want. I love this kick, the rush and buzz of joy and freedom. Just being in motion for the sheer heck of it. This is the unbeatable intensity of solitude that keeps me hooked on travelling alone.'

And there can be few places that bring the intensity of solitude into sharper focus than ❶ Antarctica. Vast, white and impossibly empty, this icy expanse has bewitched generations of adventurers and explorers, and if you truly want to know what it might feel like to be the last person left on Earth, there's nowhere to match it. 'The end of the axis upon which this great round ball turns,' (as the explorer Ernest Shackleton referred to it), Antarctica covers 14 million sq km (5.5 million sq miles) of ice and snow, and is perhaps the last place in the world that can be called wild in the purest sense of the word. Apart from a few scientific stations dotted across the ice-sheets, it's one of the few areas of Earth that humans have never properly colonised. It offers a vision of a world without people – and perhaps that's why it continues to exert such an irresistible hold on our imaginations.

In practice, unless you're mounting your own trans-polar expedition, it's hard to experience quite the same level of aloneness felt by Scott, Shackleton, Amundsen

③ ALASKA, USA

Alaska Route 11, or the Dalton Hwy, runs for 666km (414 miles), starting to the north of Fairbanks and ending at Deadhorse near the Arctic Ocean. It's a road built mainly for trucks, and many sections are rough and unpaved, so a proper cross-country vehicle such as a pick-up, SUV or 4WD is absolutely essential. There's no mobile phone coverage for most of the route, so it's important to know at least the auto basics such as changing tyres, oil and so on. Most standard rental companies in Fairbanks specifically prohibit their vehicles from travelling on the highway, so you'll need to arrange hire from a local operator such as Alaska Auto Rental (www.alaskaautorental.com) or Arctic Outfitters (www.arctic-outfitters.com).

④ SKELETON COAST ROAD, NAMIBIA

The Skeleton Coast Park is accessed via the salt road from Swakopmund, which ends 70km (44 miles) north of Terrace Bay, or via the C39 gravel road, which runs between Khorixas and Torra Bay. A good, reliable vehicle is important here, and the places to stay are at Torra Bay, Terrace Bay and Cape Cross – all must be pre-booked. Cars can readily be hired in Swakopmund, or you can arrange a fly-drive package with operators such as Expert Africa (www.expertafrica.com).

et al, but even on an organised cruise you'll feel a long, long, long, long way from home – especially as your boat chugs south, civilisation recedes towards the northern horizon, and you chart a course for the great white unknown. Most ships depart from the Argentinian port of Ushuaia, and explore the finger of land in the northwest known as the Antarctic Peninsula, although occasionally some boats are also able to explore even more remote regions around the Weddell Sea and Ross Sea.

Antarctica isn't the only place where human footprints are hard to find, however. There might be more than seven billion of us on the planet now, but pockets of wilderness remain if you know where to look. Take ❷ the Empty Quarter, for example. Covering 650,000 sq km (251,000 sq miles), an area roughly the size of France, and spanning the borders of four countries – Oman, the UAE, Yemen and Saudi Arabia – the Empty Quarter (or Rub' al Khali, as it's properly known) encompasses the largest swathe of sand dunes anywhere on Earth.

On a map, it's a big, blank splash of yellow that takes up most of the Arabian peninsula, unmarked by any defining features. But it's only when you step foot on the dunes that you realise how profoundly empty this place is. Apart from a handful of Bedouin tribesmen who have clung on to their nomadic lifestyle, no one lives in the Empty Quarter these days – so when you set up camp, you can be pretty certain that you're probably the only human soul in several hundred square miles. The explorer Wilfred Thesiger had a lifelong fascination for the place, and with its palette of fiery colours and blazing night skies, it's not hard to understand why. 'No one can live this life and emerge unchanged…' Thesiger wrote. 'For this cruel land can cast a spell which no temperate clime can match.'

❸ Alaska is another place that can rightly claim the title of true wilderness. Covering more than 1.7 million sq km (656,000 sq miles), it's the largest of the 50 US states, and also the least populous, with a population

⑤ THE RED CENTRE, AUSTRALIA

The main gateway for exploring the Red Centre is the city of Alice Springs. There are direct flights from most large Australian cities, otherwise it's roughly a 1500km (930 mile) drive from Darwin or Adelaide. Once you're there, it's easy to explore the surrounding area: you can arrange walking tours of Uluru with Aboriginal guides, drive yourself around the West MacDonnell Ranges and Alice Springs Desert Park, or arrange a stay at the Ayers Rock Resort. See www.parksaustralia. gov.au/uluru or www. australia.com for background and planning.

⑥ TIBETAN PLATEAU

Visits to nearly all areas of the Tibetan Autonomous Region (which includes the plateau) must be arranged through a travel agency authorised by the Chinese government to conduct organised tours. These will arrange the necessary visas, travel permits, tour guides and transport as part of your package. The majority of tours fly into Lhasa; the most commonly used gateway cities are Kathmandu in Nepal and Chéngdū in China. There are plenty of operators to choose from: going with a small, local operator such as Explore Tibet (www.exploretibet. com) can be a good idea if you're looking for a tailored experience.

This page: hiking in Nepal's Upper Mustang region on the Tibetan Plateau. Previous page: Namibia's Skeleton Coast.

density that's a fifth of Montana's, a 30th of Oregon's and almost a thousandth of New Jersey's. That makes it a paradise for solitary types, and if you like your skies big and your landscapes empty, then The Last Frontier has no equal. Surprisingly, however, the more popular areas, such as the spectacular national parks of Denali and Wrangell-St Elias, can feel busy (relatively speaking).

So if it's proper alone time you're after, then it's the Far North you want: from the tiny settlement of Livengood, the epic Dalton Hwy unfurls into empty wilderness for 666km (414 miles), and it's quite easy to drive the whole day without ever passing another soul.

Namibia's ❹ Skeleton Coast Road is another stretch of tarmac legendary for its emptiness. Officially designated as the C34, this sand-and-gravel highway skirts along the barren coastline of Namibia's southwest corner, from Swakopmund to Terrace Bay, and is almost entirely devoid of features save for a seemingly never-ending panorama of sand dunes and surreal shipwrecks rusting along the rocky coastline (dense sea-fogs mean this patch of coastline is an infamous graveyard for ships). In all, the road is about 460km (286 miles) long; towns

Left: a hardy dog in Greenland. Right: the Russian town of Tynda, a stop on the Trans-Siberian Railway.

and petrol stations are pretty much non-existent along its entire route, which means you'll need to be 100% self-sufficient, as well as a dab hand at mechanics – the chances of a tow-truck just happening to trundle by are somewhere between nada, zilch and zero, and this is definitely not the kind of place where you want to find yourself stranded without knowing how to change a fan belt or put on the spare tyre.

The spiritual experience of getting lost in order to find yourself is something that comes naturally to Australia's indigenous people. For thousands of years before the arrival of white men, walkabout – the act of heading into the Outback in search of self – was an important rite of passage for young Aboriginal men, marking their transition into adulthood and their ability to live off the land. And while few people these days have the know-how, or the inclination, to survive solo in the Outback, Australia is still a fantastic place to get well and truly

⑦ SIBERIA, RUSSIA

Winter in Siberia is brutal, so visiting during the summer months from May to September is the only practical option. Eastern Siberia is the most remote region, where huge tracts of forest and wilderness surround the focal points of Lake Baikal and the city of Irkutsk. This is real backcountry Russia, so it's quite a challenging place to travel: accommodation is generally basic, and it's tough to get by without speaking a little Russian, so an organised tour is probably the best way to go. Another option is to book a ticket on the Trans-Siberian Railway.

⑧ GREENLAND

There are seasonal flights to Greenland's international airport in Kangerlussuaq and the capital, Nuuk, from Copenhagen, and regular flights from Reykjavik. Travelling around is trickier. There are hardly any roads in Greenland, so most travel is via boat, helicopter or plane: Air Greenland (www.airgreenland. com) has links to most areas. Winter here lends itself to dogsledding, snowshoeing and cross-country skiing, while in summer, hiking, kayaking and wildlife-watching are prime possibilities. Just remember to bring the mosquito repellent. A great starting point is www.greenland.com.

Heading for the hills on the
Klondike Hwy in the Yukon.

lost. The ❺ Red Centre is a fitting place to start: though it's home to some famous sights such as Uluru and Alice Springs, this world of crimson sand and weathered rock formations holds great spiritual significance for indigenous people, and offers plenty of opportunity for your own solo walkabout, from a desert trek on camelback to a bush-tucker hike with local tribesmen. And, since it's about 1500km (930 miles) away from the big cities of Darwin and Adelaide, it's an area with incredibly low light pollution – making it great for star gazing.

But even the Red Centre can't match the ❻ Tibetan Plateau in terms of all-out remoteness. A three-week expedition from the city of Lhasa and more than 4500m above sea-level, this is officially the most isolated place on the planet, according to the European Commission's Joint Research Centre. Often known as the Roof of the World or the Third Pole, it's a sprawling, empty land of rugged mountains and sweeping plains, populated only by small bands of yak herders who trek up here in summer to tend their flocks.

There are no buildings of any kind up on the plateau: the herders prefer to live in yak-wool tents, which can easily be collapsed and moved around as their cattle graze. Some of them might even put you up for the night, although the delights of a late-night cup of yak butter tea are something of an acquired taste. The only way to visit at present is on an organised tour, usually beginning in Lhasa, before heading onwards to remote areas such as the lake region of Koko Nur, the salt-flats of Chaka and the soaring mountains of Minyak Gangkar.

❼ Siberia is another classic destination for solitude seekers: covered by tracts of dense forest, it's one of Russia's least-populated areas, and that's really saying something for a country that already has one of the lowest population densities on Earth. Home to lots of rare wildlife incliding the Amur leopard, Siberian brown bear and Siberian tiger – yet precious few people – it's a favourite of wildlife documentary makers, as well as adventurous travellers who are searching for a glimpse of unspoilt Russian nature.

Unfortunately, since winter temperatures regularly plummet down to -40°C, you'll need to be tougher than musk leather to survive here – there's a good reason Stalin chose Siberia as the location for his Gulags, after all. Even old Thoreau might have questioned his ethics if he found himself stuck out in the Siberian wastelands mid-winter. But come in summer, and you'll discover a wild side of Russia that few people ever get to see.

❽ Greenland's landscape has much in common with Siberia – its terrain would look familiar to any Siberian who decided to take his summer holiday here (unlikely as that may be). Most towns in Greenland feel miles from anywhere, even relatively accessible ones such as Ilulissat and Nuuk. But in terms of remoteness, teeny Ittoqqortoormiit takes top prize: it's officially the remotest inhabited community in the Western hemisphere, icebound for nine months of the year, and home to about 450 hardy people, who are considerably outnumbered by the local population of polar bears.

The town itself is little more than a scattering of colourful wooden buildings overlooking the Scoresby Sund, the largest fjord on Earth. There are only a couple of flights a week, or you can arrange your own transfer in by sea, by chopper or – if it's Arctic style that really counts – by dogsled.

Canada is another country that seems to have been tailor-made to help you lose yourself. It's the world's second biggest nation, taking up more than 40% of the North American land mass, but has a population of just 36 million people, roughly the same as Morocco.

⑨ THE YUKON, CANADA

Whitehorse is the main access point for the Yukon, with flight connections to all major Canadian cities. The city makes a useful base for exploring, although the province's size means sights are spread out. Road-tripping is the most practical option or, even better, hire a campervan, or RV. This means you can pitch up like the gold-rushers of yore, only with the advantages of a bed and a chemical toilet. The Travel Yukon (www.travelyukon.com) website has plenty of advice, and for RV hire, try Canadream (www.canadream.com).

⑩ THE ROCK ISLANDS, PALAU

The easiest way to reach the western Pacific archipelago of Palau (www.pristineparadisepalau.com) is to fly from Asia: there are direct flights from Japan, South Korea, Taiwan and the Philippines. All flights land at the main city of Koror, which is also the best place to arrange an onward adventure to the Rock Islands. Dive-shop boat trips, snorkelling tours and kayak excursions can easily be arranged with local operators based in Koror.

Aitutaki atoll in the southern group of the Cook Islands.

Unsurprisingly, it's ideal for isolation-seekers – whether you choose to get lost in the Great Bear Rainforest or cruise the empty roads of coastal Nova Scotia – but it's the wild ❾ Yukon that feels emptiest of all. The population here peaked during the Klondike gold rush of 1896-99, then declined for most of the next century; the current figure only stands at around 36,000, making this one of Canada's most sparsely populated provinces (moose outnumber people here by two to one).

It's a paradise for backcountry campers, and a place where the thrill of the old frontier still rides on the mountain winds. However, while it's relatively easy to escape other people, you might have to share your campsite with the occasional hungry bear or two. Whitehorse is a useful launch-pad, but more than 80% of the Yukon is still officially classed as wilderness, meaning you can travel in pretty much any direction and find yourself in the middle of nowhere. Paddling down

the Yukon River is an unforgettable way to experience the backcountry, while the St Elias Mountains or the Southern Lakes are pretty much people-free.

Heading into the wilderness is one way to escape the crowds. Another is to leave the mainland altogether, and head off in search of your own desert island. There are literally thousands to choose from, but unless you happen to have access to your own private yacht or feel motivated to build your own Kon-Tiki raft, finding a way to reach them can be a challenge. But there are some island chains which, although they're relatively straightforward to reach, still feel thrillingly off the beaten track. The ❿ Rock Islands of Palau, known as Chelbacheb in the local language, are such places.

Formed from ancient limestone and coral, and cloaked in tangled jungle, there are more than 250 islands in the archipelago, each with its own unique flora and fauna. Many of the islands also feature hidden lagoons and natural lakes, making them ideal for some wild swimming – or even a cheeky skinny-dip (and why not, since you're probably one of only a handful of souls on the island). The islands featured in their own series of the *Survivor* TV show, which gives some idea of the level of remoteness we're dealing with – so they're a super place to live out that long-held Robinson Crusoe fantasy.

Another far-flung archipelago that represents the stuff of desert-island dreams is ⓫ the Cook Islands, a 15-strong chain of islands spread out over 1.8 million sq km (695,000 sq miles) of the Pacific Ocean. They're divided into two groups: the southern group includes the popular islands of Rarotonga and Aitutaki, as well as lesser-visited ones such as Atiu, Mauke and Mangaia. If even these are too busy, then head for the northern group – specifically, the islands of Pukapuka and Manihiki, where the only human inhabitants are black-pearl fishermen farming natural pearls on the seabed.

Flights to these distant specks of land are erratic, so most people arrive aboard their own yacht – following in the footsteps of the American writer Robert Dean Frisbie, who settled on Pukapuka in 1924 in search of an island that represented 'the faintest echo from the noisy clamour of the civilised world'.

Amazingly, there are some islands that are even harder to reach than the Cooks, such as ⓬ Tristan da Cunha, a lonely outpost of land marooned in the middle of the South Atlantic, 2810km (1745 miles) from South Africa and 3360km (2100 miles) from South America. A British Overseas Territory, it was originally settled in 1810, when its population numbered three. It's now home to just 262 people (at time of writing), many of whom are descended from one of the island's early permanent settlers, an enigmatic Scotsman by the name

⑪ THE COOK ISLANDS

Despite their isolated location, the Cook Islands can be easily reached by air: several Air New Zealand flights between Los Angeles and Auckland stop here en route, and also serve other South Pacific Islands. Air Rarotonga (www.airraro.com) lands on most of the islands, although schedules to outlying islands (especially the northern group) can be infrequent and erratic. Travel agents on Rarotonga can arrange travel packages and accommodation. Check out www.cookislands.travel for more information.

⑫ TRISTAN DA CUNHA

Just getting to Tristan da Cunha is a challenge in itself. There are no scheduled flights, so the only option is to wangle a spot on one of the supply ships or research vessels that depart from Cape Town several times a year. The 2810km (1745 mile) journey takes between five and six days. No visa is needed, but visitors require advance permission from the island's administrator before they can make travel arrangements. Boat schedules, accommodation options and other background information can be found on the island's official website at www.tristandc.com.

of William Glass. These days, apart from the islanders, the only people you're likely to find yourself sharing the island with are twitchers: Tristan is renowned for its impressive birdlife, and unusual species to spot include rockhopper penguins, sooty albatrosses, Antarctic terns, brown noddies, Atlantic petrels, great shearwaters and spectacled petrels. Sometimes, right whales, baleen whales and humpbacks can be spied offshore.

In terms of weird and wondrous wildlife, however, there's another island chain that has been fabled since the days of Charles Darwin – **13** Galápagos. Flung out in the middle of the Pacific, more than 1000km (600 miles) from Ecuador's west coast, these jagged volcanic islands offer a fascinating glimpse of Earth's pre-Anthropocene past. Marine iguanas slither along the rocks, giant tortoises lumber across the land, blue-footed boobies hop from foot to foot on the beaches and frigate-birds glide overhead while seals flop around in the shallows.

The weirdest thing of all is the animals' complete lack of fear: they've never learned any reason to be afraid of people, so you can get astonishingly close and most of them won't bat an eyelid. And that's before you even

Left: Pinnacle Rock on Bartolomé Island in the Galápagos. Below: a blue-footed booby in the Galápagos.

start to explore under the waves, where green turtles, hammerhead sharks and manta rays glide through the depths. It's a thrilling experience to be so intimately connected with nature, and to be reminded that, though you might be far away from other people, you're just one of myriad species that call this planet home.

Another place that's great for experiencing that end-of-the-Earth feeling is **14** Iceland, although sometimes it feels as if you've left terra firma altogether and stepped on to an entirely different planet. From vast ice-sheets to volcanic craters, bubbling geysers to geothermal pools, Iceland is a land that seems as if it's in the process of being formed, a place where you can watch nature's machinery at work. And with a population density of just 3.3 people per square kilometre – putting it roughly on a par with Namibia and Libya – Iceland is also a wonderful place to feel intoxicatingly alone, whether you're driving a 4WD across the volcanic highlands or touring the

13 GALÁPAGOS ISLANDS, ECUADOR

Visits to Galápagos are strictly limited to protect the local wildlife. Flights connect to the islands from Quito or Guayaquil, landing at either Baltra or San Cristóbal. The most eco-friendly way to visit is aboard one of the officially approved cruises, which are required by law to travel with qualified naturalists, and can only follow pre-arranged routes around the islands, and land at specific sites. The non-profit Galapagos Conservancy (www. galapagos.org) has good general advice on minimising your impact while visiting the islands.

14 ICELAND

Iceland is an easy and accessible place to reach these days: the main carrier is Icelandair (www.icelandair.com), but budget airlines including Wow air, Wizz Air and easyJet have brought fares down. Once you've landed at Keflavik Airport, the best plan is to hire a car and hit Route 1, otherwise known as the Ring Road, which circles around the whole island for 1338km (832 miles). From the Ring Road, you can then take detours to reach even more remote areas such as the Snaefellsnes peninsula and West Iceland, or take a 4WD up into the volcanic highlands of the interior. www.visiticeland.com

The icy water of Kirkjufellsfoss on
Snæfellsnes peninsula, Iceland.

craggy coast of the stunning Snaefellsnes peninsula. Unsurprisingly, it's become a favourite location for filmmakers looking for somewhere to represent distant worlds – and walking over the blasted volcanic plains of Myvatn or the blue glacier fields of Vatnajökull is about as close as most people get to being an astronaut touching down on an extra-terrestrial planet.

So finding empty, faraway places is definitely one way of experiencing the addictive thrill of solitude. But it's not the only one. Are you only really alone when you're miles away from everyone and everything, with nothing but a bag and a tent on your back, an empty road ahead and the wide horizon beyond? Or are there other ways of being alone, too? Snatched moments of solitude? Flashes of freedom? Can you actually be alone, even when you're in the middle of a busy city, surrounded by traffic jams and teeming hordes of people?

It's a theme that intrigues Al Humphreys. 'I think there are many different ways of being alone,' he muses. 'Alone might be out in the hot scrub, watched by nervous deer, motionless except for the crunch of a family of wild elephants walking slowly past. Or alone might be on the roof of a cheap guesthouse at sunset, having walked for hours through the crowds and chaos – like a murmuration of starlings – to reach the centre of the city and this brief moment of sanctuary.'

Take ⑮ Los Angeles. It's one of America's biggest, busiest, most people-packed cities, a place that defines hustle and bustle. But what many people don't realise is that it's actually a city fringed by the wild – from the steep bluffs and wildflower meadows of the Santa Monica Mountains to the tranquil lakes of Franklin Canyon and the old-growth woods of the Angeles National Forest. In less than a hour you can swap the traffic-clogged freeway for the empty trail, and exchange smog for clear mountain air. And even in the city there are places to leave the crowds behind – such as the beautiful botanical gardens of Descanso or the meditation spaces at the Peace Awareness Gardens in West Adams.

Then there's the example of ⑯ Stockholm, another city where it's easy to find yourself far from the madding crowd. Surrounded by an archipelago of around 30,000 islands, this is a metropolis where finding some space to call your own is unlikely to be a problem. Some of the islands are well-populated and can be reached by passenger ferry, while the more remote ones are often uninhabited and can only be reached by canoe, yacht or motorboat. During the summer, many Stockholmers can't

⑮ LOS ANGELES, USA

Everyone drives in LA, which is convenient since it's also by far the best way to escape the city in search of solitude. The Santa Monica Mountains (www.nps.gov/samo) are about 56km (35 miles) west of Downtown; the main visitor centre is off Mulholland Highway at Calabasas, from where it's easy to reach quiet areas such as Malibu Creek State Park and Topanga State Park. The Angeles National Forest (www.fs.usda. gov/angeles) is about the same distance north of the city and can be reached via Hwy 2 and Hwy 39. There are visitor centres at Chilao, Grassy Hollow, Mt Baldy and Clear Creek.

⑯ STOCKHOLM ARCHIPELAGO, SWEDEN

With more than 30,000 islands to choose from, the task here is picking where you want to go. Ferries run by Waxholmsbolaget (www. waxholmsbolaget.se/ visitor) serve many of the larger islands, whereas the most remote can be reached via water taxi, private boat or on an organised kayaking tour. Discounted island-hopping tickets enable you to visit many of them, and there is plenty of accommodation, ranging from campsites to B&Bs. The Stockholm Archipelago (www. stockholmarchipelago.se/ en) website has all the information you'll need.

wait to escape the city streets for some wild camping, fishing and skinny-dipping out in the archipelago. Local custom says that you're free to camp on any of the islands, as long as it's not on privately owned land, you don't stay for more than one or two nights in any one place and, of course, you leave no trace of your stay.

There are times, however, when solitude isn't so much a geographical space as a state of mind. Josh Duvall is a landscape photographer who has a special interest in finding quiet corners of the world's metropolises. 'Even in the biggest cities – the most crowded, human-dense places on Earth – there's nearly always somewhere where you can escape and find your own space. It doesn't matter whether it's Manhattan or Mumbai, if you know where to look and you're happy to step a little bit off the beaten path, in my experience you'll nearly always be able to find somewhere where you can be alone.'

17 London is a great example of his theory, he explains, as it's a city spotted with pockets of solitude. 'One of the things I really like about London is its green spaces,' Duvall says. 'I often recommend that people explore the city's cemeteries: they're incredibly peaceful, there are loads, and most people never take the time to explore them.' One of his favourites is Highgate Cemetery: covering 15 hectares of prime real estate in northwest London, it's a Gothic fantasy-land of overgrown trees,

Above: the ponds on Hampstead Heath, London. Right: a robin rests in Highgate Cemetery, London.

crooked headstones and ivy-covered tombs, stitched together by a web of winding paths. And there are many more to visit across the city: Abney Park, Brompton, West Norwood and Nunhead, to name a few. And that's before you even begin to enjoy the city's numerous public parks – from classics such as Richmond Park and Hampstead Heath to lesser-known ones like Clissold Park and Victoria Park.

In other words, seeking solitude can sometimes open doors to the hidden city. Even in a super-populated megalopolis such as **18** Tokyo, somewhere synonymous with the commuter crush, there are places to escape the human traffic. In the walled gardens of Rikugien, for instance, commissioned in 1702 by the fifth Tokugawa shogun, are peaceful ponds, quiet woods and footbridges illustrating scenes from famous Japanese poems.

Koishikawa Korakuen Garden is one of Tokyo's oldest and loveliest. Dating from the Edo period in the early 17th century, it's an oasis of aloneness right in the heart of Tokyo's traffic-choked downtown. Or try Shinjuku-gyoen National Garden, an hour's walk southwest. In fact, heading for the nearest park or garden is often

one of the best strategies for finding personal space in overcrowded cities: most metropolises have a few green spaces where you can find an empty bench or a patch of grass to lie down on and savour some solo-time.

Temples, abbeys, churches and other religious spaces are also reliable places for escaping the throngs. Although you might have to share these spaces with other pilgrims, the emphasis on quiet, focused contemplation make them perfect for recharging your solitude batteries. In Běijīng, a good bet is the ❶❾ Lama Temple, the most revered Tibetan Buddhist temple outside Tibet. Construction began on the temple in 1694, and its various halls are decorated with frescoes, tapestries, prayer halls and ornate woodwork, and though the main halls can be busy, various side-halls offer a space to be alone with your own thoughts – which, after all, is what solitude is really all about.

But perhaps the best place to champion the art of aloneness is the adopted home of Henry David Thoreau himself. ❷⓿ Walden Pond in Massachusetts, USA, has changed little since the days when Thoreau lived here from July 1845 to September 1847: it's now a national monument and nature reservation, covering approximately 135 hectares of protected land, surrounded by another 1085 hectares (almost 11 sq km) of undeveloped woodland, and it's still possible to take a wild dip in the waters where Thoreau bathed every day. There's even a replica of the little one-room wooden cabin where HDT lived – the writer's own fortress of solitude, where he sat, listened, thought, wrote and simply experienced the wonder of the world spinning by.

'The man who goes alone can start today,' Thoreau wrote in *Walden*. 'But he who travels with another must wait till that other is ready, and it may be a long time before they get off.'

So what are you waiting for? You heard it from Thoreau: solo is the way to go.

Previous page: Shinjuku-gyoen garden in Tokyo. This page: the Lama Temple in Běijīng. Below: a replica of Thoreau's cabin in Massachusetts, USA.

⑰ LONDON, ENGLAND

Highgate Cemetery (www.highgatecemetery. org) is in the northwest of London. The nearest Tube station is at Archway, just over a mile away or a 20-minute walk. Entry to the East Cemetery is free, but you have to purchase a map if you want to locate the most famous graves. There's a list of the city's other cemeteries at www. londoncemeteries.co.uk. It's also free to visit all of London's public parks, including the eight Royal Parks (www.royalparks. org.uk) as well as all the smaller ones. Most are open from dawn to dusk.

⑱ TŌKYO, JAPAN

Entry to Rikugien Gardens (teien.tokyo-park.or.jp/ en/rikugien) costs ¥300 (£2) per adult. It is open from 9am to 5pm and located at 6-16-3 Hon-Komagome; the easiest way to get there is to take the metro on the Namboku Line to Komagome Station, from where the gardens are a seven-minute walk. Koishikawa Kōrakuen Gardens (teien.tokyo-park.or.jp/en/koishikawa) has the same opening hours and admission prices; the nearest metro is Iidabashi Station on the Toei O-edo Line.

⑲ LAMA TEMPLE, BĔIJĪNG, CHINA

The Lama, or Yonghe, Temple (www. yonghegong.cn) is located at 12 Yonghegong Dajie, just inside Bĕijīng's second ring road. There is a metro station nearby, or you can catch a taxi from anywhere in the city. It's open 9am to 4pm and costs CNY25 (£2.80), or CNY50 (£5.60) with an English audio-guide.

⑳ WALDEN POND STATE RESERVATION, MASSACHUSETTS, USA

Thoreau's beloved lake has been a Registered National Historic Landmark since 1965. It's located near the town of Concord in Massachusetts. There's no entry fee, but it costs $8 (£6) to park, or $10 (£7.50) if you've got a non-Massachusetts licence plate. Various trails lead from the main parking lot, including to the replica of Thoreau's cabin. You're welcome to swim in the lake, and lifeguards are on duty through the summer months.

AMUSEMENT

No one is really quite sure why we laugh. But one of the best working theories is that laughter is an evolutionarily selected trait, as it helps us bond with our own clans while also defusing tension with strangers. This is exactly why a sense of humour is so crucial for travellers. We crack jokes to keep things light on long family road trips. We use goofy hand gestures to bond with strangers in hostels, laughing even when we don't speak the same language.

'Never leave home without your sense of humour,' says Allen Klein, an author of several books on the power of laughter, who himself has been known to use a red clown nose to calm down angry passengers during flight delays.

What's more, humour, fun and laughter all have huge benefits for us as individuals. 'When you laugh because you find something funny, every system in your body gets a workout,' Klein says. 'Your heart rate and blood pressure go up and then dip below normal after you stop laughing. It's very much like aerobic exercise.'

This chapter is called 'Amusement', so we'd be remiss not to start with a place that promises exactly that, the ❶ amusement park. Some of the world's better-known parks have such ginormous crowds and eternal queues that all your capacity for merriment is sucked dry the second you slap on your expensive wristband. So forget those and stick to the old-school models. There's New

① AMUSEMENT PARKS, VARIOUS CITIES

Coney Island is in the New York borough of Brooklyn. Get there from downtown Manhattan in less than an hour by taking the D, Q, N or F train to Stillwell Avenue. Some of the parks are open year-round, though many rides are closed in winter. Blackpool Pleasure Beach is in the northern English seaside town of Blackpool, about 400km (250 miles) from London. Liverpool and Manchester are the nearest large cities. The park opens daily from early April to early November. Luna Park is at Milsons Point, Sydney Harbour. Open year-round, its hours vary.

② STATE FAIRS, USA

Most American state fairs happen in late summer or autumn, the traditional agricultural harvest season. More northerly states generally hold theirs earlier in the season, while southern states go later in the autumn or even winter. Some of the best fairs include those of Iowa, Minnesota, New York (the oldest) and Texas (the largest), but every state's has something to offer. Fairs generally run for 10 days to two weeks, with admission prices hovering around $10 (£7.50 – rides and games cost extra). Go on a weekday if at all possible, as crowds at weekends can be quite intense.

Previous page: the X-Scream
rollercoaster in Las Vegas. This page:
scenes from Minnesota State Fair.

York's Coney Island, a summer destination for more than a century. It's home to a venerable yearly hot dog eating contest; a Mermaid Parade that occasionally verges on the pornographic; and a 90-year-old wooden roller-coaster that'll rattle the teeth right out of your head.

Across the Atlantic, there's England's Blackpool Pleasure Beach, a 120-year-old roller-coaster-laden heaven that's the perfect place to wander around in your swimming trunks, getting sunburned and sticky with candy floss like you're 12 again. And over in Sydney, there's Luna Park, sitting at the foot of the Sydney Harbour Bridge since 1935. Enter through the mouth of a grinning, slightly creepy enormous face, then wobble your way around the moveable floors and distorted mirrors of a classic 1930s funhouse, take a spin on the Ferris wheel, then throw some darts at balloons to win an enormous, entirely useless stuffed whale.

Similar to the amusement park, but with a seasonal and very all-American spin, is the classic ❷ American state fair. Held in late summer or early autumn, these fairs were originally agricultural expos, with farm families coming from hither and yon to display their finest heifers and yuck it up with the neighbours they rarely got to see. Today, you can still gawk at livestock and admire blue ribbon-winning quilts, but now you can also indulge in a smorgasbord of weird Americana.

Cheer on the pig races at the North Carolina State Fair; admire life-sized cows, motorcycles and Elvis Presley busts carved entirely out of butter at the Iowa State Fair; or catch dogs performing backflips at the Wisconsin State Fair. The food is designed to entertain as well, with fairs competing to create the most over-the-top gonzo treats. Deep-fried jellybeans! Chocolate-dipped scorpion! Bacon margaritas!

Continue the merrymaking in a place where the fun is turned up to volume 11, 24/7/365. Yup, we're talking about ❸ Las Vegas, baby. A gambling and entertainment mecca built on mob dollars, it rises out of the Mojave Desert like a mirage, offering amusement at its most manic. Due to all that neon and glitter, you'll hardly know what time of day it is here, and it hardly matters. Kick-off your bacchanal at downtown's Fremont Street Experience, a five-block stretch covered in a huge arched LED canopy hosting hallucinatory light and music shows on the hour from 6pm to 1am. It's also home to SlotZilla, a 12-storey-high 'slot machine-inspired' zipline enabling you to hurtle through the air, horizontal Superman-style, above thousands of gawking pedestrians.

Calm down the adrenaline coursing through your veins with whiskey and blackjack at the Mandalay Bay, then bring it back up with a stroll along the casino's walk-through shark tunnel. Scuba diving with the sharks is only for hotel guests, so get your kicks at Circus Circus, which has a two-hectare indoor amusement park and acrobats flying overhead all day and night. Top off your evening (or morning, who are we to judge?) with the buffet at Bacchanal in Caesars Palace. Pile your plate with unseemly amounts of king crab legs, slabs of prime rib, sushi and made-to-order soufflés, then grab a table overlooking the Garden of the Gods pool complex. If you don't end your Vegas trip overstuffed, overstimulated and underfunded, you're doing it wrong.

OK, so maybe you prefer a slightly higher-brow type of amusement. If so, then August in Edinburgh is the place to be. The ❹ Edinburgh Festival Fringe, known simply as 'the Fringe', is the world's largest performing arts festival, hosting some 50,000 performances across 300 venues over the course of a month. While there are shows of all types – children's theatre, burlesque, dance, opera, chainsaw juggling (yes, really) and more – comedy is the biggest category and the biggest draw. Lots of marquee-

❸ LAS VEGAS, NEVADA, USA

You can fly into Las Vegas' McCarran International Airport from practically anywhere in the world. Many hotels offer shuttle buses from the airport, or you can take a public bus right to the Strip. Don't bother renting a car unless you plan to head into the desert; parking is expensive and difficult. Once you're on the Strip, the 6.3km (four mile) monorail is the best way to get around. Hotels in Vegas can be outrageously cheap, as gambling is how the hotel-casino complexes make their money. When large conventions are in town, prices can spike though, so check ahead. The city bustles year-round, but summer is painfully hot.

❹ EDINBURGH FRINGE FESTIVAL, SCOTLAND

The Fringe runs from early to late August, for about 25 days. Some popular shows begin selling tickets at the beginning of the year; keep tabs on the festival's website (www.edfringe. com) to know what's happening when. The full programme is usually available by early June. Edinburgh's population doubles in August, so hotels are at a premium. If you can't find a room, look into booking student dormitories or personal apartments. Edinburgh Airport is 12km (seven miles) from the city centre, with flights from Europe, the US and beyond. Or take the train from London, which, at its quickest, can take less than five hours.

name comedians have launched here, so you might well catch the next Eddie Izzard or Craig Ferguson.

Unusual venues are a Fringe signature – see acts in parks, cafes, schools and office buildings. And plan to get interactive, as past shows have involved the audience playing a made-up sport, attending an absurdist cooking class, participating in a naughty gameshow and taking shots of booze with the star of a one-woman show.

Make it an entire summer of comedy by starting a month earlier, in Montréal. Here, each July brings ❺ Just for Laughs, the world's largest international comedy festival. Wander the arty Quartier Latin with two million of your fellow comedy hounds, choosing from several hundred stand-up acts and funny films. Basically everyone who's anyone has performed here at one time or another over the past 30-plus years – Louis CK, John Cleese, Sarah Silverman, Dave Chappelle, Jerry Seinfeld and Gad Elmaleh, to name a handful.

However, sometimes the no-name up-and-comers have the best, most energetic performances (and it's certainly easier to get tickets to their shows). With so many comedians and fans wandering around, the entire city takes on a slightly giddy vibe, from the bongo players in Parc du Mont-Royale to the rainbow-draped cafes of the Village to the sidewalk bars of Saint Denis Street.

Catch stand-up of a very different sort across the Pacific. Many of us are familiar with ❻ Japanese comedy from variety show clips heavy on the groin-bashing and other painful high jinks. But there are several ancient forms of Japanese comedy performance still alive and well today. Some popular ones include *kyogen*, a sort of Japanese vaudeville, heavy on slapstick and exaggerated facial expressions; *manzai*, a double act with a clever straight man tormenting a dull-witted funny man with high-speed wordplay; and *rakugo*, a one-man or one-woman show with a traditionally dressed performer telling a long funny story and portraying various characters.

For non-Japanese speakers, penetrating the Japanese comedy world can be tricky. But it's not impossible. Catch a monthly English-language *rakugo* show in Tokyo, giggling at the antics of the performer (who has served a multi-year apprenticeship to be a master comedian) as they portray various characters from samurais to geishas to small children. Although *kyogen* is rarely performed in English, its goofy broadness and slapstick makes it possible to enjoy even without understanding the words.

In the ancient city of Kyoto, you can see *kyogen* performances at shrines, often in conjunction with a religious ritual, throughout the year. During the Setsubun 'bean-throwing festival' in early February, head to Kyoto's Kitano Tenmangu shrine to watch masked *kyogen* performers toss beans to drive away demons.

Osaka, considered Japan's comedy capital, hosts several English-language comedy troupes and stand-up nights, drawing crowds of Japanese and global aficionados.

If that doesn't make you laugh, then here's something that will: ❼ laughter yoga. Join a group of strangers in a park to chuckle, guffaw, chortle and howl. No, nobody's told a joke or even done anything particularly funny. It's just that laughter, much like yawning, is contagious. Get one person started, and it's almost impossible not to join in. And the benefits of laughter are identical no matter why you're laughing. You get the same rush of relaxation and sense of wellbeing, the feelings that drive the cliché 'laughter is the best medicine'.

The science behind this is fairly solid. According to the Mayo Clinic in the US, laughter can release endorphins, stimulate muscle relaxation and draw more oxygen to the organs. Laughter yoga's inventor, Indian doctor Madan Kataria, calls it 'internal jogging'. Kataria started informal 'laughter clubs' throughout India in the mid-

⑤ JUST FOR LAUGHS, MONTRÉAL, CANADA

The Just for Laughs festival runs for the second half of July, with the biggest names arriving in the second week. You can pay per show, or purchase two-, three- or five-show packages. There are also early-bird specials, so check the website. You can often get cheap last-minute tickets, but seats may be lousy. Montréal–Pierre Elliott Trudeau International Airport receives flights from many destinations in the US, Europe and beyond. Buses run from the airport to the city all day and through the night. www.hahaha.com

⑥ JAPANESE COMEDY, JAPAN

If you speak Japanese, head to Tokyo's Asakusa neighbourhood, home to the bulk of the city's traditional comedy theatres. Also in Tokyo, you can catch a rakugo performance in English about once a month; check an events calendar online for details. In Osaka, ROR Comedy (www.rorcomedy.com) is the heart of the English-language comedy scene. At this club, watch English stand-up every Friday and Saturday night, try your hand at open mic, or just shoot the breeze with local and expat comedians.

Overleaf: entertainers at Edinburgh Festival Fringe, Scotland. The world's largest arts festival runs every August.

1990s to spread the gospel of the giggle, and the idea has taken off worldwide. You can study with the master at Kataria's Laughter Yoga University in Bangalore. Or just join a morning laughter club near you, and start your day howling like a maniac in the grass.

Back in the USA, there's another way to revel in public goofiness: hop aboard a giant waterfowl for a ❽ Duck Tour of Boston. The 'ducks' – brightly painted WWII-style amphibious vehicles – are half bus, half boat, and look as silly as can be. They've been ferrying visitors around the historic city for more than 20 years, and are a familiar sight to Bostonians, who borrow them as parade vehicles whenever a local sports team such as the Red Sox or the Patriots wins a major championship. Take your seat beneath the canopy and listen to the 'conDUCKtor' (wisecrackers with silly costumes and names like Vincent Van Duck and Old QuackDonald) tell you all about Boston's history, including its weirder side.

In 80 minutes, you'll hit all the city's big sights – the shiny gold-domed State House, the 17th-century graves of the Granary Burying Ground, the terraced houses and gaslit lanes of Beacon Hill, the wealthy 'Boston Brahmins' shopping on tony Newbury Street, the swan boats in the Public Garden (how do the swan boats feel about the duck boats? We'll have to ask). Then they'll dip into the Charles River for a paddle around the waterfront. Your conDUCKtor will bring out your goofy side, asking you to quack out loud at people on the sidewalk or boo rude drivers. So get over your adult hang-ups about

Left: a puffin comes in to land.
Right: discover Boston on a Duck Tour.

'humiliating yourself' or 'looking ridiculous' and just do it. As Bostonians say, it's 'wicked fun'.

Speaking of silly water birds, have you ever seen a ❾ puffin come in for a landing? The little black-and-white flying dumplings hover in the air, their comically huge orange feet spread wide, a look of terror on their tiny faces. Once they touch down, their top-heaviness often causes them to plough face-first into the grass. It's inelegant but completely adorable. No wonder puffins have earned the nickname 'clowns of the sea'.

One of the best places on Earth to watch the little goofballs is the Isle of Staffa, in Scotland's Inner Hebrides. Approaching the island in a small boat, you'll see massive basalt pillars rising out of the sea, surrounding the mouth of Fingal's Cave. From here, you climb a rocky staircase on to the island's gently sloping grassy back. In summer, this is prime puffin breeding territory. Thousands of the birds hop around the tufty cliffs, dive-bombing into the

⑦ LAUGHTER YOGA, WORLDWIDE; LAUGHTER YOGA SPIRITUAL SEMINARS, BANGALORE, INDIA

You can find laughter yoga groups anywhere from Los Angeles to Hanoi to Florence to Cairo. The best way to find one is to google 'laughter yoga' and the name of your city. If you want to take it to a deeper level, founder Dr Kataria offers spiritual retreats in Bangalore throughout the year. Check the website (www.laughteryoga.org). Or train with Kataria to become a laughter yoga teacher yourself and start your own laughter yoga club.

⑧ DUCK TOURS, BOSTON, MASSACHUSETTS, USA

Boston Duck Tours depart daily year-round from the Prudential Center, the New England Aquarium and the Museum of Science. They last about 80 minutes. Adult tickets cost $40 (£31), children's $27 (£21) and kids under three $10.50 (£8). The Ducks are heated, but dress for the cold, as the river can be breezy. Fly into Boston's Logan International Airport and take the subway into town. The city's also connected to the rest of the Eastern Seaboard via Amtrak. Visit in spring or autumn; winter can be brutally cold. www. bostonducktours.com

A baby three-toed sloth gets to grips with life in Costa Rica's rainforests.

water and returning with their brightly coloured beaks brimming with fish. They're friendly little guys, so you can get close enough to snap pictures that will make all your friends go 'awwwww'. You might even spot a baby puffin – technically known as a puffling – in the burrow.

Vying with the puffin for the title of World's Goofiest Animal is the sloth. Due to their round heads and sleepy smiles, these furry tree-dwellers look as if they're children's stuffed toys come to slow, lumbering life. Catch one in the wild at the 20 sq km ❿ Parque Nacional Manuel Antonio on Costa Rica's Pacific coast. Here, the keen-eyed can spot two-toed and three-toed sloths dangling on the branches of cecropia trees, lazily munching away. You're less likely to see one on the ground – sloths only come down once a week, to poop.

The park has a special sloth trail, the Sendero El Perezoso ('perezoso', the Spanish word for sloth, also means 'lazy'), along an access road, where the sloth-sleuthing is particularly good. Once you're done sloth-watching, you can amuse yourself in a dozen other ways – listening to howler monkeys, wading in the turquoise surf at Playa Manuel Antonio, watching raccoons devour coconut crabs, hiking the emerald hills.

Puffins and sloths are inherently funny. Pigs, not so much. But take a pig and add water, and presto, comic gold. In the Bahamas, the uninhabited island of Big Major Cay is home to a colony of wild pigs that love nothing more than to paddle around in the gin-clear water, snorting happily. Join them for a splash at ⓫ Pig Beach. The porkers will sometimes swim right up to waders or snorkellers to oink hello. No one knows how the pigs wound up on Big Major Cay. Some say their ancestors were ditched there by passing sailors, while others tell tales of a nearby shipwreck where porcine survivors paddled to the nearest bit of land. Wherever they came from, the fun-loving piggies and their aqua backdrop make for one of the world's quirkiest (and most Instagram-worthy) experiences.

While we're on the subject of swimming creatures, let's cross the Straits of Florida back to the US, where Florida's ⓬ Weeki Wachee Springs State Park is home to an even rarer breed: mermaids. Since 1947, women dressed in shimmering tails have performed underwater in the crystal-clear natural springs. Eyes wide open, hair drifting like seaweed, they swim in graceful circles and wriggle bewitchingly, barely pausing to sip compressed air from tubes planted around the set. Sitting in the chilly underground theatre built into the limestone surrounding

the spring, you'll see the mermaids sip sodas and eat bananas underwater, smiling like pageant queens the entire time. Resident turtles and even the occasional manatee may float into the picture.

This is one of Florida's oldest and kitschiest roadside attractions, the kind of earnest Americana that will put a grin on even the Grinchiest face. Around the springs is an old-school pleasure park, with a riverboat cruise, waterslides and a picnic area, the kind of place that would have thrilled children in the mid-20th century, before everyone decided that amusement came only from television and tablets.

While the fun at Weeki Wachee doesn't involve you actually getting wet yourself, this definitely does: Thailand's ⓭ Songkran, aka 'the world's biggest water fight'. The Thai Lunar New Year, Songkran was originally celebrated by the ritual washing of Buddha images and sprinkling water on the hands of elders. That still happens, but so does an all-out water-gun shooting, water-balloon hurling, bucket-tossing extravaganza, with anyone on the street being fair game for a soaking (foreigners are no exception!).

---

⑨ PUFFIN WATCHING, ISLE OF STAFFA, SCOTLAND

Tours of Staffa depart from Fionnphort on the Isle of Mull; the Isle of Iona, across the water from Fionnphort; Tobermory, on northern Mull; the mainland's Ardnamurchan Peninsula; and the mainland port of Oban. Boat tours can last between three and 12 hours and cost from £30 to £70, depending on where you go – some trips go beyond Staffa. The best time to spot puffins is during their breeding season, from early April to early August. Getting to the various departure towns is a two- or three-hour drive from Glasgow and Edinburgh respectively.

❿ SLOTH WATCHING, PARQUE NACIONAL MANUEL ANTONIO, COSTA RICA

Quepos is the nearest town to the Parque Nacional Manuel Antonio. Get there by air from the Costa Rican capital of San José, or by a three-hour direct bus. Park admission is $16 (£12) for adults; guided tours cost $51 (£40) for adults and $35 (£27) for children, but they give you a better chance at seeing sloths and other wildlife, and include transport from your hotel. The dry season is December through March. During the winter and Easter high seasons, visit during the afternoon for a less crowded experience.

Getting soaked at the spring festival
of Songkran in Chiang Mai, Thailand.

In the northern city of Chiang Mai, Songkran festivities can last for almost a week. You may be sprayed by squirt-gun-toting kids from the back of a motorbike, soaked by a hose held by dancers on a sponsored float, or drenched by a passing elephant. Or you might find yourself covered in soap bubbles during an impromptu pavement foam party. Gird yourself – the water is cold. At first it's refreshing, as Songkran is in mid-April, the hottest time of year. But soon you'll be running around shivering, your hair a mess, your shirt plastered to your back. And you'll be having the best time of your life.

It'll be good for you too. 'There's an essential biological need to experience playfulness,' says Dr Stuart Brown, founder of The National Institute for Play in California. Play is important for adults, not just kids, Brown says, and can reduce stress, anxiety and depression, while boosting creativity and even enhancing job performance. Sounds like a good reason to pick up a water gun.

⑪ PIG BEACH, EXUMA, BAHAMAS

Pig Beach is on Big Major Cay, part of the Exuma Cays district of the Bahamas. The nearest island with accommodation is Staniel Cay; from here you can hire a local guide to take you to visit the pigs. Otherwise you can book a tour from mainland Exuma, which will include iguana-spotting, snorkelling and lunch. You can also take a day tour from the Bahamian capital of Nassau. To get to the Exumas, take a ferry or a quick flight from Nassau. You may want to avoid the Bahamas from June to November, as it's hurricane season.

⑫ WEEKI WACHEE SPRINGS STATE PARK, FLORIDA, USA

Weeki Wachee Springs State Park is in the pinprick hamlet of Weeki Wachee (so small there are more mermaids in the park than people in the town) on Florida's Gulf coast. It's 90km (56 miles) to Tampa and about 145km (90 miles) to Orlando; both cities have large international airports. The mermaids perform two shows, twice a day. Seating is first-come, first-served. Admission to the park is $13 (£10) for adults, $8 (£6) for kids, which includes the mermaid show, a wildlife show and a riverboat ride.

So long as we're playing in the water, we can't neglect one of the most delightfully weird swimming spots on Earth, the ⑭ Dead Sea. As you probably know, the vast lake bordering Israel, Palestine and Jordan is so saline (nearly 10 times saltier than the ocean), it's denser than the human body, making your swim-suited self as buoyant as a cork. Bob around for a while beneath the Levantine sun, taking some wacky pictures of yourself reading a newspaper while floating. The water feels heavy, almost slippery, and is so dense that it's hard to remain upright, so you'll keep springing to the surface involuntarily, like a dolphin with a few wires crossed.

In a desert across the globe, a community mocks its arid climate by holding a boat race… with no water. Alice Springs, in Australia's Red Centre, has hosted the bizarre ⑮ Henley-on-Todd Regatta in the dry bed of the Todd River for more than 55 years. It's been cancelled only once, in 1993, when rain meant there was actually water in the river. Grown adults dressed as Vikings and pirates run along the sand in bottomless boats, while others race in bathtubs, old tyres, giant hamster wheels or while being dragged on boogie boards.

---

⑬ SONGKRAN, THAILAND

Songkran, Thai New Year, falls on April 13, but most parts of Thailand celebrate on the 14th and 15th as well. The holiday is a time to visit family back in the villages, so parts of Bangkok can feel quite empty. If you're here, try the foreigner-laden Khao San Road for the heaviest partying. Chiang Mai has perhaps the most famous Songkran celebration, where splashing lasts for several days longer than elsewhere. Don't wear your nice clothes, keep your phone safe, and stay off the roads if possible – traffic deaths spike during the week around Songkran.

⑭ DEAD SEA, ISRAEL, PALESTINE AND JORDAN

You can access the Dead Sea from the resorts on the Israeli side or the Jordanian side. On both, summer is incredibly hot, while the springtime Jewish holidays of Passover and Sukkot pack the Israel-side hotels with domestic tourists. Regular shuttle buses to the Dead Sea run from Tel Aviv and Jerusalem, and buses and taxis run from Amman. There are many resorts and campsites on the Israeli side; on the Jordanian side luxury resorts cluster the sea's northeastern end. You don't need to be staying at a hotel or resort to swim, so it's possible to visit as a day trip.

Left: floating in the Dead Sea. Below: swimming with pigs in the Bahamas.

A parade kicks off the festivities, and costumes are de rigueur – pink wigs, sparkly hula skirts, mock yachtie attire. Grab some greasy food and loll in the shade beneath the gum trees to watch it all. As a grand finale, trucks decorated as boats drive around the sand, shooting water cannons and flour bombs at the audience. It's all for a good cause – the local Rotary clubs that organise the event donate the proceeds to charity.

For more quirky Australiana, gas up your Holden (the first mass-produced Australian-designed car) and set out on the great Aussie road trip. This means white-sand beaches in Queensland, fancy wine-tasting in South Australia and plenty of sausage rolls in Red Centre roadhouses. But most of all it means ⑯ Big Things.

The Big Things are a collection of novelty sculptures and buildings that have been built as roadside attractions across the country, designed to lure travellers into small towns and way stations. Heading north out of Sydney, you'll hit the sleepy city of Newcastle, where Ossie the Mossie tops the sign for the Hexham Bowling Club. A giant version of the local Hexham Grey mosquito species, he'll make you understand why writer Bill Bryson described the Big Things as looking like 'leftover props from a 1950s horror movie'.

Head north along the coast to the town of Coffs Harbour, where the Big Banana tops a retro-tastic banana-themed

⑮ HENLEY-ON-TODD REGATTA, ALICE SPRINGS, NORTHERN TERRITORY, AUSTRALIA

The Regatta is held every third Saturday in August – Australian winter. Flights to Alice Springs take about three hours from Sydney and three and a half hours from Melbourne. If you fly in, you'll want to rent a car. If you want to race in the BYO boat event, get to the Alice Springs Town Council lawns at 9.30am to register. And bring your own boat. The parade starts at 10.30am and the races start at 11.45am. Wear sunscreen and bring a hat. www.henleyontodd.com.au

⑯ BIG THINGS ROAD TRIP, AUSTRALIA

Recall that Australian seasons are the opposite of those in the Northern Hemisphere, so December is summer and so forth. The dry season of April through October is the best time to visit the Outback. Driving here can be hazardous, as you'll be sharing one-lane highways with enormous 'road train' trucks and kamikaze kangaroos. It's best not to drive after dark. In North Queensland, the wet season is November through April, and can bring both flooding and dangerous box jellyfish to the coast. Cities such as Sydney, Melbourne, Brisbane and Adelaide are lively year-round.

amusement park on the site of a banana plantation. Further on, the town of Ballina is home to both the Big Prawn and a stunning turquoise beach. To the north, the fertile lime-green hills of sunshiny Queensland are dotted with a Big Mango, Big Macadamia Nut, Big Pineapple and several Big Oranges.

Stock up on water and travel the one-lane highway into Australia's dusty, depopulated centre, where you'll find a Big Stubby (beer bottle) and a Big Aboriginal Hunter, plus thousands of kilometres of stunning desert the colour of the sunrise. Down in South Australia, you'll encounter the OG of Big Things in the state capital of Adelaide. Standing 5m tall, the kilt-clad, bagpipe-playing Big Scotsman has been watching over Scotty's Motel since 1963, making him the oldest Big Thing of all.

For a very different sort of tour, head to the Irish capital of ⑰ Dublin to follow in the footsteps of the city's beloved son, the writer Oscar Wilde. Though not all of Wilde's work was comic (his most famous poem, *The Ballad of Reading Gaol*, was about his grim imprisonment for homosexual acts), he was a renowned wit, tossing off immortal epigrams over glasses of whiskey.

Start your tour at his birthplace, 21 Westland Row, an elegant 1830s brick terrace now belonging to Trinity College. You can't go inside, so just admire the façade and move on to Merrion Square, a Georgian-era public garden featuring a statue of Wilde reclining on a boulder, wearing a green smoking jacket and a foppish smirk. Snap a picture of the grand exterior of 1 Merrion Square,

Left: the very arid Henley-on-Todd Regatta in Alice Springs. This page: the icy interior of Sweden's Icehotel.

Above: the Big Prawn of Ballina, one of
Australia's many 'big things'. Right: Oscar
Wilde reclines in Merrion Sq, Dublin.

where Wilde grew up, before heading across the street to the National Gallery of Ireland to see the portrait of William Wilde, Oscar's surgeon father. In the evening, take in a show at the venerable Abbey Theatre, which has staged several notable Wilde productions, including an all-male version of *The Importance of Being Earnest*.

As Wilde's life shows, humour can help us survive some of fate's dreariest circumstances. After being released from prison, Wilde died broke and nearly friendless in a seedy Paris hotel. But even nearing his end he was able to joke about the dinginess of his surroundings. 'This wallpaper and I are fighting a duel to the death,' he said. 'One or the other of us has to go.'

Oscar Wilde would certainly have had something to say about the wallpaper at one iconic American home: Elvis's ⑱ Graceland. An ode to the King's lavish tastes and the wonderful badness of 1970s design, the white Colonial-style mansion is the second most-visited house in America (after the actual White House). Slip on an audio tour headset and stroll past the faux waterfall of the tiki-themed Jungle Room, down a hallway with green carpet on the ceiling, and into the aggressively yellow TV room. Outbuildings are filled with Elvis memorabilia – posters of movies such as *Blue Hawaii* and *Jailhouse Rock* from the Skinny Elvis days and rhinestone-studded white jumpsuits of the later Fat Elvis era. The King

himself is buried next to the kidney-shaped swimming pool, along with his beloved mother and father.

Speaking of buildings that are entertaining in and of themselves, 200km north of the Arctic Circle is the mind-blowing ⑲ Icehotel of Jukkasjärvi, Sweden. For nearly 30 years, artists and artisans have carved the extraordinary structure anew each winter, only to have it melt away in spring. Enter a cavernous lobby awash in mint blue light, every surface crystalline ice except for the furs covering the ice couches. Sip vodka from ice glasses at the Icebar, then dance the night away on the floor of snow. Nobody looks cool dancing in a parka, so go ahead and cut loose. Sleep on reindeer skins on an ice block bed, surrounded by modernist ice sculptures (yes, you get a sleeping bag, rated for Arctic expeditions). Room themes, which change every year, have ranged from 1970s Love Hotel to Imperial Russian splendour.

In the daytime, enjoy all the amusements Lapland has to offer: dogsledding, cross-country skiing, ice fishing, or riding a snowmobile to see the Northern Lights. When you're done, sweat in the traditional sauna before plunging into icy Torne River. Because this is, apparently,

⑰ OSCAR WILDE TOUR, DUBLIN, IRELAND

Fly into Dublin Airport from cities in the USA, Canada, Europe and beyond. It's 12km (7.5 miles) to the centre, which can be reached by bus. The Holyhead to Dublin ferry connects with Wales in less than two hours. Summer is the nicest time to visit, with warm days and cool nights. Everyone else thinks so too, of course. Most of the Wilde sights are south of the River Liffey. To catch a show at the Abbey Theatre, book ahead online (www.abbeytheatre.ie).

⑱ GRACELAND, MEMPHIS, TENNESSEE, USA

Memphis International Airport connects the city with most major US destinations plus Toronto. If you're staying downtown, there's a free shuttle bus to Graceland from Sun Studio. Otherwise, drive or take a tour bus. Tour options range from the basic $39 (£30) mansion tour to a $160 (£124) VIP tour and start at the visitor's centre across the street. Buy tickets there or online. August 11-19 is Elvis Week, when thousands of fans honour the King. Avoid or gawk, your choice.

⑲ ICEHOTEL, JUKKASJÄRVI, SWEDEN

The Icehotel is open December through April. December and February are the busiest months. But a new Icehotel 365 on the same grounds is open year-round, kept cool by solar panels. In addition to the famous 'cold rooms', there are also standard 'warm rooms' in an adjacent area. The hotel recommends staying one night in a cold room and several in a warm room. The nearest airport is in Kiruna, with 90-minute flights to Stockholm. You can also get there by train from Narvik, Norway, or Luleå, Sweden. www.icehotel.com

⑳ MOLECULAR GASTRONOMY, WORLDWIDE

Getting a table at The Fat Duck in Bray, a village in southern England, is a trick. Reservations are 'released' on the first Wednesday of each month at noon, with bookings up to four months ahead. Reservations are prepaid. It's a similar deal at Chicago's Alinea. El Celler De Can Roca accepts bookings up to 11 months in advance. Noma is currently in the process of changing locations, but offers occasional pop-ups around the globe. These four are justly famous, but there are many other innovative restaurants around the world.

what the Swedes find fun. Well, when in Jukkasjärvi!

All this dogsledding and sauna-going must have made you hungry. Why not dine at a restaurant where food is also entertainment? We're talking about ⑳ molecular gastronomy, the 21st-century phenomenon of using (mad) science in the kitchen, transforming liquids into spheres, serving meat dishes that look like candy and candy that tastes like meat, and turning absolutely everything into a foam.

Chef Heston Blumenthal's The Fat Duck in Bray, England, is perhaps the king of the genre, serving you the likes of bacon and egg ice cream, created tableside with a silver pitcher of liquid nitrogen. Chicago's much-celebrated Alinea claims to not even be a restaurant, though it does serve food. If you can call edible balloons 'food' (we do; they're delicious). It's a multisensory carnival, asking you to search for beef jerky camouflaged in a twig basket, slurp liquid beets from a block of ice, or eat using two cinnamon sticks as chopsticks.

At El Celler De Can Roca in Girona, Spain, you'll be treated to modernist twists on Catalan cooking: a bowl of lobster ceviche emblazoned with a frozen tiger-face design or a sourdough ice cream that appears to breathe thanks to a hidden motor. And at Copenhagen's eternally buzzy Noma you may be served live ants with a dollop of crème fraiche. Tasty? Actually, yes. Fun? Absolutely.

Chris Blackwell's (of Island Records)
GoldenEye resort on Jamaica.

INSPIRATION

For a concept so inherently linked to revelation and illumination, inspiration is hard to pin down. It's elusive; it's tantalising; it's 'unscientific'. Indeed, the title of bestselling author Elizabeth Gilbert's book on the subject says it all: *Big Magic: Creative Living Beyond Fear*. The word 'Magic' is particularly telling.

'Even very rational, empirical people will use a certain kind of language when they talk about inspiration,' explains Gilbert, whose previous books include international bestseller *Eat Pray Love*. 'They'll say "and then this idea came to me", as if there's a sense that this thing somehow came from the outward-in.'

It's a familiar sentiment. Inspiration is something we 'seek', which then 'strikes' us. It is always, as Gilbert notes, an external force that appears in certain situations and places. The question of inspiration, therefore, becomes not so much a 'what' as a 'where'.

If inspiration is something we find 'outside the box', and the box represents our daily, accepted routines, then the best way to find inspiration is to travel. In particular, to places where it has struck before. Because in the immortal words of Jack London: 'You can't wait for inspiration. You have to go after it with a club.'

① GOLD COAST, JAMAICA

Jamaica's Gold Coast, including Oracabessa and GoldenEye, is located on the northwest side of the Caribbean Island. The best international airport is at Montego Bay, about a two-hour drive from Oracabessa. Temperatures consistently hover around 25-30°C throughout the year. Local company Jamaica Xplored (www.jamaicaxplored.com) offers James Bond-related tours of the area, taking in key sites that made it into Fleming's novels and the subsequent films. For more, see www.visitjamaica.com

② KEY WEST, FLORIDA, USA

Miami and Fort Lauderdale are the main gateway airports to Key West. Hire a car at the airport and drive south on the Florida Keys Overseas Highway to reach it – 295km (183 miles) from Fort Lauderdale or 257km (160 miles) from Miami. Key West is great to visit year-round but is at its most popular from January to March. For best prices and availability, aim to visit in November or December. Once you're in Key West, the best way to get around is by bicycle, moped or the open-sided electric tourist cars, aka 'Conch cruisers'. All can be rented on arrival.

Clockwise from top left: interior of Hemingway's house on Key West; its exterior; Key West's Schooner Wharf Bar; Key West architecture.

Ian Fleming made up his mind while WWII was still raging. Leaving Jamaica after a naval conference, he slammed his briefcase shut and turned to a friend.

'I've made a great decision,' he said. 'When we've won this blasted war, I'm going to live in Jamaica. Just live in Jamaica and lap it up, and swim in the sea and write books.' So inspired had the young naval officer been by his brief experience of ❶ Jamaica's Gold Coast that he knew he'd found the perfect place to create his novels. Good as his word, once peace was declared, Fleming bought land near the pretty fishing village of Oracabessa and built GoldenEye – the home he visited religiously every winter for the next 17 years, producing a new James Bond novel every time.

③ CYCLADES ISLANDS, GREECE

The Cyclades are most enjoyable in late spring – when the landscape is still green and the sea has warmed up enough to swim, but the crowds have yet to descend – and early autumn, when the hordes have departed and the sea is at its warmest. The main airports are Mykonos, Santorini or Paros, with international charter flights direct during the summer months, or domestic transfers via Athens and Thessaloniki year-round. Within the Cyclades group, the best way to get between islands is via regular ferry routes (see www.aferry. com for a summary of all lines and timetables). Positioned right in the centre of the islands, Paros makes a great base.

④ ISLE OF JURA, SCOTLAND

One of Scotland's Inner Hebrides, Jura is best reached via the regular car ferry shuttle from Port Askaig on Islay. It takes five minutes and departs hourly Monday to Saturday, and every two hours on Sunday. From April to September, the Jura Passenger Ferry (www.jurapassengerferry. com) runs from Tayvallich on the mainland to Craighouse on Jura (one hour; one or two sailings daily except Tuesdays). Booking recommended. The friendly Jura Hotel, Craighouse (www. jurahotel.co.uk) is a good bet accommodation-wise, or for a self-catering option see www. escapetojura.com.

Fleming found GoldenEye – and the Gold Coast in general – a near-limitless source of inspiration, from the teeming reef he swam along every morning to the magnificent Laughing Waters beach nearby (where Ursula Andress later emerged from the surf during the filming of the first Bond movie, *Dr No*). Lit in the afternoon by a warm apricot glow, the Gold Coast was an enchanted oasis for Fleming: a place of recovery, sanctuary and creativity while London shivered itself through winter and 'people streamed miserably to work, their legs whipped by the wet hems of their mackintoshes'.

A literary great from the other side of the Atlantic, Ernest Hemingway, experienced a similar creative awakening on the other side of the Caribbean – in ❷ Key West, Florida. It was here, in the little island town nicknamed 'SoHo in the sun', that the Nobel Prize-winning author produced his greatest body of work over a ferocious nine-year period. It's easy to see why the place appealed so strongly to his romantic soul.

Dangling at the bottom of the long, slender Florida Keys like a golden pendant at the end of a hypnotist's chain, the lively beach town has always been a magnet for mavericks, creatives and free spirits, and Hemingway thrived off the energy in the bars, cafes and restaurants. It's very much the same place today, with crowds gathering in Mallory Square to applaud the sun going down over the ocean every evening, while magicians, dancers and performing cats entertain them. The old creative magic is obviously still working too – with more than 50 published authors based within the island's 19 sq km (7 sq miles) at last count.

So what *is* it about these places that make them so inspiring? Gilbert writes in *Big Magic* about a Greek concept called Eudaemonia. There's no direct translation, but her explanation is 'the happiness that comes when you're engaged with your creative daemon at the highest level'. Today we'd call it the 'flow' or the 'zone'. Tellingly, Fleming and Hemingway both discovered Eudaemonia on islands, where the beach and the sea played significant roles in galvanising their creative talents. On this merit, one of the finest places in the world to seek inspiration would be among the Greek islands themselves, particularly the spectacular ❸ Cyclades, which have been attracting writers, poets and philosophers since Eudaemonia was first conceived.

The name 'Cyclades' refers to the islands forming a circle around the sacred island of Delos, with countless dazzling seascapes, white sand beaches and ancient sites between them. The best way to seek Eudaemonia here is to island hop, taking care not to miss some of the richest spots, including Chora, the clifftop city on the island of

This page: the town of Oia on Santorini, Greece. Right: a characteristic church there.

Gásadalur village on the west
coast of the Faroe Islands.

Folegandros, and Patmos – the unspoilt Greek island where you'll find the Cave of the Apocalypse, the site where St John supposedly drafted the Book Of Revelation.

Inspiration of any kind – revelatory or otherwise – isn't overly concerned by the weather. When George Orwell retreated to an island to write his seminal masterpiece *1984*, he shunned the sunshine of the Mediterranean and instead plumped for the raw, wild allure of ❹ Jura. One of Scotland's Inner Hebrides, Jura is as beautiful as it is remote, with roughly 200 inhabitants still outnumbered by deer, and only one significant road, one pub and one (extremely good) distillery to its name.

Staying on the north side of the island in a remote farmhouse called Barnhill, Orwell thrived on the silence and tranquillity that envelop Jura's heather glens, ancient forts and standing stones still: the perfect conditions to conduct inspiration when it strikes. Barnhill can still be hired out today – although, in keeping with its heroic isolation, you'll rely on a generator for electricity (on the plus side, it makes it harder for Big Brother to watch you).

North of the Hebrides, half way to Iceland, you'll find Eudaemonia is also served chilled in the ❺ Faroe Islands. These tiny shavings of land, pretty much equidistant between Iceland, Norway and Scotland, are still ignored by a number of maps, and that's exactly how the locals like it. Because the Faroe Islands are quite possibly the most peaceful place on Earth. If there was ever a land where fairy tales were writ large, this is it. The streets of the pretty capital, Tórshavn, are lined with colourful, grass-roofed houses (a legacy of the Vikings who first arrived here in the 9th century and hunkered down under their boats, using grass sod for insulation).

Outside Tórshavn, the bright timber dwellings give way to dramatic seascapes and lush valleys, mirror-like fjords and dramatic, layer-cake sea cliffs. Inspiration is everywhere you turn on this archipelago, driven in part by the Viking culture that is still alive and well here, from the traditional chain dances and ancient ballads – both performed regularly – to the native tongue itself: the closest Scandinavian language to Old Norse.

Further north still, and Iceland is galvanising imaginations on an entirely new level, particularly, at its most southerly point, around the village of ❻ Vik. Here, Reynisfjara, a spectacular, otherworldly black-sand beach encircled by bristling basalt sea stacks, has become a mecca for writers and film directors alike, inspiring scenes in movies ranging from *Interstellar* to *Star Wars: Rogue One*. (They're far from the first storytellers

to spin tales around the natural wonders here: folklore has it those giant basalt stacks were formed when three trolls attempted to pull a ship to shore, and daylight turned them to stone).

It's easy to see why Hollywood creatives are now harnessing this part of Iceland on a regular basis: its entire south coast is both evocative and uplifting, boasting colossal waterfalls such as Skógafoss and Seljalandsfoss, as well as picturesque Vik itself. The dramatic fog that often envelops this part of the island just adds to the effect (imagine the kind of foggy day that would have inspired Stephen King), particularly when ignited by the Northern Lights.

The Land of Ice and Fire might be reliably hot in Hollywood right now, but the same can't be said of its summer months. If you like a guaranteed tan to go with your volcanic island, head for ❼ Maui – where you'll also be able to enjoy one of the most exhilarating sunrises on the planet. The daybreak in question is from the summit of Haleakalā, a dormant giant on the Hawaiian island, which, mass-wise, is also the third largest mountain on the planet.

The 3055m Haleakalā's very name, meaning 'House of the Sun', bears testament to the fact that, for generations,

⑤ FAROE ISLANDS

You can fly direct to the Faroe Islands' main airport, Vágar, from a number of international hubs, including Reykjavík, Copenhagen, Barcelona, Lisbon and Edinburgh on the Faroese national carrier, Atlantic Airways (www.atlantic.fo). The best accommodation options are Hotel Føroyar (www.hotelforoyar.fo) and Gjáargardur (www. gjaargardur.fo). The 18 islands are connected by a series of short tunnels, and the best way to get around them is to hire a car, though there are also regular, reliable bus routes. For details: www. visitfaroeislands.com.

⑥ VIK, ICELAND

Iceland has become far more accessible in recent years, with more flights arriving from more destinations in both Europe and North America. IcelandAir (www.icelandair.co.uk) also offers a popular seven-day 'Stopover in Iceland' deal between the two continents, with no extra airfare. From Reykjavík the best way to Vik and the south coast is to hire a car (the drive will take just over two hours) or take one of the twice-daily buses (www.straeto.is). If you wish to take your own vehicle, the car ferry from northern Denmark is also a good alternative (www. smyrilline.com).

© Fabian Zehnder / 500px

Top left: Cappadocia. Lower left:
frescoes in Goreme Open-Air
Museum. Right: Haleakalā on Maui.

the volcano's ancient crater has been regarded as one of the most awe-inspiring natural theatres from which to witness dawn. Indeed, Mark Twain felt moved to describe it as 'a billowy ocean of wool aflame with the golden and purple and crimson splendours of the sun'.

He wasn't overselling it. To see a new day emerge from Haleakalā is to watch a giant, steaming cauldron of molten lava and gold bubble and boil before spilling out across the horizon, then racing towards you, searing across a carpet of clouds.

To be amid those clouds as the sun kindled them would be something else – and that's exactly what you can do in the Turkish town of **8** Göreme. Since the beginning of the 18th century, travellers from East and West have been flocking here, to the mysterious moonscape of Cappadocia, with its ancient cave dwellings, twisted rock spires and fairy chimneys. Today, the most uplifting way to study its mysteries – in every sense – is via the

⑦ HALEAKALĀ, MAUI, USA

Haleakalā is at the centre of Maui, the second largest Hawaiian island. The easiest way to reach it is direct to Kahului Airport from a handful of North American cities – or via Hawaii's international airport on the main island, O'ahu. To explore Haleakalā National Park in depth you'll need to rent a car, as there's no public bus service. The summit is a couple of hours' drive from Kahului. A number of operators offer organised sunrise visits to the summit, with many adding an optional mountain bike ride back down. All will pick up and drop off from your hotel. See www.gohawaii.com for more.

⑧ GÖREME, CAPPADOCIA, TURKEY

Cappadocia has two airports, Kayseri – 75km (47 miles) from Göreme – and Nevsehir, 40km (25 miles). There are regular shuttle buses from both airports, bookable via www.goreme.com. Cappadocia Cave Suites Hotel allows you to stay in Göreme's rock face in comfortable accommodation (www. cappadociacavesuites. com) , and while there are multiple balloon operators for the sunrise flights, Kapadokya Balloons (www. kapadokyaballoons.com), one of the pioneers, is particularly good.

The ancient adobe architecture
of Taos Pueblo, New Mexico.

fleet of hot air balloons that rises at dawn each day, climbing over the surreal, silent terrain as the first fingers of light claw at the darkness.

From the basket you'll see the strange beauty of Cappadocia's rocky wonderland unravel beneath you – particularly the natural spires, which were hollowed and honed by generations into everything from homes to churches. The silence from a gliding balloon as day breaks over this extraordinary place amplifies its power.

In a recent University of Pennsylvania study, psychologists Todd M Thrash and Andrew J Elliot identified three main elements that need to be present for inspiration to occur. These were 'evocation' (inspiration should be evoked spontaneously, without direct or logical intention), 'transcendence' (a moment of clarity and awareness of new possibilities) and 'approach motivation' (coming to the situation open to change and new ideas). On the other side of the USA, there's one place where all three elements have frequently and repeatedly mixed: ❾ Taos, New Mexico.

Described by English novelist DH Lawrence as the 'Land of Enchantment', this southwestern mountain outpost became a honeypot for writers and artists in the 1920s, and continues to be so today. Lawrence, the author of *Women in Love* and *Lady Chatterley's Lover*, found so much inspiration for his work while staying on a ranch here that he called it 'the greatest experience I ever had from the outside world. It certainly changed me forever.'

People still talk of Taos' magnetic pull today, a phenomenon that began when New York heiress and socialite, Mabel Dodge Luhan, relocated here in 1919, married a Pueblo Indian and set up a literary colony, inviting creatives from across the world, including Lawrence. Her legacy of artistic inspiration can be seen everywhere today, in a town packed with galleries, studios, museums and craft markets. Today it's an innovational melting pot where new-age nomadic hippies (referred to locally as 'sage monkeys') peacefully coexist with artists, natives and daredevil adventure sports enthusiasts – all seeking their own form of modern inspiration.

If Taos is the US Shangri-la, then what of the original? Since James Hilton imagined the mystical paradise-on-Earth in his bestselling 1933 novel, *Lost Horizon*, a host of Himalayan areas have laid claim to be his inspiration. But only one place – ❿ Zhōngdiàn in China's southwestern Yunnan Province – has officially gone by the name Shangri-La County since 2001.

Zhōngdiàn's claim is strong. The mountainous region covers a stunning land of snowcapped peaks and plunging parallel gorges carved by three of Asia's mightiest rivers, as well as the fine 17th-century Tibetan monastery Songzanlin – all strongly reminiscent of Hilton's descriptive passages. Yunnan was also home to early 20th-century explorer and botanist Joseph Rock, whose writings on the area are thought to have been Hilton's inspiration. Many say the Buddhist monastery of Songzanlin itself is enough to convince that this is indeed Hilton's earthly Eden, exuding as it does a powerful, peaceful sense of separation from the everyday world.

Of course, peace and tranquillity are not prerequisites for inspiration. For many, the exact opposite will get their evocation, transcendence and approach motivation all firing as one inspirational whole. Elsewhere on the Silk Road, ⓫ Samarkand is one such place.

Located in modern day Uzbekistan, Samarkand is one of the oldest inhabited cities in Central Asia, dating back to as early as the 7th century BC. It's a magic-carpet kind of place, where history hangs heavy amid the slender minarets and azure-tiled archways, all inevitably funnelling you towards monumental Registan Square.

⑨ TAOS, NEW MEXICO, USA

To reach Taos, you can fly into either Albuquerque (a two and a half hour drive) or Santa Fe (one and a half hours). However, only the former serves all major airlines and car rental companies. Once in Taos, the historic Taos Inn (www.taosinn.com), where DH Lawrence himself stayed, should be your first choice. Representing surprisingly affordable luxury, it has also hosted a number of Hollywood greats, from Greta Garbo to Robert Redford. In terms of activities and trip planning, www.taos.org is excellent.

⑩ ZHŌNGDIÀN/ SHANGRI-LA, YÚNNÁN, CHINA

Díqìng airport opened in 1999, a couple of years before Zhōngdiàn was renamed Shangri-la. Daily flights land from a handful of Chinese cities, including Kùnmíng and Chéngdū, and the airport is just outside town – there are taxis. Shangri-la also receives daily buses from some Chinese cities, though if you're looking to travel this way from a major centre such as Chéngdū, you'll need several transfers over the course of a few days. Roads around the town can sometimes be closed for political reasons or because of snow. Visit in spring or autumn – it's cold in winter.

⑪ SAMARKAND. UZBEKISTAN

Uzbekistan Airways (www.uzairways.com) flies between the capital, Tashkent, and Samarkand. Overland transfers are also available from Navoi airport, 180km (112 miles) from Samarkand. In the city itself, the best accommodation option is the Hotel Grand Samarkand (www.grand-samarkand.com). One of the most experienced Western tour operators in Uzbekistan is Cox and Kings (www.coxandkings. com). For more ideas and information, see www. welcomeuzbekistan.uz.

⑫ OXFORD. ENGLAND

Oxford is about 100km (60 miles) northwest of London. At peak times, six trains an hour depart Paddington Station in the capital for Oxford, with the express service taking around 50 minutes. The 'Oxford Tube' bus service also runs from Victoria Station 24 hours a day, with a journey time of 90 minutes. If you're travelling outside term time, the colleges themselves make excellent, affordable accommodation options. Not only are the rooms clean, central and great value, but you get the feel of authentic college life, with breakfast served in the grandeur of each college's dining hall (www. oxfordrooms.co.uk).

Samarkand's venerable walls and turrets are built on thousands of stories and legends, which have, in turn, inspired countless generations.

Despite Samarkand's proud heritage and rich history, there's another European city that has the edge on it in terms of both ancient learning *and* dreaming spires. Roughly 100km (60 miles) north-west of London, ⑫ Oxford, with its time-honoured traditions, magnificent libraries and grand colleges, has produced a ridiculous amount of the world's most inspired minds (27 UK Prime Ministers to date, compared with Cambridge's paltry 14). Founded in 1096, the oldest university in the English-speaking world also has a strong claim to be the most beautiful, with its hushed cloisters, cobbled courtyards and perfectly manicured quadrangles contributing to a reputation which saw Oscar Wilde hail Oxford as 'the capital of romance'.

From The Inklings – a group of renowned authors, including JRR Tolkien and CS Lewis, who would meet once a week at the Eagle and Child pub to discuss plotlines – to Charles Dodgson, the mathematics tutor otherwise known as Lewis Carroll who penned *Alice in Wonderland* while strolling the quads, corridors and meadows of Christ Church college, Oxford is a city with inspiration dripping from its honey-coloured bricks. And the true beauty is that little of consequence has changed. Those seeking inspiration can still walk the same alleyways, explore the same colleges and frequent the same pubs – fall down the same rabbit holes if you

Opposite: Zhōngdiàn in China; Samarkand in Uzbekistan. This page: the Radcliffe Camera library in Oxford, UK.

will – as the great minds before them, basking in the sheer creative power exuded by the place.

It's an elevating force that the founders of the city's most prominent namesake, ⓭ Oxford, Mississippi, were keen to emulate. And, strange as it might sound, they appear to have done so, with the 'other Oxford' now touted as 'the cultural mecca of the South'.

You'd think that after the Revolutionary War, Americans would want to steer clear of British influence, but that wasn't the case here, where legislators named the town after its famous English forebear in 1841, in a bid to convince the powers-that-be to build the state university here. The gambit paid off, and since then, the university town has turned into a source of literary inspiration for big-name authors including William Faulkner, John Grisham and Donna Tartt.

Faulkner, author of *The Sound and The Fury*, lived and wrote in a house here called Rowan Oak, with cedars lining the pathway to the door in a bid to forge the right creative energy (along with the tools of his trade, namely 'paper, tobacco, food and a little whiskey'). You can soak up some of it for yourself by paying a visit – and paying

The Côte d'Azur,
France, playground of
artists and authors.

particular attention to the room where he wrote a full plot outline on the wall.

While American literati such as Faulkner were flexing their artistic muscles in Oxford, Mississippi, their European contemporaries were making a beeline for the Côte d'Azur in France. Specifically the seaside town of ⓮ Juan-les-Pins, where truth often became stranger than fiction. F Scott and Zelda Fitzgerald were among the vanguard here, heading to the legendary Villa St Louis in the mid-1920s. Here, they lived on money from the sales of *The Great Gatsby* while F Scott penned *Tender Is The Night*, his last great work.

Today the villa is the Hôtel Belles Rives, a unique Art Deco treat crammed with original features and possessions of the Fitzgeralds and their glamorous Jazz Age coterie. Add a profoundly relaxed atmosphere and spectacular palm-fringed views of the sun-spangled sea and you have the perfect ingredients to inspire your own creative impulses. Just check the guest book for validation from the likes of Victor Hugo, Jules Verne, Monet and Picasso.

The creative buzz of ⓯ San Francisco erupted just 40 years later, but was incredibly different to the decadent vibe of Juan-les-Pins. Here, in the famous countercultural summer of 1967, something extraordinary happened and its repercussions can still be felt in this uniquely energising and enriching city to this day. The Summer of Love blossomed in the Haight-Ashbury area with its grand Victorian homes, but spread its flower-garlanded inspiration across a city that has been a nexus of creativity ever since. Today the psychedelic storefronts and vibrant street art remain but the visionary, out-of-the-box thinking has infected everything from the advertising industry to tech startups, lubricated by some excellent bars, breweries and wineries.

Of course, buzzing, positive port towns have always been hubs for original thinking, and one of San Francisco's closest spiritual sister-cities is ⓰ Melbourne, Victoria. Another 'city by the bay', it's likewise a hub for dynamic street art, with its sprayed, stencilled alleyways containing some of the most vibrant and important murals in the world. They adorn an incredibly interactive city, which also boasts one of the finest art gallery and cafe scenes in the Southern Hemisphere. In this extraordinary town, inspiration hides round every corner – down nondescript passageways, behind inconspicuous doors and up rickety old stairs, as much as in fabulous boutiques and hip cocktail bars. Just a

⓭ OXFORD, MISSISSIPPI, USA

Memphis is the nearest international airport to Oxford, the 112km (70 mile) drive takes about one and a quarter hours. The website visitoxfordms.com provides a thorough overview of what to do and where to stay in the 'cultural mecca of the South'. You will want to visit William Faulkner's home from 1930-1972, of course – Royal Oak was built in the 1840s and stands among 12 arboreal hectares just south of the Square. The property and grounds are open daily year-round (except public holidays and Mondays in winter), admission is $5 (£4).

⓮ JUAN-LES-PINS, FRANCE

The nearest airport to Juan-Les-Pins is Nice Côte d'Azur, which receives flights from cities across the world and is a 30-minute drive away. Nearby Antibes is on mainline train and bus routes. The Hotel Belles-Rives (www. bellesrives.com), where F Scott Fitzgerald wrote Tender is The Night, is still the best ticket in town and you can follow the lead of the author by enjoying a drink in the Art Deco surrounds of the Fitzgerald Bar. Alternatively, the Hotel Juana is an excellent property and surprisingly affordable (www.hotel-juana.com).

Left: an iconic storefront in San Francisco. This page: Melbourne and Port Phillip Bay.

Scenes from Petra,
Jordan, including the
Al-Khazneh Treasury.

short drive to the north you'll also find Montsalvat, Australia's oldest continuously active arts community. This remarkable colony, situated across a 5 hectare site of picturesque buildings and carefully cultivated gardens, was founded in the 1930s and artists, painters, sculptors, writers and musicians have been travelling here ever since.

In the general scheme of world history, of course, San Francisco and Melbourne are both remarkably recent settlements, both less than 250 years old. But cities don't have to be young or modern to be visionary and inspirational. **⑰** Petra in southern Jordan is an entire city carved out of stone by the Nabataeans more than 2000 years ago. A monumental work of art as much as architecture, the city, originally known as Raqmu, was little more than a myth in the Western world until the early 19th century, when Swiss explorer Johann Ludwig Burckhardt disguised himself as an Arab and tricked his

Bedouin guide into leading him into one of the world's greatest wonders.

If perspiration truly is the mother of inspiration, then you'll find plenty of both here on your entrance to the city. The only way in is the narrow 'Siq', a 1200m-long winding chasm bordered by 100m-high walls under the desert sun. Sometimes called the 'Rose City' after the natural colour of the rock from which it was honed, Petra is a hypnotic place whose highlights include Al-Khazneh – or 'The Treasury' – an epic hand-carved building jutting from the red cliff face in all its monolithic glory. If it reminds you of a giant movie set, that's because it has been: the Siq and The Treasury both starred in *Indiana Jones and The Last Crusade*.

You'll find another awesome example of man's ability to create infinite beauty from seemingly sheer cliff faces in Bhutan. Taktsang Lhakhang, better known as **⑱** the Tiger's Nest, is an incredible monastery, clinging to the rock face high above the spectacular Paro Valley. One of the holiest sites in the country, it's said to be where Guru Rinpoche or 'Precious Master' – also known as the 'Second Buddha' of Bhutan – materialised some 1300 years ago on a flying tigress, which had recently been his Tibetan concubine. Finding shelter in a series of caves, he meditated here for three years, before setting about converting the Bhutanese to Buddhism.

For those who left their flying tiger concubine at home, getting to the Tiger's Nest is significantly more difficult, but infinitely rewarding. It involves a steep two-hour hike from the valley floor to the Tiger's Nest 900m above (and 3000m above sea level). Emerging through the mountain mists, the sweeping views down over the happiest country on Earth are nothing short of sensational.

If the Tiger's Nest inspires with its serenity, **⑲** Patan, across the Himalayas in Nepal, excites the imagination for the opposite reason. Kathmandu's sister city – the two are separated by the Bagmati River – is lesser known, but just as boisterous and rambunctious, with one of the finest collection of temples in the world.

What makes Patan so special is that its history dates all the way back to the year 250 BC, when the corners of the ancient town were marked by stupas. A royal stronghold (Patan was formerly the residence of the Malla kings), its myriad of pretty squares, old brick lanes and courtyards are awash with life, rituals and colour. Home to some extraordinary architecture, there are breathtaking sights around seemingly every corner of its sanctuary-saturated streets, not to mention the Patan Museum, known locally as Keshav Narayan Chowk, which now houses one of the finest collections of religious art in Asia.

Inspiration can be incredibly elusive to pin down. From one perspective it can be starry-eyed, utopian –

⑮ SAN FRANCISCO, CALIFORNIA, USA

The international airport 21km (13 miles) from San Francisco is connected to the city by a 30-minute BART train. There are several ways to get down with SF's psychedelic past including Wild SF Walking Tours' Free Love Tour (www.wildsftours.com) of Haight-Ashbury's hippie heritage, which starts at 1.30pm daily. Or you might dig The Magic Bus Experience's Summer of Love (www.magicbussf. com) – a two-hour tour using video and audio to enhance visits to the Haight and other landmarks. The bus has screens that turn it into a kind of mobile cinema complete with simulated 'mystical LSD trip'!

⑯ MELBOURNE, AUSTRALIA

Various bus services, shuttles and taxis link Melbourne's busy international airport – 22km (14 miles) northwest of downtown – with the city. Once ensconced, you can get a good overview of this thriving town's artistic nooks and crannies on a Hidden Secrets Tour (www.hiddensecretstours. com), which will walk you through many of the cultural hits. The artists' community of Montsalvat is in the suburb of Eltham, accessible by road and rail. It hosts a rolling programme of exhibitions, events and workshops, and its grounds are open daily from 9am-5pm, for an admission fee. See www.montsalvat.com.au.

Left: tilting at the windmills of La
Mancha, Spain. Right: the Golden
Temple of Patan, Nepal.

some might even say extravagant and unrealistic. Or in a word, quixotic. Where better to seek it, then, than the ⑳ La Mancha region of central Spain, where the literary character behind the word itself, Don Quixote, famously tilted at windmills on his one-man mission to heroically right the world's wrongs and bring back lost chivalry. It was the historic, whitewashed windmills around Argamasilla de Alba that inspired Miguel de Cervantes when he wrote *Don Quixote*, dotted among a patchwork of buff and green fields.

Today, references to Don Quixote, his loyal squire Sancho Panza and his beautiful lady Dulcinea abound in the surrounding villages, from local dishes and sweets to theatrical recreations of his feats. But the stars of the show are the timeworn windmills, central to the best-known episode of the book when Don Quixote imagines they are giants and tries to fight them. The scene gave rise to the expression 'tilting at windmills', or fighting imaginary enemies. And it's a concept still inspiring people to return 500 years later.

⑰ PETRA, JORDAN

Petra is a three-hour drive from Jordan's capital, Amman. Its temples, stairways and cisterns were carved out of stone by the Nabataeans 2,000 years ago. Entry to the site ranges from 50 dinar for a day to 60 dinar for three days. Buy tickets from the Visitor Information Centre at the entrance to the archaeological site. Horses are allowed to transport you from the Visitor Centre to the entrance of the Siq. The rides are included in the entry fee. No one is permitted to stay overnight inside Petra, but the Mövenpick Petra Resort puts you as close as you can get. To help plan your visit see www. visitpetra.jo.

⑱ TIGER'S NEST MONASTERY, BHUTAN

The Tiger's Nest Monastery (Paro Taktshang) is about 16km (10 miles) north of Paro, which is the perfect home base when making this visit, particularly as it's also the site of Bhutan's only international airport. Most people can only visit Bhutan on an organised tour, so transportation will be arranged for you by a licenced operator. Allow a full day for your visit. You'll have to walk up to the monastery, which takes between four and five hours to do the (6.5km) four-mile round-trip hike, plus one hour to tour the monastery. Cameras are not allowed inside.

⑲ PATAN, NEPAL

Many people visit Patan on a day trip from Kathmandu across the river, so stay overnight and you'll have the squares and courtyards to yourself. Even after the 2015 earthquake, Durbar Sq is the finest collection of temples and palaces in Nepal. The neighbouring city is home to the country's only international airport, where flights arrive from destinations across Asia. You can get from Kathmandu to Patan on bike, bus, cab or tempo (an electric three-wheeler). Learn more about Patan Museum and its renovation at www.asianart.com/ patan-museum.

⑳ CASTILLE–LA MANCHA, SPAIN

Spain's third largest region has the country's lowest population density. Madrid's is the nearest international airport, the Spanish capital has fast train links with the towns of Cuenca, Albacete and Toledo. Early autumn, when temperatures have cooled, is prime time to hike in Don Quixote's footsteps, and Spain's tourism body (www. spain.info) has mapped a weekend route for you to do so ('In Search of Don Quixote'), running near Toledo through Orgaz, Mora, Tembleque, Villacañas, Consuegra and Madridejos – and past lots of windmills.

EXHILARATION

In a world full of images of exhilaration – action movies, pop videos, car commercials – it's somewhat surprising that real exhilaration is so hard to find. It is possible to go through days, or weeks, or even years without ever feeling the visceral rush of what it means to be alive.

Thank heavens, then, for travel, which serves up thrills and spills to spare in a worldwide buffet of life-affirming experiences. Scientists have shown that exhilaration promotes the release of endorphins, natural hormones that reduce pain and stress and increase happiness – so, not just fun, but good for you too. Before you sign up for a skydive or bungee jump, however, know that there's more to this elusive emotion than action movie antics. Sometimes real exhilaration is a slow and subtle smile that spreads across your face as you realise that right here and now, in this very moment, you are present and alive.

So what are the elements that make an experience exhilarating, rather than simply, well, quite nice? One essential ingredient is anticipation. Think about the last time you really looked forward to something, bubbling with delight and constantly on the verge of bursting out in an ear-to-ear smile.

Setting off on a journey is a great way to tick the anticipation box. The moment when the airplane door closes and you know that the next time you set foot on

① LUKLA, SOLUKHUMBU, NEPAL

Lukla is 140km (87 miles) east of Kathmandu, accessible by a week-long trek from Jiri or a 35-minute flight from Kathmandu. Guides and porters can be arranged through agencies in advance in Kathmandu, but Sherpas crowd Lukla's miniature airport offering their services to arrivals. The trek from Lukla to Everest Base Camp is a two-week round trip; teahouse accommodation is available all along the route. The best season for trekking is October to November or March to April; in winter, snow can block passes, and many lodges close during the summer monsoon.

② GEYSIR, ICELAND

Around 100km (62 miles) east of Reykjavik, Geysir is an easy drive, or an easy bus ride during the summer tourist season. Most people visit as part of the 'Golden Circle' loop, dropping in at Geysir, Þingvellir National Park and the thundering waterfall at Gullfoss. You can do the loop in a day, but it's more interesting to stay overnight near Geysir or Þingvellir to beat the crowds. Peak season is May to September, coinciding with the warmest weather; winter is cold and dark, with skeleton public transport, but Strokkur blows its top year-round, come sun, rain or snow.

Previous page: taking off from
Tenzing-Hillary airport at Lukla, Nepal.
Right: Strokkur geyser in Iceland.

solid ground, the adventure will have begun. Even better if you're on a small plane picking its way between peaks to the slopes of the highest mountain on earth.

There's something about flying in a light aircraft that heightens the senses; the world outside the window just seems that little bit closer. In the case of the flight from Kathmandu to ❶ Lukla, it is closer. The flight route to the start of the Everest Base Camp trek slaloms between mountaintops, before dropping on to a mountain runway not much longer than a family of yaks.

Trekking through the world's highest mountains is exciting enough by itself, but squeezing yourself into a cramped Twin Otter at Kathmandu's frenetic domestic airport just adds to the expectation. Nothing is certain

until the weather conditions have been checked and double-checked, then suddenly, with a jolt, you're off, climbing steeply into a sky that seems more full of rock than clouds. The tension builds as Lukla finally looms into view – 527m (1730ft) of tarmac inclined uphill at 11.7% – finishing abruptly at a rocky mountainside. But before you have time to think about that, there's a roar of engines, a shudder of metalwork and an involuntary cry of 'Whoa!' from the assembled passengers, and you're down, safe on terra firma, ready to start the trek to the shoulder of the world's highest mountain. We defy you not to be exhilarated.

Of course, anticipation comes in all shapes and sizes. It can be as big as the flight before a skydive or as delicate as pushing back the foliage for a glimpse of a bird of paradise. At ❷ Geysir in Iceland, nature serves up a natural spectacle that will leave you giggling with expectation long before it finally blows its top. Set in a blasted landscape of mud pools, fissures and fumaroles, Strokkur is probably the world's most reliable geyser, erupting every six to 10 minutes in a mighty surge that can top 40m (131ft). There's no telling exactly when the spout will blow, but when the water starts to bubble up into a glassy dome, it's time to step back as hundreds of gallons of water blasts suddenly skywards.

Most of the time, the forces of nature are noticeably missing from day-to-day existence. There were no avalanches on the way to work. Lunch wasn't disrupted by a meteor strike. Bedtime was marked by a book and a milky drink. Sometimes, you need to break out of the humdrum and expose yourself to elemental forces, just to remind yourself that you live in a world of fire and glorious, untamed fury.

Volcanoes have a special place in human experience. These bubbling cauldrons were the imagined homes of pagan gods and the source of the cataclysm that buried Herculaneum and Pompeii. It was no accident that Frodo Baggins destroyed the One Ring in the furnace of Mount Doom. Seeing this uncontrolled power up close in real life is almost to touch the divine.

On the island of Hawaii, lava has been bubbling up to the surface for 600,000 years, and Hawaii's ❸ Volcanoes National Park is one of the most consistent places on Earth to see real-life volcanic pyrotechnics. Eruptions are less a fountain, more a treacle flow, but the lava still burns as red as the fires that forged the planet when the universe was a whirling ball of dust and gas. The Kīlauea shield volcano – Hawaii's most reliable performer – comes into its own as night falls, when the lava glows with inner fire and the darkness is filled with the sounds of creaking rock and the hiss of steam from lava tumbling into the sea. Chances are

③ VOLCANOES NATIONAL PARK, HAWAII, USA

The aptly named Volcanoes National Park spans the domes of two massive shield volcanoes – Kīlauea and Mauna Loa – on Hawaii's Big Island, but it's normally Kīlauea that provides the fireworks. The entrance to the park is about 50km (30 miles) southwest of Hilo, served by inter-island flights with Mokulele and Hawaiian Airlines. The best way to get close (but not too close) to the lava flows is on a guided hike, but you can also watch the sparks fly from a boat or helicopter. Kīlauea rumbles year round, but conditions change daily – the Kīlauea Visitor Center can point you in the right direction for the current flows.

④ IGUAZÚ FALLS, BRAZIL/ARGENTINA

Technically, the Iguazú Falls tumble between Brazil and Argentina but visitors can access the cascades from Foz do Iguaçu in Brazil, Puerto Iguazú in Argentina (both with airports) or Ciudad del Este in Paraguay. Special (expensive) visa arrangements are in place for travellers who want to see the falls from both sides. Both Foz do Iguaçu and Puerto Iguazú have plentiful accommodation and bus services to the boardwalks and viewpoints. The falls are most impressive in the hot wet summer, from October to March, but most visitors prefer the dry winter months from May to September, avoiding the regular downpours.

© Roc Canals / Getty Images

you've never felt more insignificant, nor more in touch with the power of nature, than when listening to the way the world was made.

If you're more of a water person, rest easy. Waterfalls are another glorious metaphor for the unstoppable flow of time and our own insignificance compared to the awesome power of nature. At ❹ Iguazú Falls, water has even shaped nations, forging a foaming border between Argentina, Brazil and nearby Paraguay.

Iguazú is not just one waterfall, but an astonishing 275 cascades, merging together in a rushing, roaring chorus. Despite the tidy boardwalks and viewing platforms, there's a palpable sense of raw power, as 1756 cu metres of water plunges into the ravine with each passing second. Stand a while on the viewing platform atop the aptly named Garganta del Diablo (the Devil's Throat) and contemplate the forces that carved this fantastical landscape. You may feel a tingling frisson at the thought of exactly how long you would last if you tumbled into the white water surging into the gulf below.

For many, exhilaration is synonymous with speed. From hanging on a rope swing to riding the rapids, human beings seem to be hard-wired with an inbuilt need to go higher, harder, faster. If someone else is in control of making the split-second decisions that determine if you live or die, that only adds to the excitement.

Navigating the finger-width canyons of New Zealand's ❺ Shotover River by jet-boat is an exquisite mixture of pleasure and terror. Perils and obstacles lurk on all sides but the boat pilots who navigate these narrow channels know the waters like salmon returning upstream.

Most people only experience this kind of high-speed, don't-touch-the-sides adrenaline via the medium of computer games, but the racing boats that ply the Shotover River reach speeds of 85km/h as they zoom through canyons only marginally wider than a family saloon car. It's a spray-in-the-face, wind-in-the-eye-sockets experience, complete with near-misses, dramatic rolls and sudden 360-degree turns. By the end of the trip, you'll be river-drenched, air-blasted and shaken up like a NutriBullet, but you'll also have cheeks aching from smiling in adrenaline-fuelled joie de vivre.

You don't have to defy death personally to feel the burn. Sometimes seeing others take the leap of faith is as exciting as stepping out into the abyss. Take ❻ Lauterbrunnen in Switzerland, where daredevils leap like lemmings from the cliffs in search of the ultimate natural high. Even watching BASE jumping as an observer is to step into a world without fear.

Acrophobics will feel their hearts in their mouths just on the gondola ride to the rim of the Lauterbrunnen Valley, and you'll need a climbing harness and safety rope to reach the so-called 'exits' used by BASE jumpers. But for those brave enough to step to the edge and look down, the vicarious rush is amplified tenfold by the notion that people are voluntarily hurling themselves into the void.

Expect a racing pulse and weak knees as you watch jumpers making their final preparations, checking parachutes and wingsuits and phoning ahead for clearance from Lauterbrunnen airspace before casually stepping off the edge and plummeting down towards the patchwork of green meadows below. To actually join them in the air, you'll need some serious airtime – 300 skydives or more – and years of experience. Oh, and nerves of diamond-hardened steel – did we mention that?

If you'd rather take the helm yourself, there are other, less madcap ways to get the endorphins surging. In the desert emirate of Dubai, locals burn off steam by ❼ dune bashing, and the buzz of sending $40,000

---

⑤ SHOTOVER RIVER, QUEENSTOWN, NEW ZEALAND

Three companies run jet-boats on the rivers around Queenstown, but which you choose will depend on how much time you want to spend zipping through the Shotover River Canyons. Shotover Jet (www. shotoverjet.com), the only company licensed to run in the narrow canyon zone, offers short, fast trips from Arthurs Point, 7km (4.3 miles) from Queenstown. Longer trips leave from Queenstown and Glenorchy, at the north end of Lake Wakatipu, doubling your time on the water. December to February brings the best weather and the biggest crowds. Flights go direct to Queenstown; people also visit on overland camper tours from Christchurch.

⑥ LAUTERBRUNNEN, SWITZERLAND

The Swiss BASE Association (www. swissbaseassociation. ch) lists 15 jump zones in the mountains around the tiny village of Lauterbrunnen, which is easily accessible by narrow-gauge train from Interlaken. If you want to find the paths to the exits, chat to the jumpers hanging out in the Airtime Cafe or the Horner Pub in Lauterbrunnen and see if they mind you tagging along. The easiest route to the top of the valley is the cable car to Grutschalp, continuing on the mountain railway to Mürren. BASE jumping is a summer activity – April to June are the liveliest months for leapers.

Previous page: Volcanoes National Park, Hawaii. Left: jet-boating Shotover River.

Dune bashing in a 4WD in the
desert around Dubai, UAE.

Be sure to keep your distance from
whale sharks when snorkelling in Cebu.

worth of automobile barrelling down the side of a
giant sand dune is hard to resist. This is off-roading
with abandon, executed at high speed on the endlessly
shifting, sliding sands. The lack of traction only adds to
the sense of urgency – the slow and cautious end up
swamped, needing a haul-out from fellow off-roaders
(it would be a foolish dune basher who travels without
an emergency radio).

The first oil-explorers battled the sands in rattletrap
military jeeps, but modern dune bashers use sleek, air-
conditioned Nissans and Toyotas. There's a childlike
tingle of naughtiness about taking one of these gleaming
monsters off the tarmac and sending it skidding over the
crest of a dune – like building a sandcastle and then
knocking it down, just because you can. In a society of
strict moral codes, it's a tension-releasing act of rebellion
that won't draw the ire of the authorities.

Exhilaration doesn't have to come at a hundred miles

⑦ DUBAI, UNITED ARAB EMIRATES

*Dubai is usually dry as a
bone, so dune bashing
is a year-round activity,
but there's a chance of
rain from December to
April, which can make for
tricky driving conditions.
Conversely, July and
August are insanely hot –
not good for overheating
engines. As one of the
world's busiest air hubs,
Dubai is served by flights
from everywhere, and
agents can arrange dune
bashing trips all over the
Emirate – Bidayer and Al
Faya are easy drives from
Dubai city. Unless you're
a confident off-roader
with comprehensive
dune bashing insurance,
you may want to stick to
an organised trip with a
local driver.*

⑧ MALAPASCUA ISLAND, CEBU, PHILIPPINES

*Measuring just 1km by
2.5km (0.6 by 1.5 miles),
Malapascua is a dot
of green floating in the
Visayan Sea, about 7km
(4.3 miles) from the island
of Cebu. International
flights run directly to
Cebu City and local buses
zip up to the seaport at
Maya, where pump boats
wait to ferry visitors out
to Malapascua. Dive
operators are dotted
along the shore; thresher
sharks gather at Monad
Shoal year round and
manta rays cruise by in
spring. The best weather
on shore is from October
to April; Cebu normally
escapes the worst of the
typhoon season from
June to October.*

Watching and waiting during
migration season in the
Serengeti, Tanzania.

an hour, with only a millimetre between you and certain extinction. There are other more subtle ways to get the nerves tingling. Adrenaline rushes can, for example, be slow and hauntingly beautiful, such as the moment when you slip beneath the waves and cross the threshold into an underwater world.

Nothing gets the pulse racing like a moment of commitment, and the last glimpse of sky as you dip beneath the bubbles and descend into the inky darkness on a scuba dive is up there with the best of them. The experience is even more emotional when you know there are sharks waiting to greet you at the bottom.

On the surface, the Philippine island of ❽ Malapascua is a vision of sun, sand and surf, but the thresher sharks that gather offshore are what put it on the map. Unlike the famous great white shark dives in South Africa, the emphasis here is on gentle, respectful encounters; shark dives are a waiting game, as divers gather at Monad Shoal – a cleaning station where marine life congregates on the seabed – waiting for a flash of silver as threshers cruise in slowly from the gloom.

There are no cages to divide shark from diver, and things get up close and personal surprisingly quickly, as the fish swim in to investigate, passing centimetres overhead before zipping away into the deep blue. Observing this graceful ballet is a dreamlike experience that will leave you grinning around your regulator, while welling up at the profound beauty of it all.

If you are looking for a once-in-a-lifetime wildlife encounter on land, you probably want something more exciting than squirrels in the mist. Naturalist David Attenborough claimed a cuddle from a mountain gorilla as one of his favourite wildlife experiences, and meeting the 'hairy women' of the forest (the origin of the word gorilla – an unfortunate mix up by an ancient Carthaginian explorer) has topped travel bucket lists ever since.

Since Rwanda hiked the fees for gorilla treks, Uganda's ❾ Bwindi Impenetrable National Park has become the favoured spot for close encounters with mountain gorillas, but it's debatable who is really watching who. Visitors are under strict instructions not to approach the gorillas, but the animals are under no such obligation, and swing-by groomings are commonplace. Needless to say, lying on the forest floor while a 160kg silverback picks through your hair for ticks is an absurdly beautiful experience that will leave you questioning where the divide between man and animal starts and ends.

Uganda is just one of hundreds of places in Africa where you can feel the rhythms of nature. Every summer, ❿ Serengeti National Park in Tanzania shakes like thunder as a million hoof beats rock the savannah. The annual migration of wildebeest and zebras from the Serengeti to the Masai Mara is one of the world's greatest natural spectacles, an epic story of life, death and survival. Seeing the great migration in the flesh is one of those 'hell yeah' moments, like finding yourself teleported into a BBC nature documentary. The dust kicked up by gazillions of ungulates transforms the migrating herds into a monochrome silhouette, an endless paper-chain of horns and hooves. You'll taste the dust in the air long before you see the animals making it.

The most gripping viewpoints for the migration are the bottlenecks where the great herds brave waiting crocodiles to cross the Mara and Grumeti Rivers. Here the whole cycle of life is on display. Every kill is a tragic reminder of the struggle to stay alive, each escape from hungry jaws a joyful celebration of the will to survive. Looking on through the dust, you'll find yourself asking questions of yourself as well, as you ponder your place

❾ GORILLA WATCHING, UGANDA

It is possible to spot mountain gorillas in Rwanda, Uganda and the Democratic Republic of Congo, but with the high Rwandan fees and the security situation in DRC, Uganda is currently the better deal. Uganda's Bwindi Impenetrable National Park is 470km (290 miles) southwest of Kampala; small planes zip to the airports at Kihihi and Kisoro. Accessing gorilla territory is only possible on a trek with local guides and a permit, staying in jungle lodges such as those near Buhoma and Nkuringo. Gorillas can be spotted year round; avoid the rains from March to May and October to November.

❿ THE SERENGETI, TANZANIA

The migration across the Serengeti is a two-way trip, but most visitors come for the northbound leg from Tanzania's Serengeti National Park to Kenya's Masai Mara National Park. The herds take two routes to the Masai Mara, to the north through the Seronera Valley (busiest between July and October), and the Western Corridor, crossing the Grumeti River (from May to July). Game lodges abound and there are campsites at Seronera, Lobo, Ndabaka and Ikoma. Organised safaris are an easy option, or explore by self-drive 4WD. Flights run from Arusha in north Tanzania to the park's airstrips.

© kjekol / Getty Images

213

⑪ SYDNEY. NSW. AUSTRALIA

Thanks to its easterly timezone, Sydney is one of the first cities to welcome in the new year, and the Sydney New Year's Eve celebrations are mobbed. Accommodation is at a premium, as are flights at what is the very height of the high season. Some of the best locations for viewing the display (the Royal Botanic Garden, Taronga Zoo, Barrangaroo Reserve) have ticketed entry, and tickets sell out fast, but the official Vantage Point Map lists dozens of free viewing locations (www. sydneynewyearseve.com). Locals often stake out a spot as soon as city parks open in the morning.

⑫ LERWICK. SHETLAND ISLANDS. SCOTLAND

Lerwick lights the fires for Up Helly Aa on the last Tuesday of January, but the diminutive Shetland capital (population 7500) is not overflowing with accommodation and demand is fierce for rooms. There are no tickets, but only people who have been resident in Shetland for five years can actually take part in the processions. Watching is free, as are many of the events laid on by the guizers (performers). The Shetland Islands lie 160km (100 miles) north of the mainland; ferries run from Aberdeen and Orkney, and flights drop into Sumburgh Airport, 31km (20 miles) from Lerwick.

in this timeless tableau.

Of course, human beings have put together some pretty amazing spectacles of their own. The first firework display probably took place in China, sometime around the 7th century. Today, people use explosions to celebrate everything from the Hindu festival of Diwali to the almost successful attempt to blow up the British parliament by Guy Fawkes.

There are dozens of contenders for the world's best fireworks display, but for sheer aplomb, ⑪ Sydney's New Year's Eve display tops most polls. This may be something to do with the spectacular setting – a basin-shaped harbour framed by the barnacle curves of the Sydney Opera House, backed by a landmark bridge that doubles as launch pad for a conflagration of fountains, flares and aerial shells.

Of course, the gloriously warm Antipodean weather doesn't hurt. You certainly won't freeze as you oooh and aaah while the sky is painted by A$7 million (£4 million) worth of fireworks. This is a rush you can enjoy while sitting down in your shorts with a cold beer in hand, smiling at the realisation that, when it comes down to it, life probably doesn't get a whole lot better than this.

If your inner pyro demands you get a little closer to the action, we'd make a strong pitch for the ⑫ Up Helly Aa festival in Lerwick on the Shetland Islands. Here, anyone with Viking roots – or to be honest, anyone drawn to flickering flames – can get medieval with the torch-bearing guizers as they parade through the streets

Left: fireworks in Sydney.
This page: Bwindi Impenetrable
National Park, Uganda.

of Shetland's diminutive capital and ritualistically set a Viking longship ablaze.

Despite the remote location and grim North Atlantic weather, Lerwick throws open its arms to outsiders for the festival, and the party rages literally through the night, complete with flaming torches and rousing Viking songs. It's a heart-warming reminder that a) we're all a little pagan at heart, b) health and safety is only advisory, and c) given the opportunity, we'd all quite happily burn a Viking longship to the ground.

Sometimes the buzz comes from simply being there, in the moment, with a like-minded crowd. There's a reason the club scene is still going strong, four decades after the death of disco. The world's club capitals call out like a beacon to people who get their kicks from dancing till the morning light. In ❸ Ibiza – where every other building is a nightclub, pub or beach bar – you haven't been out unless you see the sun come up over the sand.

In the hands of the right DJ, a dancefloor adopts a hive mind. Highs and lows are set by the pulse of the beat, and the music washes over everyone like a wave. There'll be a price to pay in the morning, but after watching the

⑬ IBIZA, BALEARIC ISLANDS, SPAIN

Ibiza is Spain's nightlife capital – more than seven million party people descended on the island in 2016 alone. The town of San Antonio (Sant Antoni de Portmany) on the western coast is party central, and the top clubs here host the top DJs from around Europe and the world. The whole island is crammed with accommodation but don't expect much sleep if you stay in the heart of San Antonio. Dozens of airlines zip into Ibiza airport, just outside Ibiza town, and boats run to Ibiza Port (you may notice a theme here) from Alicante, Valencia, Barcelona and Palma de Mallorca in summer.

⑭ GOLDEN TEMPLE, AMRITSAR, INDIA

The Golden Temple sits in the heart of Amritsar's old city, surrounded by a grand marble pavilion ringed by gurdwaras and hostels. The focus of attention is the gold-covered Harmandir Sahib, reached by a causeway across a sacred tank. Hotels crowd the approach to the temple, and free meals are served to pilgrims in the langar (dining hall) behind the temple (donations are appropriate). Amritsar is served by regular trains from Delhi and flights from around India, the Middle East and Central and Southeast Asia. Shoes and uncovered heads are forbidden inside the temple.

A Sikh guard at the Golden Temple of Amritsar in India.

sun climb over the bay you can crash on the sand in the balmy Balearic sunshine.

Being up at dawn never stops feeling exciting. Perhaps it's the sense that you're rushing to meet the day, rather than hiding from it underneath the duvet. Or it could be the notion that you're stealing a march on the rest of the world, which is still in bed while you are out there seizing the day. Travel is the ultimate alarm clock, where the chance to be the first at the temple ruins is a call to action in a way that being late for a meeting never was.

Dawn has a special power in the Indian subcontinent, where sacred sites are thronged by devotees long before the sun hits the horizon. At the ⑭ Golden Temple in Amritsar, the atmosphere at sunrise is electric; the causeway to the Sri Harmandir Sahib is already crowded with devotees, and a sense of shared, passionate belief pulses through the air, like a throbbing sound just at the edge of human hearing.

Rather than joining the crush, stake out a vantage point on the marble terrace surrounding the Amrit Sarovar, the sacred tank surrounding the gilded jewel box of the Golden Temple. As devotees wash past in a continuous human tide, watch for small vignettes of spiritual life – pilgrims chanting passages from the Guru Granth Sahib, and devout members of the Khalsa (Sikh brotherhood) taking ceremonial dips in the sacred waters.

Observing profound spirituality is ceaselessly fascinating and endlessly uplifting, even for the most secular soul. In an age of smartphones and selfies, it nourishes the human spirit to see how the rest of the world does human interaction, and how people can rise above material concerns in pursuit of a shared purpose.

As dusk falls over Delhi's ⑮ Hazrat Nizamuddin Dargah every Thursday, crowds gather to fill the night with qawwalis – devotional hymns that have changed only superficially since the Mughals ruled the plains. Transporting listeners on a soaring journey, these haunting rhythms have been rising over the tomb of the Sufi saint Hazrat Nizamuddin since the 14th century. Performed over a sparse backing of handclaps, tabla beats and the drone of a harmonium, qawwalis drip with the sadness and joy of human experience. Composed in an age of hardship and suffering, these sung poems are an effusive celebration of life, praising everything from Allah and the Prophet Muhammad to lost love and the sensation of being intoxicated by the divine.

Some festivals take devotion to a whole other level, with extreme acts of penitence that seem to be the living

Previous page: Thaipusam festival in Kuala Lumpur, Malaysia. Right: jamming at O'Donoghue's pub in Dublin, Ireland.

embodiment of the idea that you only get out what you put in. There may be pain, there may be blood, but watching these rituals is a powerful reminder of what it means to really believe in something. Consider for a moment how many things you believe in strongly enough to poke needles through your tender skin?

For most of the year, the people of Kuala Lumpur live a life of quiet modernity, but every January or February, devout Hindus put down their mobile phones and pierce themselves like pin-cushions for the festival of **16** Thaipusam, one of the world's most extreme rituals of self-mortification. Skewers through cheeks and tongues are de rigueur and more committed devotees sport portable altars known as kavadis mounted on gantries of spikes.

A palpable sense of excitement grips the city as devotees affix their impalements and begin the long climb up the steps to the Batu Caves. Travellers have

been known to get carried away by the atmosphere, offering up their own skin for ritual piercing. Pilgrims enter a trance-like state, making them seemingly impervious to pain, but it is not known if this extends to tourist volunteers.

You can participate without the agony. The best festivals are not just spectacles but immersive experiences, where outsiders can step across the divide and feel for a moment what it would be like to be a local. Travellers throng to Chiang Mai in Thailand every November to join the festival of **17** Yi Peng, when thousands of floating khom loi (fire lanterns) fill the sky like jellyfish swarming in a tropical sea.

Symbolically carrying away the ills and misfortunes of the old year, khom loi are a hangover from the animist culture that existed across Thailand before the arrival of Buddhism. Luckily, the spiritual merit that comes from releasing a fire lantern is open to all, and it comes with a free side-serving of childlike wonder. The mass lantern release that you've probably seen photos of is actually a ticket event, held at the Lanna Dhutanka temple near Mae Jo University, but releasing your own khom loi is as easy as buying a lantern from a city market and joining the crowds along the banks of the Ping River. Make a wish and if the lantern is still lit when it vanishes out of sight, it may come true.

Participation often comes with a gush of endorphins. In the old-fashioned watering holes of **18** Dublin, impromptu folk jams start up with the spontaneity of bar brawls in a Clint Eastward western. Joining in is positively encouraged, if you can keep pace with the regulars bashing out reels and jigs on fiddles, guitars, drums, flutes and pipes.

Being open to all is one of the defining characteristics of folk music, but etiquette dictates that you ask the local tunesmiths before hauling out your instrument and launching into a reel. O'Donoghue's on Merrion Row and The Cobblestone in Smithfield are veteran music pubs with veteran regulars and all the craic you'll need to get your bow-arm moving.

One part of exhilaration is innocent delight – something you used to feel all the time, but don't seem to experience quite so regularly since you got the promotion and the company car and the late-night sales calls to Seattle.

Everyone fantasises about being an explorer, and playing Indiana Jones is as much fun at 50 as it was aged 10. Tramping through the jungles of Mexico's **19** Yucatán Peninsula, you can push back vines to reveal sacrificial altars, and dive into submerged caverns where warrior kings worshipped arcane gods, while howler monkeys scream a cacophonic chorus over the canopy.

15 HAZRAT NIZAMUDDIN DARGAH, DELHI

The Hazrat Nizamuddin Dargah shrine is hidden in the lanes of Nizamuddin, Delhi's historic Muslim quarter. Pilgrims flock to the shrine daily but sunset on Thursday is the time to hear qawwali singers practice their art. Autorickshaws are the easiest way to reach the dargah, but the shrine is walking distance from the JLN Stadium metro stop. Shoes are prohibited inside the mausoleum, and modest clothing is essential, as are head coverings for women. After dark, the kebab stands outside the dargah do a lively trade in mutton and chicken tikka and spiced kebabs.

16 BATU CAVES, KUALA LUMPUR

Thaipusam is celebrated on the full moon in the 10th month of the Hindu calendar, which falls in January or February depending on the year. The limestone massif hiding the Batu Caves is squirrelled away in the suburbs north of Kuala Lumpur, but you can't miss the entrance – just look out for the giant gold statue of the Hindu god Murugan. The grand parade of kavadis happens on the second day of the celebrations. Kuala Lumpur is one of Asia's biggest air hubs and KTM Komuter trains run from KL Sentral straight to the Batu Caves. Stay in Brickfields, home of KL's Indian community.

Tulum in Mexico's Yucatán, where
Mayan ruins meet the Caribbean sea.

The triangle formed by Chichén Itzá, Playa del Carmen and Tulum offers rich pickings for latter-day explorers, with plenty of lesser-known sites where you can evade the coach tour crowds. The kick of being the first on the scene at Cobá, and hauling yourself up the sundered steps of the Ixmoja pyramid to see the forest spread out like a green carpet stretching to the horizon, is instinctive and life-affirming. These are the kinds of views that greeted the first explorers: just ruins, foliage and the screech of birds and jungle insects. So give full rein to fantasy, grab your notebook, wipe the sweat from your brow, and decide what you are going to call your latest discovery.

Climbing pyramids is hot work, but fortunately, the ground around Tulum and Playa del Carmen is perforated like a Swiss cheese by submerged caverns where Mayan kings practiced occult rituals. Swimming in one of Yucatán's impossibly blue waterholes is an essential part of the explorer fantasy, so head to Cenote Dos Ojos or Cenote Azul near Tulum, and hear the hiss of steam as you dive beneath the sapphire surface.

For every Livingstone or Richard Francis Burton pushing back boundaries below the equator, there was a Roald Amundsen or Robert Peary making similar headway in the frozen north. The hardships endured by Arctic explorers are hard to imagine: extreme cold, polar bears, snow-blindness, starvation. Nevertheless, for some, enduring everything the world can throw at you and emerging victorious is the very definition of exhilaration.

The frozen wastes of **20** Finnish Lapland are a stunning place to test your inner polar explorer. In the lakes and forests around Enontekiö, you can enjoy such tests of mettle as igloo building, snow-shoeing, and ice-hole swimming (to quote Finland Tourism, 'the initial shock and momentary loss of feeling in your legs soon pass') in the eerie gloom of perpetual night.

Alternatively, you could let someone else do the hard graft and try your hand at mushing – dogsledding through the taiga forests on the rim of the Arctic Circle. Either way, you'll get to experience the electrifying sensation of being totally alone in an icy wonderland that stretches to every horizon, very much the polar (ahem) opposite to the daily commute on the 8.15am from Sevenoaks.

17 CHIANG MAI, THAILAND

Taking place one day before the festival of Loi Krathong, Yi Peng marks the full moon of the 12th Thai month (or the second month, according to the northern Lanna lunar calendar) in mid- to late-November. As one of Thailand's busiest backpacker hubs, Chiang Mai is packed with accommodation; rooms fill up fast for the festival. Tickets are required for the lantern launches at Lanna Dhutanka temple near Mae Jo University, but it's free to join the crowds downtown; the square by the Three Kings Monument and the banks of the Ping River are popular launch points.

18 DUBLIN, IRELAND

Folk jams take place nightly at pubs across Dublin, but some venues are legendary for music and craic (atmosphere, or more specifically, good times spent in good company). O'Donoghue's on Merrion Row, M Hughes on Chancery St and The Cobblestone in Smithfield tick all the right boxes. For instruments, fiddles, guitars, flutes, pipes and bodhráns (Irish frame drums) are all eminently jammable. Dublin is a busy air hub and ferries run from Holyhead in Wales to Dublin Port. Pick a hotel close to the pub so you can stagger home after an evening of stout, reels and jigs.

19 YUCATÁN PENINSULA, MEXICO

Brash holiday hub Cancún is the gateway to the Yucatán, and buses zip down the coast to the ruined cities of the Ruta Maya. Tulum and Chichén Itzá are the most famous Mayan sites in the northern Yucatán, but they also draw the biggest crowds. Escape the crush amid the pyramids of Cobá, or duck south to Muyil, where the ruins of another silent, pyramid-crowned city spill into the Sian Ka'an Biosphere Reserve. Cenotes are dotted around the jungle across the peninsula, with the biggest concentration of sinkholes around Tulum and Playa del Carmen.

20 ENONTEKIÖ, FINLAND

Hidden away 220km (137 miles) north of the Arctic Circle, Hetta is the biggest village of Enontekiö municipality, but that isn't saying much as the whole district is home to just 1900 people. Flights run twice weekly from Helsinki to Enontekiö airport, 10km (6 miles) from Hetta, but only from 19 February to 23 March. At other times, you'll need to fly to Kittilä, or take the train to Rovaniemi or Kolari and continue by car or bus. November to April is mushing season. The sun doesn't rise from November to January, but, unsurprisingly, this is peak season for viewing the northern lights.

FULFILMENT

'I can't get no satisfaction,' crooned a snake-hipped young firebrand by the name of Michael Jagger back in 1965, and if we're honest with ourselves, surely we'd all have to admit we've had that feeling once or twice in our lives.

It's one of the big questions; maybe the biggest of all. The conundrum of contentment. Of how to feel satisfied in a world that sometimes seems to be doing its darnedest to make us feel dissatisfied with our lot, envious of others and uneasy about the direction in which we're headed.

Now, some might say that this is a First World problem, and they'd be right. When compared with global warming, poverty and hunger, the question of how to feel satisfied seems like a trifling concern. And in fact, a 2017 study published in the Journal of Happiness Studies suggests that those times when we're struck by a lack of direction and endure periods of emotional confusion are all part of ultimately establishing meaning and purpose to our lives.

As that study by the University of Santiago, Chile, found, we don't have to feel good all the time to lead satisfying lives. However, in the long run, along with love, health and happiness, fulfilment is surely one of the big goals we're all aiming for. In fact, some might say it's the biggest one of all: because fundamentally, if you don't feel fulfilled, content and at ease with your inner self, then all those other life goals suddenly become that

① KOPAN MONASTERY, KATHMANDU, NEPAL

This ancient monastery is located in Nepal's capital, Kathmandu, which has regular flights to most major Asian cities. Its week-long introductory courses (£70) cover the basics: mindfulness practice, meditation techniques, concepts such as the Four Noble Truths and the fundamentals of Buddhist thinking. Dorm accommodation and meals are included in the course fee. If you feel inspired to go deeper, longer retreats lasting a minimum of 14 days can be arranged with the monastery. For details visit www. kopanmonastery.com.

② INDIAN ASHRAMS

Kaivalyadhama Ashram (kdham.com) is in the hill station of Lonavala, 82km (51 miles) south-east of Mumbai. It's an established and well-respected school that focuses mainly on traditional yoga; prices for a week-long course with a single room and shared bathroom start at £87, up to £280 for a deluxe double with air-con. It also offers longer courses and teacher-training programmes. Purple Valley (www. yogagoa.com) is in Goa, a short drive from Dabolim airport. Its one-week programmes start at £750 for a single room, though it's cheaper if you don't stay on site.

little bit harder to achieve. In the words of the Beatles' spiritual guru, Maharishi Mahesh Yogi: 'Life finds its purpose and fulfilment in the expansion of happiness.' Or, to put it another way: find your raison d'être and everything else just seems to slot into place.

Unfortunately, the question of how to go about finding your true calling is an altogether harder proposition. So, following some more of the Maharishi's sage advice, perhaps the first step is not to look outwards, but inwards.

The search for inner peace is something that's central to Buddhist practice. The concept of dukkha, or suffering, dictates that much of our unhappiness is rooted in our own desires for things that we can't have, and in order to escape that cycle of unhappiness, we need to find a way to let those desires go. That's where the practice of mindfulness comes in: learning to exist in the here and now, rather than dwelling on the unchangeable past or the unknowable future. Though you might not be able to

③ BAGAN, MYANMAR
The temple complex at Bagan is 626km (389 miles) north of the city of Yangon, which has flight connections to several Asian cities, including Bangkok. To get to Bagan, you then need to catch another flight from Yangon to Bagan's nearest airport at Nyaung U, or you can catch a slower ferry along the Irrawaddy River. The easiest way to explore the temple site is by bicycle, which are cheap and readily available for hire, or you can catch a shared taxi for about £25 a day; a private taxi is likely to cost around £50 a day. For maximum romance factor, horse-drawn carts are also available. Go Myanmar (www.go-myanmar.com/the-temples-of-bagan) has useful background.

④ UBUD, BALI
Ubud is about 40km (25 miles) north of Bali's main airport at Denpasar. Entry to many temple sites is free, although donations are welcome and better-known sites such as the Tirta Empul water temple charge an entry fee. It's important to dress modestly when visiting Balinese temples; shoulders and knees must be covered, and some sites require you to wear a sarong and headscarf. Dance performances, gamelan concerts and shadow puppet shows are easy to locate: one of the oldest dance shows is performed by Gunung Sari at the Peliatan Palace every Saturday night.

Previous page: mountainous Nepal. Right: Buddha reclining in Shinbinthalyaung temple at Bagan.

achieve the ultimate goal of enlightenment, spending a couple of days at a Buddhist temple can be a great way of simply getting your head straight and deciding what's most important.

Unsurprisingly, Nepal makes an appropriate place to begin your mindfulness journey. At the ① Kopan Monastery in Kathmandu, monks hold regular day courses that cover the basic meditation practices while exploring some of the core tenets of Buddhism, such as the Four Noble Truths and the concepts of dharma and samsara. You get to live and practise alongside the monks, and therefore be tutored in mindfulness techniques by the masters.

Another discipline that helps encourage inner peace is the practice of yoga, and there are few better places to learn the basic postures and refine your peacock pose than at an ② Indian ashram. There are hundreds of places to choose from, all exploring different styles and techniques. Which one you choose is a matter of taste. You could go for a formal school such as Kaivalyadhama Ashram in the old hill station of Lonavla, which emphasises a classical method following the form of ashtanga yoga developed by Patanjali, widely considered the father of traditional yoga.

Alternatively, you could opt for a more modern-style school such as Purple Valley in Assagao, Goa, where you can sip on detox juices and wander the tropical gardens when you're not busy practising your poses. Either way, the key is immersion: to get the most out of a yoga retreat, you need to commit – and that means ditching the phone, avoiding emails and Instagram for a while, and focusing completely on the here and now.

Sometimes, even just visiting a temple and spending some quiet time there can be enough to open your eyes to a higher state of being and an appreciation of just how lucky you are to be here at all. One of the very best places to experience that transcendental temple feeling is ③ Bagan – the greatest sacred site in Myanmar (Burma) – a vast complex of more than 2000 temples covering 67 sq km (26 sq miles).

Constructed from mud and brick between the 11th and 13th centuries, the complex opens a window to a lost world where the everyday and the divine were intertwined. Many of the temples are covered with ancient frescoes or harbour antique Buddha statues carved by long-forgotten craftsmen. Monks pad around the dusty courtyards. And watching the sun rise over the Irrawaddy River as hot air balloons take off in the dawn light is an experience that's impossible to forget: deeply fulfilling and, who knows, perhaps even life-changing.

Bali is another place that manages to combine the sacred and secular in surprising ways. Religious

practice is interwoven into the everyday here in such a fundamental way that it's impossible to imagine life without it. Most people pray and make offerings several times daily, and the calendar is littered with so many auspicious days and holy holidays, it's a wonder that anything ever gets done. But for Balinese people, their religious customs are simply part of who they are, and satisfy parts of them that other things – love, money, careers – simply don't reach.

The town of ❹ Ubud is the optimum place to experience Balinese culture; it's here you can watch shadow puppet plays, attend a traditional dance performance accompanied by a *gamelan* orchestra, explore shrines hidden away along the back-streets, and cleanse yourself under sacred fountains – hopefully emerging with a clearer, calmer, more uncluttered mind on the other side.

Martial arts have long been renowned for their ability to improve your fitness while also enhancing your sense of wellbeing. The traditional art-form of Tai Chi is arguably the best for promoting inner peace, as it combines breathing, movement, meditation and awareness into one seamless whole; it's based on movements that mimic the graceful movements of animals and birds, and is designed to use an opponent's force against him. Qi Gong is similar, but focuses less on the art of self-defence, and more on channelling the flow of *qi* (energy) around the body.

❺ Běijīng is one of the best places to learn the basics: in many public parks, such as the ones next to the Temple of Heaven and the Summer Palace, you can watch scores of people practising their Tai Chi moves every morning, and you're welcome to join in. If you get the bug, lots of local schools offer classes, including the SCIC Chinese Martial Arts Academy, where you can also learn other traditional martial arts such as Wushu, Sanshou (kick-boxing) and Kung Fu.

Another route to fulfilment that was often adopted in the past was the challenge of embarking on a pilgrimage: a physical journey that allowed ample time for spiritual contemplation. Arguably the most famous pilgrimage of all is the ❻ Camino de Santiago (the Way of St James), a 790km (490 mile), month-long trek that today still winds through southwest France and across the Spanish border to the cathedral at Santiago de Compostela, where St James himself is buried.

There are various routes that can be followed: the classic one begins in the French town of Saint-Jean Pied de Port. Accommodation en route is in rustic *gîtes* (hostels), where pilgrims get the chance to mingle with other walkers and, perhaps more importantly, discuss their reasons for embarking on the trek. More than 200,000 people now tackle the journey each year, and each has their own individual reason for doing it. But ultimately they all share a similar goal – to complete the route and achieve a long-held, life-affirming ambition. Sure, you get a nice certificate at the end too – but it's the sense of completion that really matters most.

Japan's ❼ Kumano Kodō is another pilgrimage route that seems to be made for fulfilment seekers. Criss-crossing the wooded mountains from the peninsula of Kii Hantō all the way to the Kumano Sanzan temple complex, this network of trails places the emphasis firmly on the power of nature as a route to inner peace. Along the way, you visit tiny temples and stay in traditional *minshuku* houses (which are rather like *ryokan*, only more basic). It's a walk that forces you back to basics, and after a while, if your mind is in the right place, you'll start to hear nothing but the crunch of your boots, the twittering of birds in the treetops and the babbling brook beside the trail. This is hiking, Zen-style.

⑤ TAI CHI IN BĚIJĪNG

If you just want to pick up the basics, the best idea is to head for one of Běijīng's public parks early in the morning, such as those at the Temple of Heaven and the Summer Palace, where you're bound to see people practising their moves. For a more formal education, SCIC Chinese Martial Arts Academy (www.scicbeijing. com) offers four-week Tai Chi courses at the Beijing Sport University, starting at £1700 with accommodation in a single room.

⑥ CAMINO DE SANTIAGO, FRANCE AND SPAIN

The most common route runs from Saint-Jean Pied de Port in the French Basque Country to Santiago de Compostela, a distance of some 790km (490 miles). You could extend the route by starting in other locations such as Le Puy-en-Velay, Lourdes, Arles, Vézelay or even Mont St-Michel. Organised treks can be arranged with Camino Ways (www.caminoways. com) or Macs Adventure (www.macsadventure. com), but it's possible to organise your own trip by staying at walkers' gîtes (hostels) en route. The official Confraternity of Saint James (www.csj. org.uk) website is the first port-of-call, and there's useful advice at Camino Adventures (www. caminoadventures.com).

Previous page: gamelan musicians and a temple gate at Ubud, Bali. Left: hiking the Camino de Santiago, Spain.

A sacred stone *torii* (gate) on the
Kumano Kodō trail in Japan.

But yoga moves and altered mind-states aren't the only ways to find contentment. Another method often recommended in the search for lasting satisfaction is to acquire a skill – not in pursuit of perfection, but simply for the pleasure of learning how to do something well.

Take the ancient art of Japanese calligraphy, for example. Performed for more than a thousand years, this art form (traditionally known as *shodo*) is notoriously challenging, combining precise forms with a fluidity of touch that takes years, if not a whole lifetime, to master. ❽ Kyoto is one of the best places to learn, with numerous calligraphy workshops on offer ranging from one-day primers to longer, week-long courses. But why stop there? While you're in Japan, you could also try your hand at sushi-making, flower-arranging or origami: and honestly, there are few things more satisfying than nailing that perfect peace crane, complete with sharp beak, symmetrical wings and razor-edge tail.

---

⑦ KUMANO KODŌ, JAPAN

The Kumano Kodō trail (www.tb-kumano.jp) is to the south of Osaka. The handiest base is the city of Kii-Tanabe, a two and a half hour train ride from Osaka. Once you've arrived in Kii-Tanabe, there are buses to the main trailhead at Takijiri. The classic Kiji route lasts about six days; the walk's website offers comprehensive information on the trail, along with downloadable MP3 walking guides and suggestions for places to stay. Travel specialists such as InsideJapan Tours (www.insidejapantours. com) and Oku Japan (www.okujapan.com) can arrange tailored hiking packages.

⑧ KYOTO, JAPAN

Kyoto's official website (kyoto.travel) is a good place to start your research into traditional arts and crafts. There are plenty of places around the city where you can take courses: at Wak Japan (www.wakjapan. jp) and the Kyoto Handicraft Center (www. kyotohandicraftcenter. com), experiences on offer include everything from origami and book-binding to flower arrangement, kendo, origami, sushi-making and sake-tasting. Calligraphy Kyoto (www.calligraphy. kyoto.jp) specialises in calligraphy lessons, and is run by the expert artist Chifumi Niimi.

Previous page: learn calligraphy in Kyoto, Japan. Left: taking archery lessons in Bhutan.

Archery is another pursuit that demands a level of focus that many practitioners find deeply fulfilling. In Bhutan, it's the national sport – and since this also happens to be the country that frequently tops the polls in terms of all-round happiness, it's logical to wonder whether the two things might just be linked. The capital city of **❾** Thimphu is an excellent place to learn. Lessons can easily be arranged with one of the local archery schools, although traditional Bhutanese longbows are notoriously difficult to use, and it can be discouraging to see how easy and effortless the locals make it look. Then again, simply hitting the target is reason enough to give yourself a pat on the back – even more so if you happen to score a few bull's-eyes and earn a commendatory nod from your teacher.

Cookery is another skill that's ideal for finding a sense of inner contentment. Few things feel as satisfying as creating an amazing meal from scratch for a group of friends or loved ones, and hearing their appreciative nom-noms as they dig in. And, for our money, Italian cooking is the most heart-warming, life-affirming of all: it's the definition of soul food, designed to bring people together and make them feel good. There are some great courses on offer in **❿** Italy: you could learn rustic dishes at Marika Contaldo Seguso's homely Acquolina school in Venice; pick up some Tuscan classics at the lovely Borgo Santo Pietro Cooking School; or learn how to spin the perfect base at Enzo Coccia's renowned pizza school in Naples.

Then, of course, there's the fine art of **⓫** French patisserie to consider. La Belle France is a nation that has turned having a sweet tooth into an art form, and if you've always wanted to learn how to make the perfect croissant or craft a world-class éclair, then it makes sense to go directly to the people who know how to do it best. Le Cordon Bleu school in Paris has been training the world's best pastry chefs for more than a century, and it's still the place to train in the classical art of patisserie. Unfortunately, it doesn't come cheap, and pastry-making diplomas take almost a year to complete – so if you're looking for something that requires a little less commitment, then the École Ferrandi is a great bet, as it offers shorter tailored courses, many of which are taught in English.

One of the most rewarding things about learning a new skill is that, by definition, it's not easy. Difficulty – the act of stepping outside your comfort zone, facing up to your own limitations and hopefully overcoming them – is another route that's often recommended for those who want to feel a bit more fulfilled. The tricky part can be choosing which challenge to set yourself

One obvious option is to get physical. The classic idea chosen by many is to complete a marathon: 26.3 miles (42km) of muscle-shredding effort that requires a combination of physical fitness, mental strength and good old-fashioned grit to finish. The training is hard enough, but being brave enough to actually turn up on the day for the race itself is arguably the toughest challenge of all. So you might as well choose a marathon that's going to be fun. The **⓬** New Orleans Rock 'n' Roll Marathon takes place while the city's in party mood: beads dangle from the trees, spectators hand out beignets and chunks of king cake, and brass bands line the route, playing old jazz tunes to encourage the runners onwards to the finish line. Best of all, the Big Easy's pan-flat geography means there are hardly any hills, perfect if you're a marathon first-timer.

Another satisfying challenge is to tackle a **⓭** long-distance trail. The satisfaction that results from completing an exceptionally long hike is different to

❾ THIMPHU, BHUTAN

Paro, about 50km (30 miles) from Thimphu, is Bhutan's only international airport, welcoming flights from several Asian cities to a nerve-racking landing high in the Himalayas. The main roads into the country link Bhutan with the Indian states of West Bengal to the southwest and Assam to the southeast. All visitors, other than those from India, Bangladesh and the Maldives, must obtain a visa from a local tour operator or licenced travel agent such as Transindus (www.transindus.co.uk), which will also plan your itinerary. Your hotel or tour guide can put you in touch with archery tutors.

❿ COOKING IN ITALY

Cooking courses at Venice's Acquolina school (half-day €170; full-day €290, www.acquolina.com) are hosted by chef Marika Contaldo Seguso and include course fees, lunch and shopping at Rialto market on the full day. The courses offered by Borgo Santo Pietro Cooking School (from €240 per person, www.borgocookingschool.com) cover everything from pasta-making to chocolate and truffles. Week-long courses at Enzo Coccia's pizza school (€700, www.pizzaconsulting.com) teach you all the secrets of making Neopolitan-style pizza.

⑪ PATISSERIE, FRANCE

If you truly want to understand the secrets of French cake-making then Paris' Cordon Bleu school (www.cordonbleu.edu/paris) and École Ferrandi (www.ferrandi-paris.fr) are the finest schools in France, if not the world. You'll need dedication, though: the courses cost €22,800 and €22,000 respectively, and last up to nine months. Courses at La Cuisine Paris (www.lacuisineparis.com) require less commitment; its French Pastry Classics course costs €99 and lasts three hours. Other classes concentrate on the minutiae of choux buns, tarts, millefeuilles and baguettes.

⑫ NEW ORLEANS LOUISIANA, USA

The marathon (www.runrocknroll.com) takes place in early March. It costs $84.99 to register for the main event, or you can opt for a shorter half-marathon, 10K or 5K races. Every person who finishes receives a complimentary medal, T-shirt and finisher jacket. Accommodation isn't provided, so you'll need to arrange a hotel or B&B during the event – places get booked up fast, so get planning early. New Orleans International Airport is 18km (11 miles) west of the city's downtown.

Top left: New Orleans, USA.
Top right: French patisserie.
Right: learn to cook in Italy.

almost any other physical test; it can be exhausting, both physically and emotionally, but the sense of achievement of being able to look down at a map at the end point and know that you've walked the route from start to finish powered by nothing but your legs and your willpower is hard to beat. There are hundreds of trails to choose from throughout the world: the 53.5km (33 mile) Milford Track on New Zealand's South Island will take you just a few days, whereas the 4265km (2650 mile) Pacific Crest Trail on the northwest coast of the US is likely to take even the fittest hiker around five months to finish. Appropriately, it's also the one that inspired Cheryl Strayed's much-lauded searching-for-self memoir *Wild: From Lost to Found on the Pacific Crest Trail.*

Epic bike rides are another trial that tend to leave a lasting feeling of fulfilment once they're over. There are scores of expeditions to choose from, ranging from relatively mild (New Zealand's 85km (53 mile) Old Ghost Road, for example) to the utterly madcap, such as the 11,370km (7065 mile) Tour d'Afrique, which is more of an epic journey.

Somewhere in-between lies the ⑭ Route des Grandes Alpes, a 684km (425 mile) route that winds through glorious Alpine scenery and follows several classic stretches that have often been used by course-setters in the Tour de France. Along the way, you'll be tackling some seriously punishing *cols* (mountain passes), but just knowing you've completed the same route blazed by elite cyclists of the likes of Miguel Indurain, Fausto

Spy seven species of wild and free dolphins in the Azores.

Coppi, Eddy Merckx and Chris Froome is guaranteed to imbue you with an enduring sense of achievement.

Then, of course, there's the issue of braving your deepest fears. If there's something that's always filled you with dread or brings you out in an icy sweat, then facing up to that, and conquering it, might well be a way of finding a special kind of accomplishment that other methods simply can't reach. One of the most common fears of all, of course, is acrophobia – the terror of heights. And if you really want to master it, what better solution could there be than heading up in a tiny propeller-powered plane and chucking yourself out of it? **15** Hawaii is a glorious place to do it; you'll see the whole archipelago spread out beneath you as you fall.

A slightly less adrenaline-fuelled solution might just be to reconnect with the natural world. In the words of the greatest naturalist of our times, Sir David Attenborough: 'An understanding of the natural world

⑬ LONG-DISTANCE WALKS, VARIOUS

The 53.5km (33 mile) Milford Track (doc. govt.nz/milfordtrack) only opens from late October to April for all but experienced hikers. It lasts four days; you must register in advance to book trail shelters and the various boat and bus transfers. The track is accessed by boat from Te Anau Downs, 160km (100 miles) from Queenstown airport. Walkers tackling the 4265km (2650 mile) Pacific Crest Trail (www. pcta.org) must register for a Long-Distance Permit; numbers are strictly managed. Five months is the minimum time to complete the whole trail, although you could tackle shorter sections.

⑭ ROUTE DES GRANDES ALPES, FRANCE

The Grande Traversée des Alpes (www. moveyouralps.com) website has a full section on cycling this legendary bike trail, covering route advice, places to stay, key sights and, most importantly, the 17 mountain passes that you'll need to conquer. Most of the passes are open from May, but usually close in October due to snowfall. The best months for cycling are mid-June to early July and September, when the weather is balmy but not too hot; avoid August if you can. The full route starts on the shores of Lake Geneva and culminates in Nice.

A mother and baby orang-utan
forage for food in Sabah, Borneo.

and what's in it is a source of not only a great curiosity but great fulfilment.' And there can be little doubt that there's something incredibly special about immersing yourself in nature: it's a great way of reminding yourself just how precious our planet is, and just how lucky we all are that we get to see it at all.

The biological wonderland of **16** Borneo is a great place to find that feeling: it's home to an astonishing diversity of species, many of which are found nowhere else on Earth. Most impressive of all are the orang-utans, the 'people of the forest' – those shaggy-haired crimson primates that are currently found only in the rainforests of Borneo and Sumatra. Staring into their chocolate-coloured eyes, it's impossible not to feel a sense of mutual recognition – as though they're gazing at you as much as you are at them. It's a profoundly moving experience that will change the way you view these majestic animals forever, and the Borneo Rainforest

Lodge in the Danum Valley Conservation Area is a wonderful location to experience it, combining luxury lodgings with impeccable eco-credentials.

17 Seeing cetaceans such as dolphins is another activity that frequently figures near the top of many people's bucket lists, and achieving that kind of dream is undoubtedly a life-changing moment. One of the finest locations in the world to encounter dolphins is the Azores archipelago in the mid-Atlantic: between May and September, seven species of dolphins can be found in the warm waters around the islands, and local guides are experts in giving you the opportunity to see them while also acting in an ecologically responsible way. If you're lucky, you might also get to see sperm whales and even orcas.

For many people, however, the single cast-iron way to discover deep and lasting realisation is to stop focusing on themselves, and to do something in order to help other people. The 19th-century lawyer, Freemason and writer Albert Pike perhaps put it most succinctly: 'What we have done for ourselves dies alone with us,' he wrote. 'What we have done for others and the world remains and is immortal.'

It's the very same reason why people in altruistic professions, such as medicine, teaching and charity work, tend to feel more satisfied with their lives: there's the sense that even when you're having a bad day, even when you're wracked by worry and shot through with self-doubt – well, at least you're doing something to make the world a better place.

And one of the best ways to tap into that particular source of wellbeing is to volunteer for something. There are literally thousands of projects to choose from around the world, covering everything from conservation work to humanitarian aid – but the sense of satisfaction you gain from simply doing some good is really hard to beat. Or, as Dr Martha Friedman puts it: 'Success based on anything but internal fulfilment is bound to be empty.'

One way you could pledge your time is to work for an ecological project, such as those run by **18** Rainforest Concern in Ecuador, which aims to conserve threatened rainforest habitats and the precious wildlife they contain. You could find yourself conducting scientific research in the cloud forest, teaching conservation topics in a local school, or working to replant deforested areas.

Rainforest Concern also manages projects protecting leatherback turtles in Costa Rica and maintaining

15 HAWAII, USA

Hawaii receives regular flights from mainland USA and Japan. There are several certified sky-diving operators located on the island: Skydive Hawaii (www. skydivehawaii.com) is one of the largest, and charges $250 (£196) for a 12,000ft (3660m) tandem dive. It's based in Waialua, 48km (30 miles) northwest of Honolulu. Pacific Skydiving (www. pacificskydivinghonolulu. com) is a better option if you want to stay near the capital: it's based in Waikiki, on the south side of Honolulu, and charges $179 (£140) for a 14,000ft-15,000ft dive (about 4200-4500m), with a freefall that lasts roughly a minute.

16 BORNEO

The Danum Valley Conservation Area is in Sabah province, in the northeast corner of Malaysian Borneo. It covers 438 sq km (169 sq miles) of pristine rainforest, which has never been occupied or disturbed by man, and as such is a precious habitat for many of the island's most highly endangered species, including sun bears, orang-utans, gibbons and pygmy elephants. There's only one place to stay in the reserve: a 4-day, 3-night adventure package at the Borneo Rainforest Lodge costs MYR4970 (£910) per person, including a double room, meals, guides, activities and airport transfers.

Previous page: the unique landscape of Madagascar. Left: local women pounding rice in Madagascar.

wildlife reserves in Chile. Working on dedicated conservation projects such as these is a tremendously rewarding experience and might even inspire you to explore conservation as a career.

Another worthwhile organisation working along the same lines is ⓳ SEED Madagascar, a grassroots charity that aims to help this incredibly biodiverse island develop in a sustainable way that benefits wildlife as well as local people. Its projects are incredibly varied, ranging from working with local schools to conducting field studies, educating locals on conservation issues and even digging wells for rural villages. Working within the community, especially alongside a locally based charity, is another reliable strategy for ensuring your volunteering experience feels really constructive.

Large multinational charities often offer a wider variety of projects, but sometimes feel a bit impersonal to volunteers, and it's harder to see the effects of the work you're doing. Projects such as those run by ⓴ Iko Poran, based in Rio de Janeiro, stem directly from

the needs of the community and address specific challenges identified by local councils. As such, they can offer a more satisfying experience as they focus on a specific, achievable goal, with really tangible results – so that you can head home confident your work will have a lasting impact on the community you've visited.

However, you don't have to travel halfway around the world in order to do good work. In many ways, volunteering within your own community is one of the best ways to guarantee a truly enduring sense of fulfilment; after all, it's the place you know best and the place you care about most, so helping to make it better through the work you do might just be one of the most rewarding experiences you could ever have. Ask around for ideas, and keep your eyes and ears open. Every community has its own individual needs; the key is to identify the important issues, dedicate your time and energy to them, and stay positive and enthusiastic even when times get tough.

With a bit of luck, you'll sleep a little more soundly at night, feel a bit more at ease about your own place in the world and, who knows, maybe make a few new friends along the way.

And what could be more fulfilling than that?

⑰ SEEING DOLPHINS, THE AZORES

The Azores receives regular direct flights from Lisbon and Porto, and an increasing number from other European cities. The Azores offers a huge range of cetacean species to spot, from unusual Risso's dolphins to sperm, blue, fin and sei whales. Species vary according to the time of year but there will generally be some cetaceans to spot; April to October is the prime time. There are lots of tour operators, offering mainly half-day trips. You can also visit a whaling museum and watch towers on the islands.

⑱ RAINFOREST CONCERN

Rainforest Concern (www.rainforestconcern. org) is based in the UK town of Bath. Its leatherback turtle conservation project on the Costa Rican coastline is operated in partnership with the Pacuare Reserve (www.pacuarereserve. org), about 150km (90 miles) east of the capital San José, while its project in the Ecuadorian cloud forest is run in collaboration with the Santa Lucía Reserve (www.santaluciaecuador. com), about 80km (50 miles) north of Quito. Contact the organisation directly for programme details and current prices.

⑲ SEED MADAGASCAR

London-based SEED Madagascar (madagascar.co.uk) runs projects across the island, covering conservation, English teaching, construction and community work. Most involve a minimum commitment of two weeks, up to 10 weeks for the Pioneer Madagascar programme, which involves visiting several projects. Costs range from about £695 to £1995 for the minimum donation to the project, but you'll need to cover your own expenses and air-fare. Accommodation, facilities and communications on Madagascar are basic, so be prepared.

⑳ IKO PORAN

Non-profit Iko Poran (www.ikoporan.org) was founded in Rio de Janeiro in 2002, and has a number of community-driven projects running across Ecuador, Peru, Costa Rica and Brazil with which you can get involved, as well as others in Nepal, Tanzania, Uganda, Kenya, Ghana and Thailand. It charges an initial registration fee of $229 (£179), but the programme fees are paid directly to the project, ensuring the money goes where it's needed. Nearly all programmes include meals, accommodation, supervision and in-country support.

ADVENTURE

 'Adventure,' says Ed Stafford, the first person to walk the length of the Amazon, 'is honest, humbling, tough, frustrating and unbelievably addictive.' Adventure comes in many forms but when it strikes it's hard to resist. In the early 20th century, Gertrude Bell mapped the Middle East after she had previously climbed Mont Blanc. More recently, American author Will Ferguson hitch-hiked Japan following the cherry blossom sakura for his book Hokkaido Highway Blues. However you are calibrated for adventure, stepping even a little outside your comfort zone is enough gain confidence in your capabilities.

When Gabriel Langlands felt that life in England was growing a little stale he set off on his motorbike for the ❶ Lofoten Islands of northern Norway in the Arctic Circle. He made it as far as the tip of the archipelago, the island of Røst. Each winter, arctic cod (*skrei*) arrive to spawn in the surrounding seas, luring hundreds of fishing boats. It's a tradition that goes back 5000 years, the difference being that in 3000 BC the people would row over from the mainland to fish in the deadly winter seas.

The catch is hung on wooden frames to dry outside in the salty wind. By summer, says Langlands: 'It is as hard as a board and a quarter of its original weight; light and durable for transport and trade, and almost entirely protein.' Langlands got a job hanging the cod

❶ LOFOTEN ISLANDS, NORWAY

The main islands – Austvågøy, Vestvågøy, Flakstadøy, Moskenesøy – are linked by bridges or tunnels. There are also bus services and cycling routes. But you'll need to take a four-to-five-hour ferry trip from Bodø on the mainland if you want to go all the way to Røst. Leknes is Lofoten's local airport, receiving direct flights from Tromsø and the Norwegian capital Oslo. There's a wide range of accommodation on the Lofoten Islands, from camping, cabins and hostels to hotels and self-catering; options on Røst are very limited. The weather warms up from May until September.

❷ THE SAMI, SWEDEN, FINLAND, NORWAY

The Sami live across the northern swathe of Scandinavia, so transport options really depend on which part you're visiting. Generally, international travellers will arrive at the capital cities of Oslo, Stockholm or Helsinki, which are in the south of each country. So you'll need to travel north by train or plane. The tourist season starts in spring, from April onwards.

250

Previous page: a Sami tent in Sweden.
Left: cod drying on racks. Right: Reine,
a fishing village in the Lofoten Islands.

in snow-laden gales, bloody icicles hanging off his elbows, working without sleep until he hallucinated the fish bursting into flames in his hands: 'I would wake in the night and observe resignedly that my bedclothes were made of cod.'

But you don't have to go to the same extremes to seek adventure in the Lofoten Islands. The cod quotas are filled in April and by late spring Lofoten is a much more comfortable place to be. The islands arc out from the mainland, becoming less inhabited the further you travel along them. You can get around by car but it's even better to tour by bicycle or sea kayak. In the summer, when the sun doesn't fully set, the still waters look like liquid gold. Coldwater surf breaks, perhaps the world's most northerly, attract adventurous surfers. Walkers explore these mountainous islands on day hikes.

If you want to immerse yourself even more deeply in the culture of the north, spend some time with the semi-

nomadic ❷ Sami people of northern Sweden, Finland and Norway. In Finland, the best places to meet Sami people include Inari, Enontekiö and Utsjoki, where as soon as the weather becomes tolerable in March and April you can take part in ice-fishing or watch traditional ski races, such as the most northerly ski marathon in the world between Hetta in Finland and Kautokeino in Norway, following a traditional postal delivery route.

As soon as May arrives, the Sami year starts with the birth of the season's reindeer calves, which are marked by their owners the following month. By this time the males and non-pregnant females have begun the annual migration to their summer feeding grounds. At the Sápmi Nature Camp, near Gällivare in Swedish Lapland, you can sleep in a Sami tent and eat locally harvested food in a recreation of a traditional Sami homestead – so no wi-fi, nor running water. Just remember that today the vast majority of Sami have modern lives, often in Nordic cities, living in houses and using snowmobiles for herding reindeer. There's often a gulf between the romantic idea and the reality.

However, one place where tribal life is very real, occasionally with violent consequences, is Papua New Guinea. The huge island of New Guinea, north of Australia, is one of the world's last frontiers of adventure. It wasn't until the 1930s that European explorers ventured into ❸ the Highlands of central Papua New Guinea, encountering large tribal villages, fascinating creatures such as birds of paradise and a very challenging landscape. Tribal life is central to everyday existence in this part of Papua New Guinea, governing, for example, the origin of porters or guides you'll need for such adventures as hiking the Kokoda Track or climbing Mt Wilhelm. The most visible facet of tribal life is at the annual Highland shows near towns such as Mt Hagen in the Southern Highlands and Goroka in the Eastern Highlands, which is perhaps the most accessible place to meet local tribes, who perform traditional dances.

However, for a taste of true Papuan adventure you'll need to lace up some walking boots to hike the Kokoda Track across the Owen Stanley Range in the east of the island, which is a rite of passage for many Australians due to the battles with the Japanese here in WWII. Or, to go a lot further off the grid, paddle a dugout along the Sepik River in the remote northwest, where you'll pass stilt villages, cinematic jungle scenery and crocodile-headed canoes. You'll need a guide; the river becomes less frequented the further upstream you go.

You'll also need a guide if you're to explore ❹ Nagaland in northeast India, sandwiched between Assam and Myanmar. There used to be several headhunting tribes in these little-visited highlands but

③ THE HIGHLANDS, PAPUA NEW GUINEA

The town of Goroka is the gateway to the Eastern Highlands province and hosts one of Papua New Guinea's most colourful tribal shows over the Independence Day weekend in September. Book accommodation in advance. You can take a flight to Goroka from the capital Port Moresby. From Goroka, roads lead to Mt Hagen and the north coast towns of Lae and Madang. As you continue west towards the Sepik River the level of adventure increases and the majority of travellers will require the services of a guide – see Lonely Planet's Papua New Guinea & Solomon Islands book for the latest tips.

④ NAGALAND, INDIA

Kohima is Nagaland's capital and the gateway for reaching the Naga villages of Kisama, Kigwema, Khonoma and Tuophema. You can book a car and driver for a day trip to these villages. You can reach Kohima by bus in three hours from Dimapur, which has an airport that receives flights from Kolkata and a few other cities. To visit northern Nagaland you will need your own sturdy vehicle (there's little public transport) and a local guide. Note that there is periodic political instability in this region and that you should take the latest travel advice.

Women in tribal costume at Mt Hagen in Papua New Guinea. Overleaf: a Nagaland man wearing a Konyak headdress.

© Matt Munro / Lonely Planet

the practice, which traditionally signified strength, was outlawed in 1953 (the last recorded instance was a decade later). However, exploring Nagaland is far from easy even today. Periodic security issues due to a long-running independence campaign may mean that the region is closed to outsiders. Should you get in, a sort of misty Shangri-la awaits. Hilltop villages, such as Khonoma, just 20km (12 miles) west of the Naga capital Kohima and home of the Angami tribe, are surrounded by terraced rice fields and forest. The Angamis held off British soldiers for 50 years in the 19th century but today they're better known for preserving their local environment and their settlement – surrounded by 200 species of tree, 45 species of orchid and 25 types of snake – is known as a 'green village'. Locals use about 250 plant species for medicine, food and clothing.

The further east and north you go in Nagaland, the wilder it gets. Along the border, in places like Longwa, many local people, bedecked in feathers, horns, teeth and shells, are animists and neither they nor their villages have changed much in centuries. Just reaching these places is an adventure.

Pre-dawn in ⑤ Tikal, Guatemala, and the loud barks of howler monkeys reverberate through the darkness. It's cold and misty because winter is the best time to catch the sunrise at this Mayan site, first settled around 700 BC. But the reward for beating most of the tour parties to the entrance is seeing the sky lighten, then the first warming rays of sun spread across the forest canopy, picking out the tops of the stone temples that were built from the 7th to 9th centuries. The mist now lingers in wispy patches above the jungle.

Of all Central America's Mayan ruins, those of Tikal are among the most evocative, perhaps because of the trees that reclaimed the huge city from its heyday a millennium ago, perhaps because of the role it played as the Rebel base in *Star Wars*. Or maybe because, if you're lucky enough to have the place to yourself at dawn, it's easier to imagine yourself as an explorer, entering the Gran Plaza for the first time, or climbing the slippery stone steps of a temple. Most dawn watchers head straight for the top of Templo IV, the tallest building at Tikal. But it's just as thrilling to explore the Gran Plaza with the now wide-awake and foraging coatimundis and turkeys.

For a lot more wildlife, but no Mayan marvels, head for the wild Osa Peninsula in nearby Costa Rica. Much of this southwest corner of Central America's most conservation-conscious nation is dedicated to ⑥ Parque Nacional Corcovado, where, in addition to monkeys and sloths, larger beasts such as tapirs are often sighted and signs of elusive spotted cats including water-

loving jaguars and the smaller ocelots and oncillas can sometimes be seen.

Of all Costa Rica's many world-class national parks, Corcovado is one of the most impenetrable and hard to reach. It's south of the popular and accessible Manuel Antonio and the jungle is thicker and hotter, the beach-side hammocks and cabanas replaced by basic ranger stations and arduous insect-accompanied hikes. But the reward is exploring one of the most biodiverse places on earth. Wildlife watching is centred on the trails around Sirena Ranger Station. Birds such as toucans and macaws will feature, plus peccaries and tapirs, maybe all four species of Costa Rican monkey – spider and squirrel, mantled howler monkeys and white-faced capuchins, and their airborne predator the huge harpy eagle. The sea and river crossings here may mean entering the territory of bull sharks and crocodiles, although ticks and bullet ants are likely to be more of a hazard – nobody promised that adventure would be painless.

Head further south still and the sliver of mountains, glaciers, lakes and coast that is Chile has inspired notable adventurers. At its tip, ⑦ Torres del Paine, meaning 'towers of blue', is perhaps the most famous

⑤ TIKAL, GUATEMALA

Tickets are required, purchased at the entry gate for 150GTQ (£16), though children under 12 go free. If you enter after 3pm your ticket is also valid for the following day so you can overnight in one of the three inns or the campground inside the site. The closest town is Flores, about 40km (25 miles) to the south of the ruins. There are six minibuses daily from Flores or you can take a taxi. You can also reach Tikal from the village of El Remate and Santa Elena, where the local airport receives flights from Guatemala City and Belize City, which have international connections.

⑥ PARQUE NACIONAL CORCOVADO, COSTA RICA

The Costa Rican capital San José is the main access point to the country. Corcovado is in the far southwest and can be access by several routes. From Puerto Jiménez, La Leona ranger station can be reached via Carate (take a 4WD minibus or taxi). There are also options from Bahía Drake. If you don't avail yourself of a charter flight direct to Sirena Ranger Station you will need to use 4WD transport and prepare for some hiking and river crossings. November to April is the dry season but here it's a relative term; expect wet weather any time and pack waterproof bags.

This page: a view of Templo IV at Tikal, Guatemala. Opposite: a squirrel monkey in Corcovado National Park, Costa Rica.

⑦ TORRES DEL PAINE, CHILE

Direct flights with LATAM to Puerto Natales, the closest transport hub to the park, depart Chile's capital Santiago, where most international visitors will arrive (you can also fly to Punta Arenas). From Puerto Natales daily buses go north to the popular park entrances at Laguna Amarga and Serrano, or the Lago Sarmiento entrance. There's less public transport in the winter (May to August). Once inside, pick up maps at the CONAF visitor centre. Overnight options range from campgrounds and huts for those hiking longer trails to luxury lodges. For details see www.torresdelpaine.com.

⑧ BANFF, CANADA

The nearest international airport is at Calgary, from where there are frequent shuttle buses to Banff. There's also a slightly cheaper and slower Greyhound service between Banff and Calgary. Access passes (daily or annual) to Banff National Park can be obtained from Parks Canada (www.pc.gc.ca). There are 13 campsites in the park (July and August are the busiest months when reservations will be required). Fees are variable. Some campgrounds may also provide camping equipment, including tents. Banff town has lots of accommodation and eating options.

Above: crossing Cascade river in Banff National Park, Canada. Right: Torres del Paine National Park, Chile.

of its national parks but it is soon to be joined by 16 more to create a 'route of parks' the length of this South American nation. In 1968, Doug Tompkins, later to found the North Face clothing brand, made a road trip to Patagonia with his friend Yvon Chouinard in a Ford van stuffed with climbing gear and surfboards. They surfed deserted breaks, slept under the stars and eventually climbed the challenging Patagonian peak Mt Fitz Roy. On their return to the US, both men founded outdoor clothing companies, The North Face and Patagonia.

They never forgot what they found in Chile, though, and Doug Tompkins dedicated a large portion of his fortune to buying and conserving wilderness in the country, pursuing a mission of 'wildlands philanthropy'. Tompkins died in a kayaking accident in 2015 but his wife, Kristine McDivitt Tompkins, recently returned thousands of square kilometres to the Chilean government to be inaugurated as national parks. Chouinard noted that this put Chile up with Costa Rica as the countries with the highest percentages of protected lands: 'These are tourist-ready parks, with trails and cabins and infrastructure.'

The 5000 sq km Parque Pumalín, about two thirds of the way down the country, is one of the first of Tompkins' private projects to become a Chilean

Left: Bell Gorge in the Kimberley,
Australia. Right: driving through
Western Australia's outback.

A watchful barred owl in
Olympic National Park, USA.

national park, protecting some millennia-old stands of alerce trees. Already it has numerous outstanding trails, including a hike to the crater of Volcan Chaitén, which last erupted in 2008.

8 Banff National Park, Canada's oldest, may not have active volcanoes, but it does have a new and active herd of plains bison. The 16 wild bison (including 10 pregnant females) were reintroduced in February 2017 and the first calves were born a couple of months later. Their new home will be this spectacular park in the Rocky Mountains, with glacial blue lakes, canyons, forests, mountains and meadows. Banff, together with near-neighbour Jasper National Park, is a Unesco World Heritage site.

Both parks support mountain towns (Banff and Jasper) that have become much-visited adventure hubs, yet as the vast Rocky wilderness is on their doorsteps it's not hard to escape the crowds by lacing up some hiking boots or setting out into the backcountry by paddling, mountain biking or skiing. Paddlers should try Banff Canoe Club for advice and rental canoes; bikers should check Parks Canada's cycling guide, and hikers can pick up maps and the latest trail news from the park visitor centre. One of the classic multiday hikes in the park is the 74km (46 mile) Sawbuck Trail to Lake Louise. But if you're heading into the wild country between Banff and Jasper beware of a hairy companion: in 1811 surveyor David Thompson noticed monstrous tracks that measured 36cm x 20cm. Local people knew what had made them: sasquatch, or bigfoot.

Fictional creatures of another variety patrol the town of Forks on the edge of **9** Olympic National Park in the Pacific Northwest of the USA. It's where author Stephenie Meyer set her *Twilight* series of teen novels. However, unless you're a fan of the fanged protagonists, this far corner of Washington State makes a better destination for adventure lovers than vampire hunters. Dark and dripping with moss and moisture, the Hoh Rainforest in the park is one of the USA's last remaining parcels of temperate rainforest. Explore it on hiking trails, such as the 27km (17 mile) Hoh River Trail, which navigates the maze of twisted trees all the way to Glacier Meadows on Mt Olympus.

If you're ready for a more substantial adventure, some 210km (130 miles) of the Pacific Northwest National Scenic Trail, which crosses Montana, Idaho and Washington from Glacier National Park, wends its way through the park and along Olympic's Wilderness

Coast (the longest stretch of untouched coastline in the contiguous 48 states). The west is the park's wild side and, due to the invigorating sea air, driftwood-decorated beaches, whales and eagles, is undeniably a great place to reconnect with your wild side too.

The vast continent of Australia, still inhabited in the main only around its fringes, is synonymous with incredible stories of adventure. Many perished in the Outback, be they explorer or escapee from Australia's 19th-century colonial prisons. Today, adventure in Australia is a little safer, but only slightly. Taking on a 4WD route such as the Gibb River Rd through **10** the Kimberley in the north of Western Australia is still a serious undertaking, requiring emergency water, food, spare fuel and wheels, as well as a precise plan in case of breakdown.

Temperatures are rarely less than roasting and in the wet season the dirt road is frequently bisected by rivers or washed out by floods. But the Kimberley's elemental beauty is enhanced by its brutality. It's as if the ancient red rocks are cracking under the heat. The slightest bit of water causes trees to flourish, attracting brightly

9 OLYMPIC NATIONAL PARK, WASHINGTON, USA

The closest international airport is Seattle. It's a two and a half hour drive to the northern entrance to the national park – the most accessible – which is just south of Port Angeles. There's a visitor centre (www.nps.gov/olym) at this entrance and accommodation around Lake Crescent, in addition to the park's campgrounds, to which you can hike or boat. On the west side of the park, between the forest and the Pacific are small towns such as Forks where there's a visitor centre and where supplies can be had. Accommodation books up fast in July and August. Winter weather is rough.

10 THE KIMBERLEY, AUSTRALIA

Western Australia's capital, Perth, receives international and domestic flights. From here you'll need to take another flight to Broome in the northwest of the country. You can rent a high-clearance 4WD (complete with two spare tyres, tools and the knowledge to use them) from an outfit such as Britz (www.britz.com. au). The starting point of the Gibb River Rd, the sun-baked town of Derby, is just another 220km (137 miles) from Broome. From here the real adventure begins as you drive towards Kununurra on red dirt roads, past waterfalls, gorges and very few people. Bring extra water and food.

⑪ CRADLE MOUNTAIN-LAKE ST CLAIR NATIONAL PARK, AUSTRALIA

To reach this park in the north of Tasmania, travellers can take a domestic flight to the state capital Hobart and drive north in a rental car, or a flight to Launceston or ferry to Devonport (from Melbourne), which are closer. It's a two-hour drive to Cradle Mountain from Launceston, or a three-hour bus ride. Summer, from November to April, is the best time to attempt the Overland Track through the park; book your place in advance. Most people park their car at Lake St Clair and take a bus back to Cradle Mountain to start their walk.

⑫ SOUTH ISLAND, NEW ZEALAND

Queenstown and Wanaka are the adventure hubs of New Zealand's South Island. There are stacks of eating and sleeping options in both towns. Queenstown receives direct flights from Auckland, Wellington and Christchurch, and from some Australian cities (including Sydney and Melbourne). There are bus services departing Queenstown for Wanaka and other destinations. Peak season is December and January, and advance accommodation reservations on the Routeburn Track are required from the end of October to end of April (www.doc.govt.nz/routeburntrack).

coloured parrots. And water holes such as those at Bell Gorge and Windjana Gorge are appealing spots for a swim, if there are no freshwater crocodiles about. Under the stars here it's easy to imagine that you're a pioneer. Indeed, although long revered by Aboriginal people, it wasn't until 1983 that the 350-million-year-old geology of the Bungle Bungle Range in the east Kimberley, now part of Purnululu National Park, was 'discovered' by Westerners.

⑪ Cradle Mountain-Lake St Clair National Park in the heart of Tasmania is another Australian location in which to feel adventurous. Off the southeast coast of the mainland, Tasmania does things in its own distinctive style. Forget desert, this island is all about primeval rainforest, buttongrass moorland, snow gums, myrtle and beech forest, lakes and rivers, and wildlife such as quolls and the Tasmanian devil. At Cradle Mountain, so-named for its distinctive shape, your first wild encounter is likely to be with a wandering wombat or a Bennett's wallaby. Of all Australia's national parks, this is one where the wildlife is very visible.

It's also the home of one of Australia's iconic walks, the Overland Track, a six-day hike to Lake St Clair from Cradle Valley that meanders past Dove Lake and the 1617m Mt Ossa, Tasmania's highest peak, to Lake St Clair and the headwater of the Derwent River. The region has 275 days of rainfall per year and frequent snowfalls, so it's best to be prepared. There are lots of shorter but equally uplifting walks starting from the

Left: a quoll and boardwalk at Cradle Mountain in Tasmania. This page: hiking the Routeburn Track, New Zealand.

Cradle Mountain Visitor Centre if you're only interested in a day-long adventure. Indeed, it's not the length of a walk that has the most beneficial effect on our mental wellbeing but just the fact you're walking: research published by the National Academy of Sciences in the US suggested that a regular 40-minute stroll was enough to grow the hippocampus region of the brain and cause an increase in the number of neurons (which is good for memory).

In many respects, Tasmania's landscapes are closer to those of New Zealand than the Australian mainland. Across the Tasman Sea, on the ⑫ South Island, Mt Aspiring National Park and Fiordland National Park have a pair of New Zealand's 10 Great Walks – the Milford Track and the Routeburn Track. Of these, the 32km (20 mile) Routeburn is the slightly less famous path.

Walking up from the trailhead to the Routeburn Falls Hut for the first night, the anticipation will be intense, not least because if it's the summer season you will have had to book your place on the trail long in advance (experienced winter walkers must brave blizzards and avalanches instead). The next day you will climb over

⑬ PIHA, NEW ZEALAND

Piha is an hour's drive from Auckland. If you're on a road trip you will probably have organised your own wheels, whether that's a rental car or a campervan. In any case, there's no public transport to Piha. In New Zealand most towns have a campground or holiday park with powered sites where you can plug your vehicle in. There are also 250 vehicle-accessible campsites around New Zealand run by the Department of Conservation. Rental rates from the half-dozen main operators for campervans are highly seasonal and you'll need to book months ahead for the best summer prices.

⑭ WILD COAST, SOUTH AFRICA

It's 1050km (650 miles) from Cape Town on the Western Cape to East London on the Eastern Cape, so it's better to take a direct flight if time is short (there are three or four departures daily). The N2 is the main road north to Port Edward. It doesn't run along the coast so you will need to take side roads down to the ocean and the coastal settlements, which perhaps preserves the wildness of the coast. Between East London and Port Edward are tiny Xhosa settlements, lodges (such as Bulungula Lodge near Coffee Bay; www.bulungula.com) and the occasional backpacker hostel or holiday resort in which to stay.

Roadtripping around Piha on New Zealand's North Island. Overleaf: Lubanzi on South Africa's Wild Coast.

the highest point of the hike, Harris Saddle – take the detour up Conical Hill for views of the Hollyford Valley, the treeline running like a high-water mark beneath the snow-caped peaks. Then descend along precipitous valley trails and through gnarled beech forest to Lake Mackenzie and Lake Howden.

See even more of New Zealand behind the wheel of a camper van on a road trip around the North Island, starting from the surf town of ⑬ Piha on the west coast, where the sand is black, the waves fierce and the wind strong. The town's surf club was founded in 1934 and Piha, though only 40km (25 miles), from Auckland, has long embraced the adventurous side of life. The great thing about visiting as part of a camping road trip is that you can tap into the vibe for as long as you need. Stay a weekend or a week, before hitting the highway and heading on north or south as the wind blows. You may not be getting completely back to nature in a campervan (though you will be surrounded by it in the Waitākere Ranges Regional Park around Piha) but you'll feel a little less cosseted than in a hotel or guesthouse.

In South Africa it's possible to get further off the beaten track with a vehicle. The ⑭ Wild Coast extends for 350km (217 miles) from East London to Port Edward on the cape's east coast. There's no coast road so trippers divert off the motorway to secluded sites such as the backpackers' hotspot of Coffee Bay, and the idyllic town of Port St Johns at the mouth of the Umzimvubu River.

On a road trip it helps (though is not always essential) to have a road in front of you. Over in ⑮ Oman a network of newly surfaced roads has opened up the country's mountainous interior. Former capital city Nizwa, once also a major trading post between Oman's ports and Dhofar's frankincense production, has grand buildings, such as the souk and the fort, that blend into the surrounding Al Hajar Mountains. From this base it's now possible to drive deeper into the interior or visit Oman's highest mountain, Jebel Shams, just to the northwest. The Arabian Peninsula has long attracted Western adventurers, perhaps most famously Richard Burton who travelled to Mecca in the 1850s, taking the trouble to learn Arabic fluently and get circumcised.

Perhaps the world's most famous pilgrimage is the Camino de Santiago (see p116), from the French border in the Pyrenees to the city of Santiago de Compostela in Galicia, Spain. One of the most popular routes begins in ⑯ St-Jean Pied de Port in southwest France, and this beautiful town in the foothills of the Pyrenees

Top right: St-Jean Pied de Port in France. Bottom right: Nizwa's fort and Wadi Ghul in Oman.

is the gateway to many adventures in the region. It's a distinctively Basque place, where Espelette peppers dry in the sun on the fronts of houses. The nearby commune, St-Etienne-de-Baïgorry, borders Spain and offers countless classic hikes in the waves of green-clad mountains. Try the one-day Iparla ridge walk, watching out for eagles and vultures soaring above. For cyclists, roads in the Pyrenees tend to be steeper and narrower than those of the Alps, which adds to their challenge. One of the classic cycling adventures is to pedal the length of the Pyrenees, a feat called the Raid Pyrenean.

However, adventure need not always be about physical exertions in the great outdoors. There are places that can inspire an equally interesting sense of adventurousness without the blood, sweat or tears. One such place is the city of ⑰ San Sebastián set in a sandy bay just across the border in Spain, where you can embark on a culinary adventure like no other. San

Sebastián is one of the world's most out-there dining destinations, famed for its Basque inventiveness and its own imaginative take on Spanish tapas morsels, called *pintxos*. In the city's old quarter, squeezed on both sides by water, streets are lined with *pintxos* bars serving such snippets as calves' cheeks braised in red wine, hake throats and pigs' ears. Many of the bars have their own specialities so the most adventurous gastronomes hop from one bar to the next, venturing further down the culinary rabbit hole with each bite in this wonderland.

Ordering something when you're not quite sure of what will turn up, such as *callos y morros* (tripe and snout), requires a certain intrepid spirit. That feeling is magnified when you don't even speak the language. Venturing to a seething city like ⑱ Hong Kong, which for most people will be an intensely unfamiliar experience to their usual home, is undoubtedly stimulating if not actually scary. The language barrier is one hurdle but the cultural differences may also be challenging. Yet it's an immense confidence boost to find out that you can cope, that you can understand and make yourself understood in one of the most complex and densely populated cities on Earth. Dive in – order Cantonese dim sum, take in a gig or a Chinese opera – and you will surely swim. To help you, Hong Kong also happens to have a superb public transport system.

Another example: a musical adventure. You can explore the sounds the USA's Deep South or go even further, to somewhere such as ⑲ Bogotá. Colombia's chaotic capital, home to eight million people, is known for a unique music scene, electro-cumbia, which fuses electronic music with the folkloric rhythms of Latin American cumbia. Bogotá might not be the prettiest Latin American city nor the easiest to acclimatise to, but in terms of nightlife it's one of the most vibrant and creative. Head out to music store and cafe RPM Records for the latest tips on where to begin your musical journey.

Adventure is anything that challenges us and provides a learning experience about ourselves and the world around us. It's an inoculation against feeling stuck in a rut because it helps us envisage an existence beyond the daily routine, it sparks new dreams, goals and builds the confidence to achieve them. And when you do return to daily life, you'll feel invigorated and better equipped to deal with everyday challenges, from minor setbacks and uncertainty to profound life changes.

If there's one place that inspires more of a feeling of adventure than any other, it's the mountains. 'Between my legs I could see a whole lot of nothing,' writes Robert Macfarlane in his debut book *Mountains of the Mind*, as he climbs the Matterhorn in Switzerland for the first time, having been inspired by Maurice Herzog's

⑮ WADI GHUL, OMAN

New roads have improved access to Oman's Grand Canyon. Follow signs for Jebel Shams from the Nizwa-Bahla road, about 30km (19 miles) from Nizwa. You can drive to the top of Jebel Shams mountain but you'll need a 4WD. From Muscat it is about a three-hour drive. To explore Al Hajar Mountains, you can base yourself in Nizwa (which has the most accommodation and eating options), Oman's second most popular tourist destination. There are buses from Muscat. Late autumn, winter and early spring (October to April) is the prime time (book in advance). Several outfits offer adventure experiences.

⑯ ST-JEAN PIED DE PORT, FRANCE

There are flights to the local airport at Biarritz from where St-Jean Pied de Port is about an hour's drive inland. Larger regional airports are Toulouse and Bilbao across the border in Spain. If you don't have access to a car, there's a train service from Bayonne that takes just over an hour – France's excellent rail network means that it's easy to get to Bayonne. Accommodation in St-Jean Pied de Port is at a premium from July to early September. Basic rooms, dorms and campsites cater to the pilgrims but there are also summer self-catering properties in the area.

Left: culinary adventures in San Sebastián, Spain. Right: the profile of the Matterhorn in Switzerland.

1951 book *Annapurna*. 'I kicked another crampon in, and a big slab of rotten snow lurched off from beneath my foot and cart-wheeled away towards the glacier, disintegrating as it went. I hung there, my arms raised above me, watching the snow rumble. A tingling began in my buttocks and then scampered to my groin and my thighs, and soon my whole midriff was encased in a humming, jostling swarm of fear. The space felt vast and malevolently active, as though it were inhaling me; pulling me off into its emptiness.'

The Matterhorn held a magnetic appeal, perhaps because of its singularly toothy shape, for generations. It was first climbed in 1865, although as Macfarlane notes, 'four of the successful summiteers fell to their deaths during the descent'. But mountaineers are a minority among us; adventure in the ⑳ Zermatt region can more readily involve hiking, mountain biking or skiing and then marvelling at how the peak changes with the light from somewhere serving good rösti and chilled beer.

⑰ SAN SEBASTIÁN, SPAIN

There are regional flights to San Sebastián (most from Madrid or Barcelona but also London), but Bilbao receives more international flights. It's an easy bus trip from Bilbao to San Sebastián or you can rent a car for more independence – the drive is roughly 100km (60 miles). Travellers with more time or an adventurous streak can also make the journey by train from Biarritz via Hendaye. Once in San Sebastián, there's a wide range of accommodation options from small hotels and pensións to larger beachfront hotels. Availability is limited in the high season (July, August).

⑱ HONG KONG, CHINA

Hong Kong's international Chek Lap Kok Airport on a reclaimed island makes for a particularly spectacular arrival. From the airport, the Airport Express train goes to Kowloon station. There are also taxis and buses. Accommodation in Hong Kong's Central and Kowloon area is expensive, but see www.lonelyplanet.com for the best value options. The MacLehose Trail spans 100km (60 miles) in 10 sections across the New Territories, starting from Pak Tam Chung, about 35km (22 miles) east of Hong Kong. Winter, from November to March, is the least humid time.

⑲ BOGOTÁ, COLOMBIA

Several airlines, including the national carrier Avianca, offer flights to El Dorado Airport in Colombia's capital. From there it's easy to take a taxi to your hotel (there are also airport buses if you're sure where you're going). Taxis are also an efficient way of getting around. Most people stay in the centre of the city, in neighbourhoods such as the cobbled old town of La Candelaria, or to the north, home to boutique hotels and the entertainment districts of Zona Rosa and Zona G. Temperatures are consistently mild; the driest periods are June to August and December to March.

⑳ ZERMATT, SWITZERLAND

Zermatt is the terminus for the Glacier Express train from Bergün. You can't drive into Zermatt. Park at the Matterhorn Terminal Täsch and take the shuttle train. Switzerland has an extensive rail network and trains depart from Brig for Täsch. Around 3000 experienced climbers take on the Matterhorn each year. The rest of us take summer hikes around Zermatt – the Glacier Trail has great views of the Matterhorn. There are hostels and hotels in Zermatt but many open only from July to October. In winter, skiers take over. International flights to Switzerland arrive at Geneva, Zurich and Basel.

REFLECTION

Reflection is about taking time to consider experiences. We're often more productive when we've stepped outside our daily routines and detached from work. It's part-meditation, part-musing – and it's not as easy as it sounds for people who are by habit always 'on'. Mindfulness, as defined by the University of California's Greater Good Science Center in Berkeley, means maintaining 'a moment-by-moment awareness of our thoughts, feelings, bodily sensations and surrounding environment'. There is evidence that meditation lowers stress and anxiety, and even that it boosts immunity levels. It has its roots in the Buddhist faith but is today as secular as you want it to be. However, being in a suitable and stimulating place is a good starting point.

For Lonely Planet contributor and travel writer Pico Iyer, Kyoto in Japan (also see p232) – a beautiful city of temples and shrines where, as he puts it, 'people have been sitting still for 800 years' – was where he discovered the art of stillness: 'I began to feel that if you were lucky enough to walk around the candlelit temples of Tibet or to wander along the seafronts in Havana with music passing all around you, you could bring those sounds and the high cobalt skies and the flash of the blue ocean back to your friends at home, and bring some magic and clarity to your own life.

① BHUTAN

The country's international airport is Paro, which receives flights from India, Nepal, Singapore and a few other countries; most people will need transfer flights. Entrants to Bhutan are required to pay a daily fee (with a surcharge for solo visitors), which covers food, accommodation and a guide but not every extra. Trongsa monastery is an eight-hour drive east of Paro, and is open to visitors from 6am to 5pm daily (4pm in winter). The Tiger's Nest monastery is much closer to Paro and it's possible to hike up in about three hours (open daily, from 8am to 1pm and 2pm to 5pm October to March, and until 6pm April to September).

② YÚNNÁN, CHINA

Several international airlines fly to Kūnming. It's an enjoyable place from where to start your Yúnnán trip but you can also fly direct to Dàli, Lìjiāng and Zhōngdiàn from several domestic airports. Buses link most of Yúnnán's cities but the timetables can be impenetrable. Tour operators can take some of the guesswork out of the process. Yúnnán has a temperate climate with a dry season that runs from November to April. See Lonely Planet's website or guidebooks for the latest reviews of guesthouses and hotels in the region.

Except… one of the first things you learn when you travel is that nowhere is magical unless you can bring the right eyes to it.' And the way to develop appreciative and attentive eyes is just by sitting still.

A monk's day starts at 4.30am at ❶ Trongsa monastery in Bhutan, a country with a population that's about three-quarters Buddhist. First on the schedule are morning prayers, then lessons and lectures through the day, punctuated by periods of reflection on what has been learnt. Meditation is a core part of the Buddhist faith (mindfulness might be its secular version) and Bhutan has been a Buddhist nation since the 8th century. Prior to that the Bhutanese practised Bonism, a religion that worshipped nature. So, there can few better places in which to explore the art of reflection than this mountain kingdom.

Its *dzongs* – fortress monasteries – were often sited at key locations in every district. Punakha Dzong is at the confluence of two rivers, and Taktsang, more famously known as the Tiger's Nest monastery, is on a cliff more than 3000m above sea level. Why? Because it's where Guru Rinpoche arrived on the back of a flying tiger, and then spent three years meditating before beginning his mission to convert the Bhutanese to Buddhism.

Trongsa Dzong, in the centre of the country, north of the national park named after former king Jigme Singye Wangchuck, is nicknamed 'the Door to Heaven' and it's an ideal place in which to begin your journey into the art of stillness and reflection. It stands above a river and is surrounded by forested mountains in which to walk.

❷ Yúnnán province in China has been touted as the inspiration for the imaginary Shangri-la of James Hilton's 1933 novel *Lost Horizon*. This mountainous region on the border with Laos and Myanmar is beautifully shaded in the Himalayan hues of pale grey, green and lilac. Among these gorges and lakes live many of China's ancient tribal people, such as the Mosuo of Lugu Lake, one of the world's few matrilineal communities, and the Naxi, whose historic capital is Lìjiǎng, reconstructed in a rather more touristic style after an earthquake in 1996.

The Yúnnán town of Zhōngdiàn went so far as to rename itself Shangri-la and, lying at 3200m above sea level, it certainly has the feeling of a remote mountain kingdom. The Tibetan Buddhist faith is strong here, with a huge prayer wheel adorned with golden buddhas dominating the town centre. You can seek further blessings at Ringha Monastery, festooned in prayer flags and illuminated by burning pools of yak butter. From Zhōngdiàn, the road to Deqin soars into the clouds as it climbs through forests of pines, eucalyptus and rhododendrons, with wild azaleas brightening entire meadows. The road reaches another monastery, Dongzhulin, which straddles a lofty ridge just a few miles from Tibet. It's an extraordinary and tranquil location – even with the chanting monks.

Many cultures have long known that a walk in the woods can be very relaxing, enabling not just our feet to wander but also our minds. What is also becoming clear, thanks to scientific research, is that forests can offer us even deeper health benefits, including higher immune levels and lower levels of the stress hormone cortisol. Several cultures have traditions that embrace forests: Japan has *shinrin-yoku* (or forest bathing – slowly soaking up the arboreal atmosphere), and in Germany forest kindergartens are becoming very popular. Germany's ❸ Thuringian Forest Nature Park is nicknamed its 'green heart', not least because of its location in the centre of the country, equidistant between Berlin, Munich and Cologne, and is the setting for its longest hiking trail, the 169km (105 mile) Rennsteig, which traverses the diagonal ridge through

③ THURINGIAN FOREST, GERMANY

The closest transport hub is Eisenach, equidistant between Frankfurt and Leipzig. There's a local train service (www.sued-thueringen-bahn.de) that loops around the region but the best option is to have your own transport (cars can be rented from the usual operators at airports). It's a three-hour drive into the forest from Frankfurt, for example. The Rennsteig runs for 169km (105 miles) along the Thuringian ridge from Hörschel to Blankenstein. It's divided into six manageable sections. The 13 visitor centres in the Thuringian Forest Nature Park offer maps and accommodation ideas. Visit from late spring to autumn to enjoy the outdoors at their best.

④ HAMPSTEAD HEATH, LONDON, UK

Hampstead Heath is in the north of London, with both local rail and Underground stations (Hampstead) on the south side. Few cites are as easy or affordable to reach as the UK's capital with international flights arriving at Heathrow, Gatwick, Stansted, Luton or City airports, all of which having good connections with the city centre. There are dozens of hotels close to Hampstead Heath but most out-of-town visitors will stay somewhere more central and make a day trip to the heath. Men and women have separate bathing ponds and a mixed pond is open in the summer.

Previous page: temple bells in Yúnnán, China. Right: the Thuringian Forest in Germany.

© Matt Munro / Lonely Planet

Left: Hampstead Heath in London. This page: sailing off Samson in the Scilly Isles.

the forest. It's a popular destination for Germans seeking to get their nature fix, but thanks to the park's size it's easy to find some seclusion in which to absorb the forest's sounds, scents and sights. And if you need a bit of company, there are art and craft courses at Thuringia's forest visitor centres.

If you're lucky, you don't even need to leave your city to immerse yourself in nature. ❹ Hampstead Heath in north London remains one of the British capital's more natural spots – although if you look at John Constable's landscape paintings from the early 19th century you can see that it was once a much wilder place. The heath is a mix of open grassland, woodland and the famous swimming ponds, which open at 7am allowing for a meditative early-morning, open-air dip in the soft water. Dog walkers dominate the main paths across the heath but they're easy enough to avoid. In the autumn you can have the extra excuse of venturing off the paths by hunting fungi (if you go without a guide be sure you know what you're picking before you taste it).

Seeking out a window in your routine for reflection is all about finding the time and committing to it. Scottish poet, dramatist and Hampstead resident Joanna Baillie (1762-1851) often hosted Romantic poets including William Wordsworth. She loved the outdoors and would invite her guests to 'come early enough to have a ramble on the Heath before dinner'. In her poem 'London', the 'distant traveller' views the city at dusk from the high ground of the heath: 'With sad but pleasing awe his soul is filled, Scarce heaves his breast, and within is stilled.'

Immersing yourself in water automatically slows the body's heart rate and can be a very calming experience. It may also activate the brain's slower theta waves, most usually associated with sleep or deep meditation. If there's a lake of tranquillity it would likely be ❺ Lake Saimaa in Finland. Lakes play an important part in Finnish life – this is a country of 188,000 lakes (of which Saimaa is the largest at 4400 sq km (1700 sq miles), and the fourth largest lake in Europe). Finns fish and boat on them in summer, skate on them in winter and relax around their edges all year round. Finland has a population of just 5.5 million, so it's easy to lose yourself in the natural world, foraging for wild berries in summer or fungi in autumn.

The main reason to head to Finland for reflection, however, are its saunas – all 3.3 million of them. All along the shore of Lake Saimaa you can steam in same-sex cabins then take a bracing plunge into the lake. For Finns, the sauna is relaxing and meditative – and as sociable as you want it to be. In this highly secular society, the sauna takes on the role of temple or church, just steamier. And around Lake Saimaa there are still a few ultra-traditional smoke saunas, which fill with wood smoke, much prized for the quality of their *löyly*, a word that describes the steam inside a sauna and also translates as 'spirit' in Old Finnish. 'Sauna is an essential place for cleansing and purifying our minds,' says Finnish actor Jasper Pääkkönen, a partner in a new public smoke sauna in Helsinki named Löyly. At Lake Saimaa, try Anttolanhovi smoke sauna. In winter, its nearby pier has a hole in the ice at the end, awaiting those who wish to jump in afterwards. Birch whisks cost extra.

The ❻ Isles of Scilly is another watery wonderland, where you can meditate on life surrounded by the glinting reflections of the sea. The islands lie of the southwest coast of Cornwall and are famed for their peace and quiet – with very few cars, the gulls are perhaps the noisiest things here. Five islands are inhabited, the largest being St Mary's and Tresco, but there are 140 islets in total and you can potter between

⑤ SAIMAA, FINLAND

Saimaa lies in the heart of Finland's Lakeland region and is about a four-hour drive from the capital of Helsinki and its international airport. Most Finns stay in cabins (with sauna) but there are also campgrounds and other types of accommodation (see www.visitsaimaa. fi for ideas). Days start getting longer in May and drawing in again from August. Many outdoor activities are focused on the water, with half-day introductions to kayaking and canoeing and longer guided excursions (daily or overnight). Sauna etiquette: men and women go separately, typically naked – but it's fine to wear a swimsuit.

⑥ THE ISLES OF SCILLY, UK

Flights to the Scilly Isles land on St Mary's island, departing from Newquay and Land's End airports in Cornwall, and from Exeter in Devon during the summer. The alternative is the two hour 45 minute Scillonian III ferry service from Penzance during the summer (don't forget sea sickness medication if you need it). Boats are also the only way to get between islands in the Scilly archipelago – check the St Mary's Boatmen's Association and Tresco Boat Services for details. There are several hotels on St Mary's but fewer on St Martin's and Tresco. With limited supply, prices are high.

Taking a dip in the placid waters of Lake Saimaa in Finland.

Left: moai on Easter Island (Rapa Nui); below at the Tongariki site. Right: Machu Picchu in Peru.

them by boat. The water – a beguiling blend of turquoise and emerald – is clean, clear and, in August at least, just warm enough for swimming. When your mind is not being lulled by the lapping waves, go beach-combing along the swathes of white sand, or rock-pooling around the headlands. Best of the beaches? Try tranquil Pelistry Bay on St Mary's or Periglis on St Agnes. Beautiful Rushy Bay on Bryher island is backed by wild grasses and flowers. Author Michael Morpurgo, who has set several stories on Bryher, describes the Scilly Isles as 'a cluster of distant rocks lying in a translucent green sea, hurled there maybe by some defiant Cornish giant to sink a fleet of invading ships'.

If it's real giants that set your brain whirring then you'll need to go a lot further, to one of the most remote islands in the world: ❼ Easter Island (Rapa Nui). Set in the middle of the South Pacific, though accessed via Chile, Easter Island's isolated setting makes its giants

⑦ EASTER ISLAND (RAPA NUI), CHILE

There are daily flights to Easter Island from Santiago, the Chilean capital, on LATAM, plus a weekly flight from Tahiti. Unless you have a large yacht, arriving by ocean is not an option. Once on the island, most people stay in Hanga Roa, the island's main settlement, where there are hostels, hotels, campgrounds and cabins. Peak season runs from January to March. The shoulder seasons of April to June and October to December are also pleasant periods; winter in July and August is cold. Easter Island is all about eco-travel – see Lonely Planet for tips on hiking, biking and horse-riding on the island.

⑧ MACHU PICCHU, PERU

International visitors take flights to Cusco and travel onwards to nearby Aguas Calientes. From this staging post, buses run daily up to Machu Picchu or you can hike the 8km (5 miles) uphill (remembering the effects of altitude). The Inca Trail from Cusco to Machu Picchu is another option for hikers, covering 43km (26 miles) and taking four days; advance bookings are required during the peak season, which runs from May to September with June to August especially busy (including Inti Raymi, June's solstice celebration). There's accommodation in Aguas Calientes but it's not the prettiest place.

284

The gardens of the Palacio de Generalife in the Alhambra, Spain.

all the more mystifying. They're the *moai* – huge stone monoliths carved before AD 1500 to resemble humans – that were part of the Rapa Nui people's tribal worship of its ancestors. Hundreds were carved in quarries, some 10m tall, then somehow transported to sites all around the island. The statues have some common characteristics: their heads are oversized, and most face inward towards the island's communities. The islanders coloured the *moai*'s eyes with white coral and gave them black obsidian pupils.

Some believe that the statues were representations of the Polynesian people's ancestors, imbued with their spirits. Another theory suggests that the *moai* tradition inadvertently brought about the island's environmental collapse, with the demand for tree trunks to move the moai causing deforestation and leaching of the exposed soil's nutrients meaning that the population of 20,000 people was unable to feed itself. Other theories suggest that the local population was destroyed by the arrival of Europeans who introduced rats and diseases such as smallpox, others point the finger at Peruvian slave raiders in the 19th century. Whatever the truth, it's a thought-provoking place to be.

8 Machu Picchu in Peru has a similar effect: one of reflection as you wonder how and why the Inca people built this royal retreat on an Andean ridge. It's the details that astound, such as the window of the Temple of the Sun that frames the constellation of Pleiades (a symbol of crop fertility); the earthquake-proof precision engineering of the buildings; and the rainwater collection system that irrigated the city. Ponder all this and the fact Machu Picchu was made in the 15th century and then abandoned within 100 years, as a llama calmly grazes a few feet from you. It wasn't until 1911 that American academic Indiana Jones, sorry, Hiram Bingham III, rediscovered the remarkably intact ruins after receiving local guidance (which suggests that Peruvians hadn't lost Machu Picchu after all).

In Granada, Spain, the **9** Alhambra is an equally meditative experience, especially if you visit in the quieter months to avoid the greatest volume of sightseers. This will aid your appreciation of this sublime example of Moorish architecture. Construction of the Alhambra, a fortified collection of palaces and gardens, began in the 13th century, at the peak of the Islamic rule of Spain. It was dedicated to indulgence as much as defence. What lies within its massive red stone walls that overlook modern-day Granada is undoubtedly

beautiful: from the intimidating exterior, your feelings will change as you enter and pass through hedges of cypress, glimpsing gardens and rectangular ponds. Entering the Palacios Nazaries, you'll be amazed that every wall is decorated with intricate stonework, etched with calligraphy and stories, poems and Islamic verses. Arched windows and carved doorways guide your gaze to tranquil courtyards and reflecting pools. It is as if the whole site has been designed to inspire meditation and rumination. The Moors used maths to create visually entrancing designs – the courtyard proportions are based on rectangles generated by irrational numbers, such as the square roots of two, three and five. In 1492, 800 years of Muslim rule came to an end in Spain when Muhammad XII of Granada signed away his land to the Catholic king and queen.

10 Jaisalmer's fort in the desert state of Rajasthan, India, is also decorated with impossibly intricate stone carving. This is a working city and intensely commercial so you won't get much of a chance to sit still and think quietly unless you can find a quiet spot on a rooftop of an evening – and then look up to see the stars come out

9 ALHAMBRA, GRANADA, SPAIN
Granada lies towards the east of Andalucía. It has a small airport that receives some direct regional flights from low-cost carriers. The resort city of Málaga, a couple of hours' drive to the southwest, has an abundance of flights and there is plenty of choice for renting a car from the airport. There's also a wide range of accommodation available in Granada from guesthouses and hostels to luxury paradores in historic buildings. Granada is lively all year round, although advance bookings are advised for the summer high season of July and August.

10 JAISALMER, INDIA
Set in the far east of Rajasthan, Jaisalmer is most usually reached by train (daily services from Jodhpur take five to six hours, from Bikaner six hours) or public bus (from Delhi via Jodhpur, Ajmer and Jaipur). You may also be able to take a taxi from Jodhpur, Bikaner or Udaipur. For accommodation, as ever in India, beware the promises of the touts: the cheapest rooms often lead to the hard-sell of a camel safari. See Lonely Planet's website or guidebooks for the latest recommendations. Winter is the most comfortable time to visit; it's very hot from April to August.

⑪ MCDONALD OBSERVATORY, TEXAS, USA

The observatory is 27km (17 miles) northwest of Fort Davis, which is in the far west of Texas. It's 298km (185 miles) from El Paso (the nearest international airport), and more than double that to Austin and San Antonio. Rent your own wheels as public transport is limited. Star parties take place on Tuesday, Friday and Saturday evenings. Reservations are required and they often sell out weeks in advance, especially during holiday periods. Book at www. mcdonaldobservatory. org. Special Viewing Nights on the big research telescopes are also available on select dates.

⑫ DUBLIN, IRELAND

As a growing international business destination, Dublin's airport receives flights from the US and mainland Europe, in additional to many regional services from the UK. It's an easy 12km (7.5 mile) taxi or bus ride into the city centre (there's no train). Dublin is buzzing all year round, although the summer months (May to September) are more conducive to being outside (though there are plenty of pubs for when it's wet and windy). There's a huge choice of accommodation from hostels to boutique hotels but you may need to book in advance on public holidays.

above you, as the heat dissipates and the bustle of the city whirs below you. You might get more opportunity for quiet reflection of the night sky on a camel-back tour of the desert (although, again, this is a highly commercial experience).

For a closer look at the stars, however, you'll need to visit an observatory. In east Texas, the ⑪ McDonald Observatory at Fort Davis hosts night-time star parties at its Rebecca Gale Telescope Park where stargazers can dive into the infinite depths of the night sky. The Observatory is part of the University of Texas at Austin's Department of Astronomy and if anybody can help unravel the mysteries of space, it's the astronomers here. They recently developed a technique for looking for the faintest galaxies in the early universe – back when it was a mere billion years old, or about 10% of its current age. And the newly upgraded Hobby-Eberly telescope, one of several perched on the surrounding peaks and the third largest 'scope in the world, is designed to discover the secrets of dark energy.

If there's a place to let your mind wander, it's among the stars at an observatory like this. And then you can pepper an expert with questions, such as how many supermassive black holes are there in our galaxy? In fact some of the sights, stats and theories of astronomy are so mind-blowing that attending a star party may well be a life-changing experience. Many observatories around the world welcome members of the public, from New Zealand to Hawaii, and there are a growing

number of International Dark Sky Parks and Reserves to visit (see www.darksky.org), where light pollution is kept to a minimum.

We may not be able to answer all the questions that the universe poses, but much of the wealth of human knowledge we have gained so far is kept in books, meaning that libraries are wonderful places for some reflective time. They often contain wonders, such as the 1200-year-old Book of Kells in the library of ❷ Trinity College in Dublin.

Looking at the ruins of the Library of Celsus at ❸ Ephesus in Turkey, it's clear how respected knowledge was in the ancient world. A century and a half of excavation at this Greco-Roman city on what is now Turkey's Aegean coast has revealed Europe's most complete classical metropolis (with 80% of the city yet to be unearthed). Ephesus was founded in the 10th century BC and it grew (through one conqueror after another) to be a Greek capital dedicated to the worship of the goddess Artemis – her temple at Ephesus was one of the seven wonders of the ancient world. The Library of Celsus dates from the 2nd century AD and was the

Previous page, left: starry skies above the McDonald Observatory, Texas.
Right: Trinity College Library, Dublin.

ancient world's third largest library (after Alexandria and Pergamum), protecting 12,000 scrolls in what was clearly an immensely beautiful building designed by the Roman architect Vitruoya. The library is named after a Greek-born Roman consul and governor who funded the library, under which his sarcophagus rests. Ephesus is an extraordinary place to explore by yourself or with a guide.

In the ancient world, libraries were as much cultural memories as places to store scrolls. Their scholars were required to memorise texts, in effect becoming living libraries, pre-dating Google by centuries. Memory is a big part of who we are, and the power of taste to rekindle memories has long been known (Marcel Proust's madeleine for example). Wine, with its infinite variety, is a key to unlocking memory and creating new ones. The country of ❹ Georgia was one of the first in which grapes were first cultivated by people (in about 6000 BC), and now unfailingly enchants first-time visitors with its wine, its food, its mountainous landscape and its people.

It's sundown at a house in Tbilisi, Georgia's capital. There's a table covered with plates of Georgian food – *khachapuri* (bread stuffed with cheese), tomatoes, cheese, skewers of lamb, salads with walnuts – and a jug of wine. The *tamada*, or toastmaster, pours everyone a cooling glass of a light, ruby-red, homemade wine and begins by offering a toast to peace, as is the custom, followed by toasts to family and loved ones. There's nothing quite like a Georgian banquet to make guests feel like part of an age-old tradition.

Wine has been made in Georgia for thousands of years, from grapes picked from each household's vines then sealed and stored in red-clay *qvevri* – large vase-shaped vessels – buried in the cellar. In this tiny nation of less than five million people, wine is central to the culture, which makes drinking it a great way to not only meet local people but also reflect on the meaning of life. Enough Georgian wine fresh from a *qvevri* can have a transcendental effect. Start your journey in Tbilisi but if you wish to discover the soul of Georgian wine you will need to go to the region of Kakheti in the eastern hills, where nearly two-thirds of the country's wine originates.

❺ English pubs also offer opportunities for reflection, over a pint of beer or two, if you select your pub carefully. You're looking for somewhere quiet but still friendly and sociable, where there's a hubbub of voices and some conversation at the bar while you're waiting to be

⑬ EPHESUS/ IZMIR, TURKEY

The ruins of the Greek city of Ephesus now lie an hour's drive south of the coastal city of Izmir (itself once the classical Greek city of Smyrna) in western Turkey. It's possible to fly direct to Izmir from a few European cities (London, Berlin) but most people will make the short hop from Istanbul. You can get into town with the local buses, trains or taxis. From Izmir you'll need to take a taxi, rental car or a private tour south to Ephesus. July and August can be very hot for wandering the ruins.

Left: tasting an orange wine made at the Alaverdi Monastery Cellar in Georgia.

⑭ GEORGIA

Kakheti, Georgia's wine-producing region is just to the east of the capital Tbilisi, the international gateway to the country. The village of Sighnaghi makes a good base for exploring the region (the capital of which is Telavi). Marshrutkas (minibuses) run daily to the 18th-century hilltop village of Sighnaghi from Tbilisi (two hours) or you can take a shared taxi. Driving standards are not good. There's an expanding range of accommodation options, from guesthouses to hotels, in the village. The best season for wine exploration is the grape harvest from August to October.

Previous page, left: the ancient
library at Ephesus, Turkey.
Right: scenes from an English pub.

served, but still somewhere you can muse at your heart's content. Things you don't want: a television, games machines, muzak. You're most likely to be looking for a local country pub but neighbourhood pubs in even cities as large as London can be perfect. Ask around for local recommendations, though the Campaign for Real Ale's best pubs of the year list is as good a place to start as any. The old stone George & Dragon in Hudswell, North Yorkshire, the 2017 winner, overlooks the Swale Valley and is owned by its village community.

If beer or wine aren't to your taste, then a cup of tea can provide an equally meditative moment – especially if you travel to the source. In the highlands of central Sri Lanka, some of the world's finest tea leaves are grown and harvested in the plantations around **16** Nuwara Eliya. This is a mist-shrouded land of green-clad hills, waterfalls and rickety colonial buildings. It's where English colonists retreated in the heat of summer, sipping

tea and watching cricket in incongruous style in the tropics. Before you find your perfect place for reflection, take a tour and a tasting at a tea plantation: whole leaf orange pekoe teas are the highest grade and will be a revelation if you're used to teabags.

After all that drinking, it might be wise to have some food for thought. One city as famed for its cuisine as its academic atmosphere is **17** Bologna in northern Italy. Often overlooked for more famous Italian cities, this rust-red university town (the oldest in the Western world) is perfect for a reflective retreat, although you might leave a little heavier. Consider its regional products – legs of prosciutto di Parma ham, great wheels of aged Parmigiano Reggiano cheese, balsamic vinegar – and its most misrepresented dish: tagliatelle with ragù (aka spaghetti Bolognese).

The old part of town, solidly handsome rather than pretty, is filled with restaurants and taverns in which to immerse yourself. They are the places where Umberto Eco, the superstar Italian scholar whose first novel *The Name of the Rose* was a bestseller, would entertain his students at the University of Bologna with wine and intellectual repartee. Eco, a multi-lingual professor emeritus, was interested in semiotics – how we interpret the world through signs and symbols. His hit debut novel, a medieval whodunit about a monk investigating a series of gruesome murders at a monastery, manages to weave philosophy and theology into the tale. Ponder on the ideas as you stroll the Roman historic centre sheltered by its 40km (25 miles) of porticoes.

Many artworks have the power to provoke thought but few do it in such a beguiling way as Japanese artist Yayoi Kusama's 20-strong series of **18** Infinity Rooms. She began these complex installations of mirrored rooms in 1965 with *Phalli's Field* and *Love Forever* (1966) and developed the monumental themes in *Aftermath of Obliteration of Eternity* (2009) and *The Souls of Millions of Light Years Away* (2013). The effect is more than reflective – being alone in an Infinity Room is meditative, immersive and mind-blowing.

Sometimes, to find space for reflection, we simply need to get out of the city. For example, if you cross San Francisco's Golden Gate Bridge and wend your way north through the scrubby hills of Marin County you'll arrive at **19** Point Reyes National Seashore. Here, the sea fogs rise to reveal elephant seals on surf-smashed beaches, wild elk roaming the headlands and many enticing footpaths leading through this invigorating landscape. It's easy to escape people the further you go from the car parks. Bring a picnic, such as fresh bread and local Mt Tam cheese harvested from the Cowgirl Creamery shop in Point Reyes Station, then find a washed-up tree trunk

15 THE PUB, ENGLAND

The best pubs in England are within staggering distance of a bed. Fortunately, this doesn't rule out many. A lot of rural inns will have a bedroom or two available, some dating back to the days when travellers would need to pause their journey overnight. In towns and cities there will usually be accommodation nearby, from B&Bs (beware the bad-tempered landlady) to hotels. Just ensure you have the late-entry key or code. Pubs are enjoyable all year round – in the summer try to select one with a garden, in the winter one with a log fire.

16 NUWARA ELIYA, SRI LANKA

Head to Sri Lanka's Highlands by train, bus or even bicycle. The bus station is at the central roundabout and receives buses from Colombo (six hours), Ella (three hours), Kandy (four hours) and other towns. Trains arrive at a station 9km (5.5 miles) outside town from east (Badulla) and west (Kandy, Colombo). Many hotels will pick you up. There's a wide range of accommodation, including colonial-style hotels in varying states of repair. Beware draughts! December to March is prime time to visit the hill country, but remember that nights can be chilly.

Elephant seals hauled up on a beach at Point Reyes National Seashore, USA.

Left: Varanasi, viewed from the Ganges river.
Right: Bologna, Italy. Previous page: Yayoi Kusama's
The Souls of Millions of Light Years Away installation

to sit on and watch the waves roll in. Was that a whale? Possibly. From late April to early May, mother grey whales and their calves swim close to shore.

As life begins, so it must end. At ❷⓿ Varanasi in northern India, that ending comes in one of the most remarkable cities in the world. The Ganges River, sacred to Hinduism, flows past this city. Steps lead down to the water's edge and pilgrims continuously arrive to wash away their sins in the river. In the wan early light, when the city's ancient and grimy walls merge into the grey sky and murky water, it's a decidedly otherworldly place to be. It's also the end of life's journey for many of Varanasi's devout visitors, who come here, ill or in old age, believing that to die here offers *moksha*, liberation from Hinduism's cycle of rebirth. Their bodies are burned on pyres at some of the ghats beside the river, smoke rising into the sky.

As Pico Iyer says in *The Art of Stillness*: sometimes 'you need to step back to see the larger picture'. Or, in Ferris Bueller's wise words: 'Life moves pretty fast. If you don't stop and look around once in a while, you could miss it.'

⑰ BOLOGNA, ITALY

Emilia-Romagna's capital receives low-cost flights from several European airports but travellers coming from further afield will typically transfer through Rome (from where there is also a frequent high-speed train service taking a couple of hours). There's a bus from Bologna's Marconi airport into the city's central bus station which takes about 20 minutes. Accommodation ranges from budget albergos to palazzos; stay close to the old, buzzing Quadrilatero quarter. Spring and autumn are great times to visit Bologna, when it's pleasant to be outside, but note that the city shuts down in August.

⑱ YAYOI KUSAMA'S INFINITY ROOMS

The Infinity Rooms tour the world's great art galleries (in 2017, Washington DC's Hirshhorn Museum brought together six of them) so if one or more arrives at your local gallery or city be sure to book a ticket to infinity. Details of Yayoi Kusama's exhibitions and other happenings are posted on her website www.yayoi-kusama. jp). Some of her work is permanently displayed in Japan (though not the Infinity Rooms), for example on Naoshima island, as featured in Lonely Planet's Culture Trails book.

⑲ POINT REYES, CALIFORNIA, USA

Point Reyes Station, the main town in this corner of Marin County, is just over an hour's drive north of San Francisco via the Golden Gate Bridge and Hwy 101 (bonus!). So it's possible to base yourself in the city and make a daytrip from there or the East Bay (Oakland, Berkeley and so on). If you're roadtripping, there's no reason not to stay locally and enjoy the food and drink. Grey whales swim past from January to May and the fog rolls in during the summer months (June to August).

⑳ VARANASI, INDIA

You can fly to the city with Jet Airways and Air India from regional airports. From the airport, 26km (16 miles) northwest of Varanasi, take a taxi or autorickshaw. Most people arrive by train: there are long-distance services from New Delhi and Kolkata and frequent trains from Allahabad, Gorakhpur and Lucknow, also the source of regular buses. Varanasi is a maelstrom of touts and scams (see Lonely Planet for the lowdown on the latest) so you may prefer to book a room in advance. Take care when arranging boat tours and photographing near the ghats (don't photograph the 'burning' ghats).

INDEX

The Place To Be
November 2017
Published by Lonely Planet Global Limited
CRN 554153
www.lonelyplanet.com
10 9 8 7 6 5 4 3 2 1

Printed in Malaysia
ISBN 978 17870 1125 0
© Lonely Planet 2017
© photographers as indicated 2017

Managing Director, Publishing Piers Pickard
Associate Publisher & Commissioning Editor Robin Barton
Art Director Daniel Di Paolo
Editors Nick Mee, Yolanda Zappaterra
Print Production Larissa Frost, Nigel Longuet

Lonely Planet Offices

Australia
The Malt Store, Level 3,
551 Swanston St, Carlton, Victoria 3053
T: 03 8379 8000

USA
124 Linden St, Oakland,
CA 94607
T: 510 250 6400

Ireland
Unit E, Digital Court,
The Digital Hub,
Rainsford St, Dublin 8

Europe
240 Blackfriars Rd,
London SE1 8NW
T: 020 3771 5100

STAY IN TOUCH lonelyplanet.com/contact

Authors Oliver Berry (Alone, Fulfilment), Joe Bindloss (Exhilaration), Janine Eberle (Enlightenment, Passion), Emily Matchar (Amusement, Joy), Jonathan Thompson (Inspiration)

Cover photo Philip Lee Harvey (Sukamade Beach, Meru Betiri National Park, Indonesia, see p36)